CW00922239

Jürgen & Marianne Cieslik

The History of the Teddy Bear and his friends

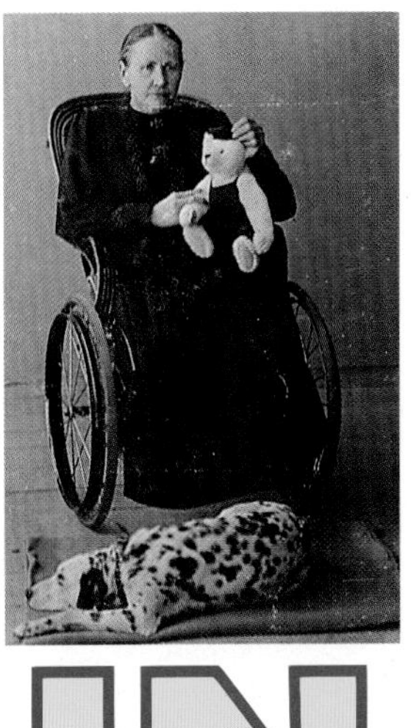

BUTTON IN EAR

MARIANNE CIESLIK VERLAG

Authorized publication
of the Margarete Steiff GmbH,
Giengen-on-the-Brenz

Translation by Laraine Freisberg
Layout and Production by
Jürgen & Marianne Cieslik

Lithos: Schreck & Jasper, Bonn
Printed in Germany by satz + druck
gmbh, Düsseldorf
ISBN 3-921844-18-5

This is the novel story of an enterprise which began in a family sewing-room and, in the space of 110 years, developed into a company of world renown. It is the remarkable story of a woman of enviable strength and cheerful disposition, who, in spite of a crippling disability, proved through her example that even the cruellest blows of fate may be mastered through perseverance and determination. It is also the fascinating story of a trademark which has come to symbolize the finest quality in toys – the Steiff Button-in-Ear. It is the story of the Margarete Steiff Company, in Giengen-on-the-Brenz. The company responsible for the life-like plush animals which have found their way into the hearts and homes of countless children and collectors. The company responsible for the unequalled popularity of the beloved Teddy-Bear in the world of toys.

Foreword

Steiff – a name which has conjured up its own special magic for millions of people all over the world, with Teddy-bears, dolls and plush animals which they have been manufacturing for over a century. Certainly a good enough reason for this extensive work detailing the history and products of the Margarete Steiff Toy Company and their famous "Button-in-Ear" trademark.

Almost four years ago we were approached by the Steiff Company and asked to take on this mammoth task. Four years appears to be a long time, but appearances can be deceptive! Numerous documents and articles relevant to our work as toy-historians were made available to us, and all these had to be studied, sorted and cataloged. Even the company archives, kept firmly under lock and key for decades, were opened for our research – to make this work based on all the original Steiff records as authentic as possible.

We studied all these documents meticulously and transferred the old catalogs onto our files. An additional stroke of luck was the fact that Steiff themselves have painstakingly saved almost every single article they have ever manufactured in specially built wooden cabinets. Thus we were able to examine, compare, measure and photograph dolls, Teddy-bears and animals (all in mint condition), in these exemplary archives. In addition, we studied over 30,000 old photographs before making our selection for this book. Among those choosen are some especially valuable color photographs which were taken in Steiff's own studios prior to 1914.

We did not confine our research to Germany; we also sought records, details and dates in England and America, in order to make this work as informative as possible. Often with unexpected and exciting results! The leading role played by the Steiff Company in the development of Teddy-bears, dolls and plush animals, is far more important than previously realised.

Thanks to our own extensive archives on the German Toy Industry, we were able to establish the exact economic and historic background of the industry, prior to the appearance of the first Steiff products.

Through our work, which involved absolute trust and cooperation between the Steiff Company and the authors, the Margarete Steiff Book, "Button-in-Ear" has come into being. Naturally we could not incorporate each item made by Steiff in this book; for they are over ten thousand in number! This would have far exceeded the limits which we were set. We were therefore often faced with the difficult task of having to choose which articles to use in order to present the reader with as comprehensive a picture as possible.

It is important to the history of the company to point out that the existing handwritten records prior to 1940 refer exclusively to three people: Margarete Steiff, Richard Steiff and Paul Steiff. Their invaluable influence, immeasurable creativity and sound knowledge of their market made them the central force of the toy factory. It was through their combined efforts that the Steiff Company developed into the world-famous enterprise it is today.

Margarete Steiff once remarked "Only the best is good enough for children" – a sentence which has remained the motto of the company for over a hundred years, and clearly expresses the company's philosophy. However, Steiff toys have also worked their magic on the adult world. Tens of thousands of adults around the world have become dedicated collectors of the noble trademark from Giengen. Teddy-bears and dolls, but also Steiff plush animals achieve impressive record prices at auction today.

Until now, no-one knew exactly when certain Steiff articles first appeared on the market or how to definitely establish, the date of manufacture. Through this book this will now be possible. Naturally there will still be questions which cannot be answered. For example it is impossible to provide absolutely exact dates or times during which Steiff buttons and labels were used for in times of need (especially during and after a war) old stock had to be used to supplement the lack of available materials.

It must also be mentioned here that a thin strip of paper sewn onto many Steiff articles is visible on several photographs in this book. These are internal labels mostly bearing a catalog number or the date on which a patent application was made. We deliberately did not remove these labels, as they will help collectors to recognise clearly the authenticity of these original objects.

We wish to thank all those people who have helped us with our work. Individual thanks are due to Dorothy and Jane Coleman for excerpts and copies from "Delineator" and "Playthings". Florence and George Theriault for their efforts in clarifying American folk-lore; Meinhard Meisenbach for his generous assistance; Laraine Freisberg for the English translation of this book; Carsten Freisberg for his successful struggles in preserving the translation on computer; and Green Tiger Press (Cal./USA.). Special thanks are due to the head of the department for product development at the Margarete Steiff Company; Jörg Junginger, the great-grand nephew of the company's foundress. Without his helpful advice, informative guidance and sound knowledge of company policy, we would not have found our way through the maze of photographs, documents and catalogs; or uncovered so many important details in the Steiff family history.

We wish to thank the following people for lending us photographs or actual items: Phillip's Auctioneers, London (Illus. 113); Sotheby's Auctioneers, London (Illus. 51, 70, 71, 117, 840); Jörg Juninger, Giengen (Illus. 281, 729, 732, 733, 785, 830-834, 884-887); Save the Children Fund, London (Illus. 108); Adelheid Kienzlen (Illus. 672, 673); Ullstein Bilderdienst (Illus. 560). All other photographs Jürgen & Marianne Cieslik, or old photographs from the Steiff archives.

We have taken great care to mention all persons or institutions who have helped us with this book. If we have forgotten someone, please forgive us, the omission was certainly not intentional.

Jülich, June 1989

Jürgen & Marianne Cieslik

Table of contents

Illus. 1: *Margarete Steiff.*

Giengen, 1847. This little town on the River Brenz had a relatively small population of some 2,300 inhabitants, yet it had a flourishing reputation in the agricultural market and was already well established in the textile and pottery industries. It was here that the building contractor, Friedrich Steiff, lived with his family. His small household was competently managed by his wife, Maria Margarete, nee Haehnle. The couple had two daughters, Marie, and Pauline, aged three and two years respectively. Their third child, another girl, was born on July 24 in Giengen. Apollonia Margarete Steiff was a healthy baby and enjoyed a normal infancy.

Approximately 18 months after her birth, the Steiff family was struck by tragedy. Shortly after the birth of her brother Friedrich, the toddler Margarete contracted polio. She was to suffer the effects of this insidious illness for the remainder of her life. Her left foot was completely paralysed, her right foot was partially lame, and she only had restricted use of her right arm.

How would this tiny child cope with such severe disability? At the turn of this century, at the request of friends, Margarete Steiff put pen to paper and recounted some of her earlier experiences. This "diary" of recollections is the only document in existence today, which provides us with information about the difficulties she suffered in childhood and adolescence.

Margarete Steiff was able to recall many episodes of her childhood. These recollections are the key to her successful life. She wrote, not without irony, of her earliest years, which were plagued by paralysis, "... apart from this (polio) I was, and remained, remarkably healthy, suffering very little from any of the other illnesses usually associated with childhood."

The worried parents, Friedrich and Maria Margarete, left no stone unturned in their efforts to help their sick daughter. Doctors were consulted, operations undertaken, spa treatments and physio-therapy tried – all with little success.

A trip to a doctor in the nearby town of Ulm is one of Margarete Steiff's earliest recollections. She cannot recall their mode of travel but she writes, "... then we went into the 'Gasthof zur Gans' (a local restaurant) where I was allowed to have a fat, juicy Bratwurst; and it is because of this sausage that I remember the trip. I don't remember the doctor we visited!"

Illus. 2: *The house where Margarete Steiff was born.*

Illus. 3: *Memorial unveiled for the 100th birthday of Margarete Steiff.*

Margarete Steiff was to depend on the help and friendship of other people for the rest of her life. Since she could not walk, she would have to rely on others to carry her. As a little girl she was taken around in a small hand-pulled cart. She preferred to be pulled along by her sisters or the other children of the neighborhood so that she could feel herself to be a part of their pranks and games.

"... in spring it was wonderful in my little cart. All the children gathered around me and I organized games in which I was the center of attention! However, the older children often ran off and then I was left babysitting the tiny tots. I always had room for two or three of them in the little cart and our neighbors were happy to have me looking after their children."

Her childhood seems to have been happy and uncomplicated in spite of her illness. The security and the familiarity of her small-town environment, with its unprejudiced neighbors, understanding relatives and childhood friends is largely responsible for the fact that the little girl was not unduly aware of her paralysis nor over burdened by it. Instead she was able to accept her suffering philosophically, and used it to develop great strength of character. ▶

In 1856, when she was nine years old, Magarete Steiff travelled to Ludwigsburg with her mother, to consult a certain Doctor Werner. The doctor took great pains with his young patient. She was taken into his family and writes: "... and I was given more freedom here than at home, so that I was not at all homesick. Doctor Werner took a great deal of trouble with me." Margarete now underwent a complicated operation, which involved the cutting of two tendons in the left foot and a tight plaster casing to straighten her leg; but the operation was unsuccessful.

A visit to a spa in Wildbad followed: "I travelled to Wildbad from Ludwigsburg by bus, together with Doctor Werner's wife and a lot of other children. During the journey she (Dr. Werner's wife) mended my badly torn clothes. At the Werner's house sliding around was not quite as strictly forbidden as it was at home ... hence my tattered skirts."

Her dresses and skirts did not suffer a better fate during her stay in Wildbad! "... we had a very easy-going house-mother and I was allowed the freedom to slide around on the stage or in the garden with the others. I wasn't really concerned about the way my clothes looked. I used to play hide-and-go-seek too."

Numerous treatments were prescribed for the young girl, including swim-therapy at the Katherine Hospital. Several nurses accompanied the children on these trips. The children were piled into a large pull-along wagon. Margarete recalls: "In the afternoons we were taken into the beautiful grounds, where the lovely, cool, ferns and the majesty of the pine trees made a lasting impression on me."

It was in Wildbad that the group had a slight accident when the nurses pulled the wagon around a corner too quickly. The wagon toppled over and the children fell head-first into the water. "Since help was at hand", writes Margarete, "we escaped with minor shock. We were tucked

Illus. 4: *Teenage photograph of Margarete Steiff.*

straight into bed and were rewarded with treats from all sides. For a few days we were the most important people in Wildbad!"

This was not the first time that the young Margarete had survived an accident in the water. One afternoon, when she was just four years old, she was out playing with her brother and sisters on the banks of the River Brenz. A neighbor arrived to take the children home in his wagon and he had to swerve swiftly to avoid colliding with a horse-drawn cart. The little hand-wagon tipped over and the children fell into the river. "As there were lots of people around, we were soon fished out", notes Margarete, "I remember someone asking me what I would have done if I hadn't been fished out. I told them that I would have swum to Basdot (to an aunt) at the water-mill. I don't recall being scared."

After a second spell at the spa in Wildbad in 1857, it became obvious that a cure was improbable. The little girl accepted the news bravely. She later confided in her diary: "It was a long time to spend searching for a cure. Finally, I told myself that as God had obviously intended that I should not walk, I must accept His will. And from the time I was 17 or 18 years old I refused to get excited about any newly proclaimed cure or medicine. The fruitless search for a cure does not allow a person to achieve peace of mind."

The travelling involved in the numerous visits to spas and hospitals meant that Margarete's education was often disrupted. Although the children received substitute schooling in Wildbad, there appears to have been no systematic program. At Doctor Werner's house, in Ludwigsburg Margarete was first introduced to the English language. Later, when she became involved with the export of her products to England and the United States, she was to regret that her knowledge of English had not progressed beyond those first basic lessons.

In her hometown, Giengen, the young Margarete, known to family and friends as Gretchen or Gretel, enjoyed her local school very much. She writes: "... and I refused to stay home, no matter how awful the weather was ... although I could easily have taken a day off."

Every morning her family or the neighbor's children would pull her along to school in her little cart. A woman who lived near the school-building was trusted with the task of carrying the little girl up the school steps. Sometimes the janitor or teachers would help, because the other children could not always be relied upon: "... It was not at all unusual for my friends to deposit my little cart in front of the school-building and rush off to their classes if they were late."

Margarete enjoyed her lessons and worked hard. Her parents decided that she should be confirmed a year earlier than was usual and so the young girl was kept busy all day: "... In the winter time I was at school from 8 o'clock in the morning until 5 o'clock in the afternoon. Confirmation lessons were between 11 and 12 o'clock, and then at noon the other children came back to school and brought me my lunch. I never had much of an appetite though, so I just carried on learning with the others. School finished ▶

around 2 o'clock and then the strongest in the class would carry me over to the Sewing School."

Here, in the needlework classes of Frau Schelling, Margarete began learning her future profession. Dressmaking, knitting, crochet-work, embroidery and all other forms of tailoring were taught at this school. Apparently Margarete's later talent was not immediately obvious! She writes: "... I was a great worry to my two sisters. They were so capable and talented, whereas I seemed to make every mistake that it was possible to make. They gave up hoping that I would ever produce anything worthwhile with my needle."

It was not really surprising that Margarete experienced difficulty with her sewing, since needlework requires the use of two steady and capable hands. "These needlework lessons were very difficult for me", recalls Margarete. "My right arm hurt after I used it for even a little while, and I had absolutely no co-ordination in my left hand. I much preferred to crochet or to do other easier handwork."

However, Margarete persevered, and later went on to the needlework classes held in the Giengen Town Hall. "I allowed myself to be taken there for many years because it was such fun." The girls at this school used to tell stories and hold debates during their needlework lessons. There was a great deal of laughter and singing and the young Margarete loved the social contact with the other girls of her own age. It was here that she formed her lifelong friendships.

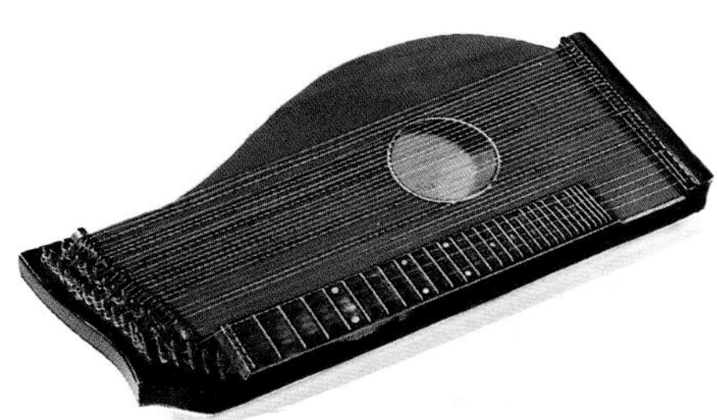

Illus. 5: A family heirloom – the Zither!

In time Margarete's sisters, Marie and Pauline, left the family home and went to work as housemaids in middle-class families. (After the two girls got married they were to spend many years overseas.) Margarete says: "... this was a difficult time for my mother, because she was so worried about my future."

The young girl did not suffer loneliness, however, "... now there was only my brother Fritz at home. He looked after me faithfully, became my closest confidant and I shared his lessons."

The neighbor's daughter and other friends called to collect Margarete in the evenings. They took her out for walks, mostly against her mother's wishes, since Mrs. Steiff preferred to see her daughter in bed by 7 o'clock in the summer. Her friends always brought her home after these "walks in the moon-light". They carried her into bed and locked up the house for her, rather than disturb the sleeping family. Margarete tells us: "... afterwards I always felt better. It was wonderful to get a breath of fresh air after all the sitting around inside the house."

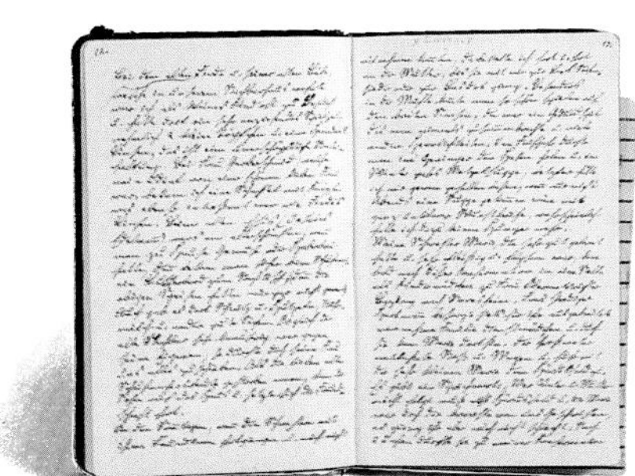

Illus. 6: Margarete Steiff's diary.

Mrs. Steiff was extremely strict and also overworked. She had to run the household, work in the family business, and look after her children, Fritz and Margarete. She suffered from pains in her legs and often had to rest. It was for these reasons that she tried to keep her disabled daughter as close to home as possible. Too much freedom meant more work and more "looking-after" for the mother.

Margarete writes: "... So I had to fight for all my rights. Mother could almost have been called an enemy of pleasure or leisure in any form. These two words did not exist in her vocabulary. Only work, and still more work! Today I am really grateful to her for teaching us to be content with what we had and for not spoiling me, as was the case with other mothers who had children like me. For mothers who spoil their suffering children do not prepare them to cope with the hardships of life."

She continues: "I never was quite as good or obedient as my sisters. 'Oh! That naughty Gretel' one often heard."

When her brother left for an engineering school in another town, Margarete's parents allowed her to "fulfill her dearest wish". She was allowed to take lessons on the zither. She derived so much pleasure from this instrument, that she was soon competent enough to be able to teach others to play. She was allowed to keep the money she made from these lessons, and writes: "... we children were allowed to keep every penny we earned, so our savings grew slowly but surely. We kept our expenses to a minimum too."

Margarete's savings soon allowed her to buy a sewing-machine; the first in the small town of Giengen! "Now we had to work hard", she ▶

Illus. 7: Machine – private collection.

wrote. There appears to have been plenty of work, especially before holidays and local celebration days. The family often worked until the early hours of the morning. Margarete recalls one Whitsun holiday: "... it was Whit Sunday morning and we did not get to bed until 6 a.m. The hard work and tedious sewing didn't bother me at all, but Pauline's health was ruined by it."

Margarete Steiff was popular with almost everyone because of her easy-going, happy disposition. She was usually the first to be asked to help out if an extra needlewoman was needed at short notice. This was no doubt because of her cheerful attitude. Margarete's godmother Apollonia asked her to help with the trousseaux of each of her four sons: Michael, Melchior, Hans and George. Apollonia was married to the felt merchant, Haehnle, and Margarete always enjoyed her visits to their home. "I didn't go home for a whole week. There was so much work to do, I had to sleep over. I earned at least 42 Kreuzer (Mark 4. 20), plus board for the week. My salary increased depending on the difficulty of the job. Later I was also allowed to embroider the names in cross-stitch ... so for many months, there we sat in the little parlor, working and singing."

The wife of the local pastor also hired the now competent seamstress to help with the trousseau of her daughter.

Margarete was collected every morning, but she often had to be home in the early afternoon to give lessons on the zither. On these afternoons, the pastor's son Paul Gross would take her home in her wagon. "With my permission, he (Paul Gross) stood on the back of my wagon. In this fashion we raced past the vicarage, past the Roessle (an inn), and down the narrow streets. I soon had to pay for my dare-devil attitude though. At the bottom of the hill the wagon overturned and I fell out and broke my lame left foot. My face was badly bruised, too."

Margarete continues: "The people who picked me up were very severe with their criticism. 'This had to happen, you simply wouldn't listen' ... I must admit that I had often been warned about my adventurous spirit ... but it was so wonderful to be able to move as fast as others sometimes ... so I had to put up with the pain. When I recovered I was able to return to my work at the vicarage."

The number of customers grew. At the age of 25, Margarete began to undertake more fashionable work. "I never really enjoyed it. I much preferred to make childrens' clothes", she writes. Her skill with her sewing machine improved and she made things easier for herself by using little tricks. She states proudly: "In the meantime I discovered that I could work the machine with my left hand if I placed it back-to-front before my chair. This was quite a discovery!"

Margarete Steiff travelled a great deal during these years. She visited relatives and friends. Her wheelchair was sent on ahead by wagon and she herself travelled by Post-Coach. She accepted help from everyone and remarks cheerfully "... with my famous lack of shyness, I accepted all that was done for me ... with gratitude naturally, but also as my undisputed right."

Her trips took her to the nearby towns of Augsburg, Geislingen, Neckarsulm and Ulm. Other trips followed and Margarete's self-confidence and independence increased accordingly. On one occasion when she travelled alone to Stuttgart, the letter announcing her visit arrived after she did! As a result, there was no-one at the station to meet her, but she recalls, "... I simply called one of the men working at the station and asked him to take me to Frau Vollherbst. She got a terrible shock when I turned up so unexpectedly."

Adolf Glatz, who was married to Marie Haehnle (a cousin and friend of Margarete Steiff's) was the son-in-law of the felt supplier in Giengen, and it was he who suggested to Margarete that she open her own the felt factory. Margarete writes: "In 1877 I started ... I opened my Felt Store and began making felt underskirts which had just come into fashion, for the firm of Christian Siegle in Stuttgart; I was also able to make and sell a few privately. I was very successful, even in the first year and I was able to employ a few people to ▶

***Illus. 8**: "Modenwelt" magazine, December 1879. This is the magazine which published the pattern for Margarete Steiff's first elephant (5in.).*

***Illus. 9**: An elephant pin-cushion (4in.) attached to a felt base was offered in Steiff's catalog, 1892.*

***Illus. 10**: A present for sister-in-law, Anna Steiff. The initials A.S. are picked out on the elephant's back with stick pins.*

work for me." The money which she saved was re-invested and fairly soon her dressmaking business was thriving.

She continued to make dresses for her relatives and friends because otherwise, she says, "... I would have made them very unhappy." The felt she used for her work was constantly improving in quality and was soon being used for other items of clothing. "Soon I had a large number of customers and provided all my relatives and friends with felt skirts, dresses, childrens' coats etc. and I was able to find work for even more people."

The company's first employee was Katherine Schnapper, and records for 1877 show that a sum of 3,065 Marks was spent on the felt used by the company in that year.

The official history of the Margarete Steiff Toy Company begins in the year 1880, although the youthful and enterprising Margarete had started her dress-making company, with her own children in the family, and I tried out the pattern in various sizes. One day I took an elephant to the Haehnle's house where I still went to sew childrens' clothes from time to time. I put the toy in the hands of the tiny, young boy ... who is the company director today ... and I said he could keep it as a reward if he didn't cry for one whole day. I should mention here, that he was always crying ... buckets of tears! I'm afraid though, that even the promise of the coveted elephant could not control his tears for long, and I ended up giving it to him, just to keep him quiet."

What inspired Margarete Steiff to produce the soft-filled elephant and the other toys which followed? Her paralysis meant that she was confined to her wheelchair, and could only undertake a minimum amount of travel. Giengen was situated a long way from the larger cities, and therefore she was forced, like many of the other toy manufacturers, to use the maga- elephant with a saddle-blanket. Later additions to the nursery menagerie were: 1879, a pig and a horse; 1880, a cat; 1883, a camel and 1884, a standing bear.

With only a short lapse of time the German magazine "Modenwelt" published the patterns from the U.S.. These do-it-yourself patterns began with a 5in. elephant on December 8, 1879, just in time for Christmas. Pattern Number "105-106. Elephant of cloth. To be used as a toy." It was this elephant that started Margarete Steiff on the road towards her soft-filled toy empire.

"Modenwelt" recommended a gray worsted material for the body of the elephant, kapok for the stuffing and a cashmir blanket. The tusks should be two bone knitting needles and it was suggested that black porcelain buttons be used for the eyes.

The pattern was easily followed and Margarete Steiff did not need long to complete her first little elephant, although it was not made exactly as

Illus. 11: Steiff pin-cushion elephant (3in.) on a heavy felt base. Saddle-cloth of red felt is fastened under the elephant's middle.

Illus. 12: The elephant as a jubilee symbol is synonymous with the Steiff story. Front: white velvet (circa 1900); middle: Jubilee elephant with gold placard, impressed "1880 – 1930"; right: gray plush elephant, "75 years – 1880 – 1955". All 3in. tall.

employees, almost three years earlier. Obviously the official date adopted has been based on the date of manufacture of the first toys.

The last two paragraphs in the recollections of Margarete Steiff are devoted to her first toy, which she sewed herself in 1880: a little elephant made of felt.

"At this time I came across a pattern for a toy elephant. Felt was the ideal material for this toy, and the filling would be of the finest lambswool. Now I could make these (the elephants) as gifts for the zines and newspapers which were available. The fashion magazines of the period printed the latest patterns for needlework, knitting, embroidery etc. as well as the usual fashion plates.

These fashion magazines also exchanged patterns with their international counterparts, and were thus able to cut costs. The first "sew-it-yourself" patterns were published in the U.S. magazine "Delineator". In 1879 a pattern for a cloth mouse was published as well as patterns for a rabbit and an suggested. She used other materials: felt for the body, and lambswool as a filling. She made many of these little toys, and gave them to friends and acquaintances as a small "thank-you", a token of her appreciation. The elephant quickly found its ideal place in many homes – as a pin-cushion!

At this time the sewing of these felt animals was still considered a pleasurable diversion. But in 1880 Margarete Steiff actually sold eight of these small toys. Records show that five of them went to Lina ▸

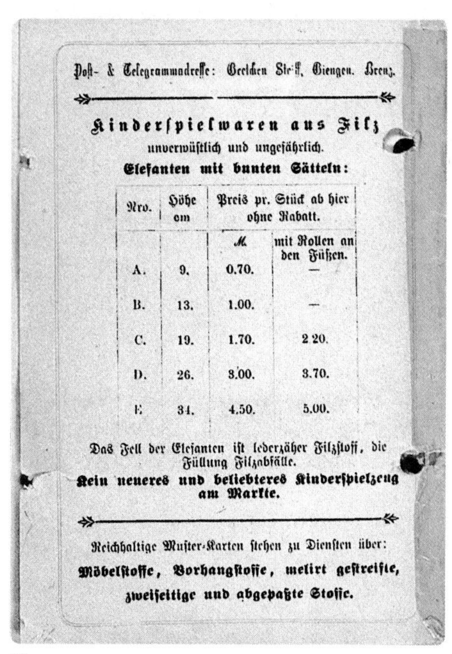

Post- & Telegrammadresse: Gretchen Steiff, Giengen. Brenz.

Kinderspielwaren aus Filz
unverwüstlich und ungefährlich.
Elefanten mit bunten Sätteln:

Nro.	Höhe cm	Preis pr. Stück ab hier ohne Rabatt.	
		M.	mit Rollen an den Füßen.
A.	9.	0.70.	—
B.	13.	1.00.	—
C.	19.	1.70.	2 20.
D.	26.	3.00.	3.70.
E.	31.	4.50.	5.00.

Das Fell der Elefanten ist lederzäher Filzstoff, die Füllung Filzabfälle.
Kein neueres und beliebteres Kinderspielzeug am Markte.

Reichhaltige Muster-Karten stehen zu Diensten über:
Möbelstoffe, Vorhangstoffe, melirt gestreifte, zweiseitige und abgepaßte Stoffe.

13

Preis-Liste
des
Filz-Versandt-Geschäfts
von
Gretchen Steiff
in
Giengen a. Brz.

Garantirt reinwollene Produkte
der
Vereinigten Filzfabriken.

14

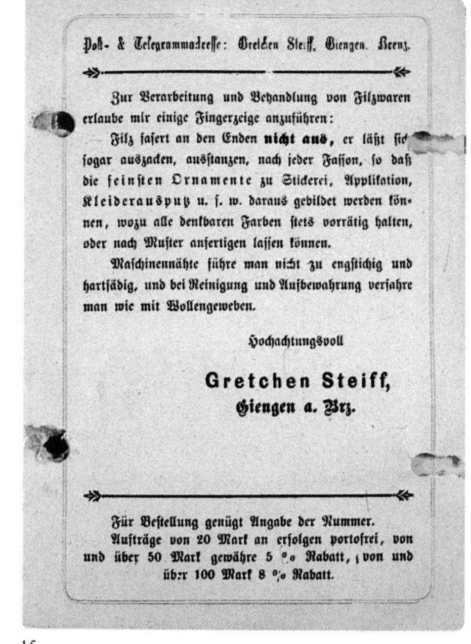

Post- & Telegrammadresse: Gretchen Steiff, Giengen. Brenz.

Zur Verarbeitung und Behandlung von Filzwaren erlaube mir einige Fingerzeige anzuführen:

Filz fasert an den Enden **nicht aus**, er läßt sich sogar auszacken, ausstanzen, nach jeder Fasson, so daß die feinsten Ornamente zu Stickerei, Applikation, Kleiderausputz u. s. w. daraus gebildet werden können, wozu alle denkbaren Farben stets vorrätig halten, oder nach Muster anfertigen lassen können.

Maschinennähte führe man nicht zu engstichig und hartfädig, und bei Reinigung und Aufbewahrung verfahre man wie mit Wollengeweben.

Hochachtungsvoll

Gretchen Steiff,
Giengen a. Brz.

Für Bestellung genügt Angabe der Nummer.
Aufträge von 20 Mark an erfolgen portofrei, von und über 50 Mark gewähre 5 % Rabatt, von und über 100 Mark 8 % Rabatt.

15

Post- & Telegrammadresse: Gretchen Steiff, Giengen. Brenz.

Garantirt reinwollene, einfarbige & melirte Garderobefilze
180 cm breit.

Qualitätsprobe einfarbig:

Qualitätsprobe melirt:

Für Bestellung genügt Angabe der Nummer.
Aufträge von 20 Mark an erfolgen portofrei, von und über 50 Mark gewähre 5 % Rabatt, von und über 100 Mark 8 % Rabatt.

Post- & Telegrammadresse: Gretchen Steiff, Giengen. Brenz.

Garantirt reinwollene, einfarbige & melirte Garderobefilze
180 cm breit.

Nro.	Farben:	Melangen:	Nro.
320			137
232			138
294			142
133			158
113			159
143			156
304			
40			
335			
202			
166			
	pro Meter 4 M.	pro Meter 4,20 M.	

Für Bestellung genügt Angabe der Nummer.
Aufträge von 20 Mark an erfolgen portofrei, von und über 50 Mark gewähre 5 % Rabatt, von und über 100 Mark 8 % Rabatt.

16

17

***Illus. 13 – 16**: The first Price list of the "Felt Mail Order Co.", of Margarete Steiff, was issued in 1890. Pieces of felt were glued to a fold-out card to illustrate the color and quality available. On the back page, under "Childrens' toys", elephants with colored saddle-cloths were offered.*

18

***Illus. 17**: A Biedermeier doll from Margarete Steiff's estate. The doll's complete outfit is made of felt. She is wearing a blue dress, covered by a coat with cape.*

***Illus. 18**: Sewing basket with pin-cushion. Steiff catalog, 1892.*

Illus. 19: *Margarete Steiff in the center of a group of fellow workers in the garden of the newly built "Felt Toy Company", cica 1895.*

Haehnle and two to Marie Spiess. For the next year or two production of the little elephants was still minimal: in 1881, 18; and in 1882, 11 examples were made.

The magazine "Modenwelt" continued to print patterns for its readers. In 1881, bear with guide; 1882, poodle; 1883, donkey; 1888, monkey; 1890, camel and lion; 1891, lamb with crocheted "coat"; 1892, parrot on a ring; 1897, an ox and 1898, terrier. All these animals were introduced into Margarete Steiff's 'program'! She altered the materials and accessories, but the basic patterns remained the same.

In 1892, the still relatively small company in Giengen applied for a Patent "for the making of animals and other figures to serve as playthings." The Patent Number was DRP 66996 (The letters DRP stood for **D**eutsches **R**eichs **P**atent). The articles would be soft-filled and the patent would ensure that the company could proceed without fear of imitation.

However, far away in Thueringia, another toy manufacturer decided that someone was encroaching upon his territory! A certain Emil Wittzack, owner of a toy factory in Gotha, claimed to be the "discoverer of soft-filled toys". He was able to prove that as early as 1879 he had produced felt deer and felt rabbits. He protested against Margarete Steiff's application for a Patent and although he managed to have it revoked, the company in Giengen did not suffer any serious consequences. The felt business of Margarete Steiff continued to provide a healthy basis for her company. The Steiff company still has a Price-List from the year 1883. This states: "Price-List of the Felt Mail-Order Company of Gretchen Steiff, in Giengen-on-the-Brenz, guaranteed pure-wool articles of the United Felt Factories.." The advantages of this material are listed in the Price-List: "Felt is the cheapest clothing material on the market and also the best, as long as it is made of pure wool. I offer (under guarantee) pure wool materials, which are especially suitable for coats, jackets, night-dresses, childrens' suits, ladies' underskirts, caps, capes, blankets, carpets, embroidery work, curtains, drapes, etc.." Color samples accompany this Price-List.

On the last page of the Price-List, one notes a possible new line of development for the small company: "Felt toys for children – robust and safe. Elephant with colored blanket."

This item was offered in a standing version, with and without metal wheels on the feet, in several sizes: 4, 5, 8, 10 and 14 inches. "The elephant is of soft felt material which is as supple as leather. The filling is of left-over felt pieces. There is no newer or more desirable child's toy on the market."

Margarete's brother, Fritz Steiff, who had by now completed his studies and was a qualified master builder, was instrumental in helping the small company to find its feet. He had married, and was now the father of six sons. Five of ▶

these six sons would later steer the Margarete Steiff Company to undreamed of success and prosperity.

Fritz Steiff quickly realized the opportunities which would become available to his sister through the sale of large quantities of these toy elephants. He wanted to help his hesitant sister, to show her that effort and determination would pay off. He persuaded her to make him a sackful of little felt elephants which he intended to sell at the nearby market in Heidenheim. He carried out his plan with huge success and obtained many new orders. His success generated new inspiration and motivation within the small company.

In 1883 the energetic Fritz arranged for Margarete Steiff's products to be displayed in an Export-Showroom in Stuttgart. Year by year, as both the production and turnover increased, so too did the variety of toys offered. The Steiff toy menagerie grew bigger and bigger.

The company's first large kapok stuffed elephants stood unsteadily on their shaky legs – sometimes the legs actually "gave way". Fritz first developed a wooden frame and then later used a metal one to lend support to the bodies of the animal. New toy animals were added to this line and thus the manufacture of pull-along and ride-on toys began.

At this time the little company was still based in the parents' home. Whilst Margarete Steiff personally taught and watched over her few employees, Fritz Steiff continued to push his sister to take over a larger building which would allow them to meet the demands of the steadily increasing number of customers. Before long a new building was put up, and the company moved into Muehlstrasse, in 1889. The house had a corner shop with two windows, ideal for the display and ▶

Illus. 20: *From the catalog, 1892.*

Illus. 21: *In the center of this view of Giengen, the Steiff house with its round alcove and inscription "Felt Toy Factory", can be easily recognized.*

sale of individual toys and bolts of felt. The words "Felt-Toy-Factory" were painted in large letters on one wall of the house.

It was at this time that Margarete Steiff became acquainted with the younger sister-in-law of her brother Fritz. Johanna Roeckh and Margarete Steiff hit it off immediately and established a friendship which was to make them inseparable for the rest of their lives.

The Steiff mail-order company flourished. Felt, felt articles and toys were in demand. Statistics of these early years confirm the upward trend in the company's turnover. The toy program was developed still further. The elephant was joined by a monkey, donkey, horse, camel and pig, as well as a dog, a mouse, a cat, a rabbit and a giraffe. The program was now so extensive that the company was able to print its first illustrated catalog.

Although they were confronted by many difficulties, the Steiff Company were determined to increase both the size and the technical performance of their animals. Not only the raw materials but also the necessary tools had to be procured. No easy task for a physically handicapped employer! But brother Fritz helped to solve all the teething problems, step by step. On March 3, 1893, the small factory was entered in the business register at the Chamber of Commerce. Four employees and ten home-workers were registered. The turnover was 12,000 Marks for felt and 28,000 Marks for toys.

A year later, a travelling salesman from Waltershausen (Mr. Ph. Morschheuser) was employed and given samples to promote. He visited stores where toys were part of the inventory and soon found many new customers. The Berlin Wholesale Company Soehlke Nachf. (Soehlke and successors) whose owner was Paul Wetzel, took especial note of the products of the ▶

Illus. 22 + 23: *Cover of the 1892 catalog. On the title page the factory building can be seen on the left, whilst on the right two young boys can be seen fighting over a camel on wheels. Underneath, a camel printed in gold emphasizes: "Muster-Geschützt" (registered trademark). The camel was therefore the first trademark of the "Margarete Steiff, Felt Toy Factory".*

Illus. 24:
Catalog pictures, 1892.

toy company from Giengen. Wetzel had a reputable showroom which was continually visited by overseas buyers. From 1897, Margarete Steiff also displayed her products in the salesroom of G. F. Herzog in Berlin.

With inherent intuition, warm-heartedness and steely self-discipline Margarete Steiff pursued her goals. She soon became the accepted role-model of her fellow workers; who admired her self-discipline and perfectionism.

Records for 1897 show a turnover of 90,000 Marks. There were ten female workers on the pay-roll, as well as thirty home-workers. The new year began with zealous preparation. It was the first time Margarete Steiff had decided to have her own stand at the Leipzig Spring Fair. (Steiff products had been displayed by an exhibition company in Leipzig since the year 1893.)

A young man who was to greatly influence the development of the toy factory in the future was also at this Fair – Richard Steiff – one of the six sons of Margarete's brother, Fritz Steiff, whom Margarete had to thank for so much of her success.

Richard Steiff enjoyed a good relationship with his aunt. From his earliest years she had recognized his creative ability and his perfectionism. His father sent him to the Art School in Stuttgart where he produced a great deal of artwork. After a finishing term at a school in England, one of his first tasks was to represent the company at the Leipzig Fair.

We should point out here that from 1897 onwards, the Steiff company was continuously represented at the Leipzig Fair. Their first display was in an Exhibition Hall in Hainstrasse 2. From 1899 through 1908 they could be found in Neumarkt 8, from 1908 through 1923 they moved to the Exhibition Palace Monopol, and from 1923 onwards the Steiff display was in the central Exhibition Palace.

Richard Steiff returned from Leipzig with his order book full. He had established international contacts, realized the possibilities of the overseas market and cajoled his aunt into further expansion. In the years which followed Richard Steiff devoted himself exclusively to the design and manufacture of soft-filled toys. His designs were

Paul (1876) *Richard (1877)* *Franz (1878)* *Lina (1879)* *Eva (189*

***Illus. 25**: Margarete Steiff was particularly close to her nephews and nieces – the children of her brother Fritz.*

mostly for animals. This can be seen clearly in the catalogs of the period which offered a variety of plush animals previously unknown. The creation of the Teddy-bear in 1903 is perhaps his greatest personal achievement, and one with which he has made "Toy-history". A further design in 1908 was for the Roloplan (a cloth kite without a tail, which could be slotted together). Later he worked on the building of mechanical display pieces with the artist Albert Schlopsnies. In the early 1920s Richard Steiff resigned from the company after a disagreement on who should head the family business. He moved to the U.S.A., and once there, he acted as a critical and stimulating observer of all ongoing developments within the company. In 1898 Margarete Steiff took two other nephews into the company. Paul Steiff, born in 1876 and Franz Steiff, born in 1878.

Paul Steiff had already finished a long apprenticeship. From 1891 until 1894 he was a draughtsman in a company which built church organs, and like his brother Richard, he had been a student at the Art School in Stuttgart (until 1898). He worked in the Steiff factory during the school holidays and his aunt soon recognized his graphic ability. He joined the Pattern Dept. and was responsible for multiplying patterns, and decreasing and increasing the standard-sized patterns. In 1902 he travelled to America at the request of his aunt, and spent over a year there in an attempt to secure the position of the Steiff Company on the American market. On his return he took over the Quality Control and Design Departments. He also continued sketching animals, and his artistic ability was highly visible and much admired in the Steiff toy menagerie for many years.

Franz Steiff had now completed his studies. He had specialized in the art of weaving, and because of his skill in the production of plush animals he was soon indispensable in the family business. He devoted himself to the internal organisation of the company; he was responsible for the buying of materials and for the increase in sales. He spent many years working in England. Franz Steiff also established the overseas warehouses. 1899, London (Herbert Hughes); 1900,

Hugo (1884) *Otto (1885)* *Marie (1887)* *Ernst (1890)*

Illus. 26: *The original Steiff building, 1889.*

Illus. 27: *Shell construction of the first glass building, 1904.*

Illus. 28: *The completed building, 1903.*

Illus. 29: *The second glass building.*

Florence (G. Pansier); 1901, Amsterdam (H. Kamp); 1908, Lisbon and Vienna (Rodrigues and Schnoetzinger). Between 1906 and 1908 the Giengen factory was filled to capacity, and Franz Steiff organized branches to supervise the home-workers in the nearby villages and towns. The famous "Button-in-Ear" trademark was just one of his ideas. In 1908, after a short illness, his early death at thirty years of age, was an unexpected blow to the family.

Otto Steiff joined his brothers in 1902 after completing his studies at a Business College in Cologne. He had previously visited England, and during 1908 and 1909 he used this experience successfully to promote the Teddy-bear in Britain. In 1911 Otto Steiff founded a subsidiary company, Steiff Frêres, in Paris. The company went into liquidation during the First World War. In 1912 he began laying the foundations for the Margarete Steiff & Co. Corporation in New York, which would take over the distribution of all Steiff products within the the United States. In 1913 the Geo. Borgfeldt Company took over as Steiff's agent in the States and Otto Steiff concentrated solely on the advertising of Steiff products.

The last of Fritz Steiff's sons to join the family business was Hugo Steiff, in 1906. He had been at an Engineering School and it was his job to supervise all future building projects. In 1925 it was Hugo Steiff who introduced the conveyor belt to the factory. He had originally ▶

***Illus. 30:** Scaffolding for the new building.*

intended it to be used solely for the production of the Steiff scooter. However, it resulted in such an impressive increase in turnover, as well as a decrease in costs, that at the end of 1925 the conveyor belt was also instituted for the soft-filled animals. This meant that there were no longer half-finished products lying in storage and that large areas of storage space in the warehouse became available.

The inventory of the factory grew and grew. The huge increase in turnover and production brought new problems for the family – the old factory rooms were bursting at the seams!

It was Richard Steiff who initiated the plans which were drawn up for three new factory buildings in 1902. These buildings are still part of the company today. They are long, flat buildings, two to three stories high, and have double walls made entirely of glass. In 1930 an archivist noted that these buildings were: "like giant hot-houses with their construction of iron, wood, and glass."

In a detailed article in 1970, the magazine "Bauen und Wohnen" (Building and Living) deplored the fact that even today no-one could be certain of the name of the architect of these buildings. However, one thing is certain – Richard Steiff was the instigator. Since there is no documentation available, the magazine states regretfully: "this (lack of documentation) is no doubt the reason these wonderful buildings have not found their way into the history of ▶

31

***Illus. 31:** Factory view, circa 1912.*

***Illus. 32:** The Toy Factory in the 1920's.*

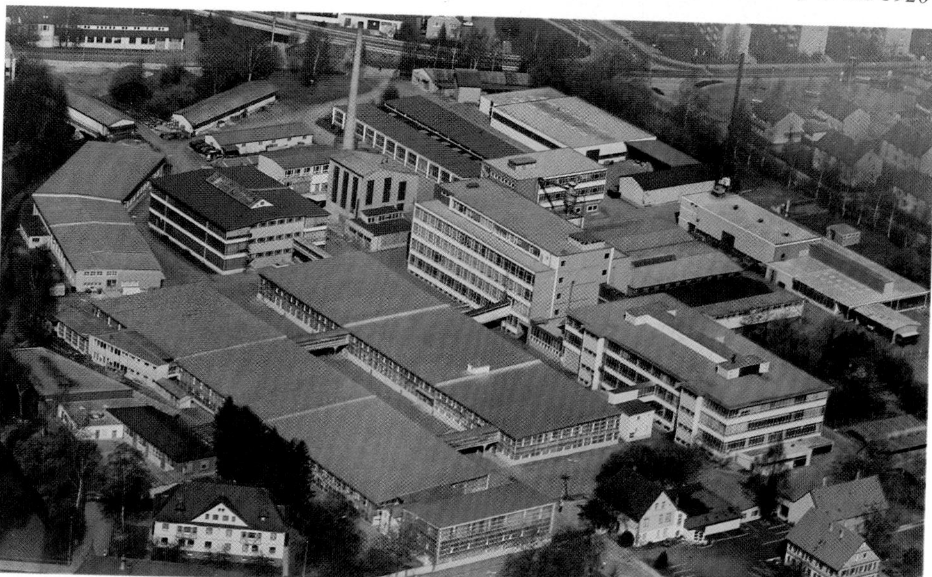

***Illus. 33:** Steiff today, in the eighties.*

34

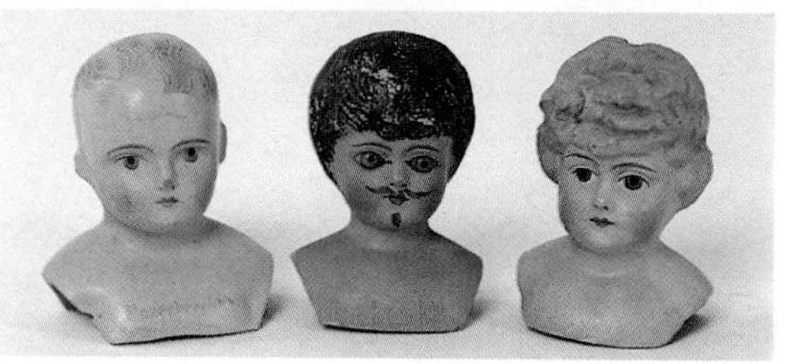

35

***Illus. 34**: The only remaining doll from the Steiff program, pre 1900. This doll is 10in. tall, completely original and was offered simply as "Kind" (child). The head and shoulderplate are of composition stamped "unzerbrechlich" (unbreakable) and "waschbar" (washable); the body is of felt with sewn on limbs. Clothing is also felt.*

***Illus. 35**: Various composition shoulderheads of the type used by Steiff.*

***Illus. 36**: Seven monkey dolls (catalog 1897). Three soldiers and a coachman, all 12in. tall. The paper tag attached to their clothing is marked with an "elephant" and the words "Made in Germany" or "Ges. Gesch. Unzerbrechlich" (Registered Patent. Unbreakable).*

***Illus. 37**: Single page from the Steiff catalog of 1897. Coaches and carriages were supplied by the Maerklin Toy Company, from nearby Goeppingen.*

36

37

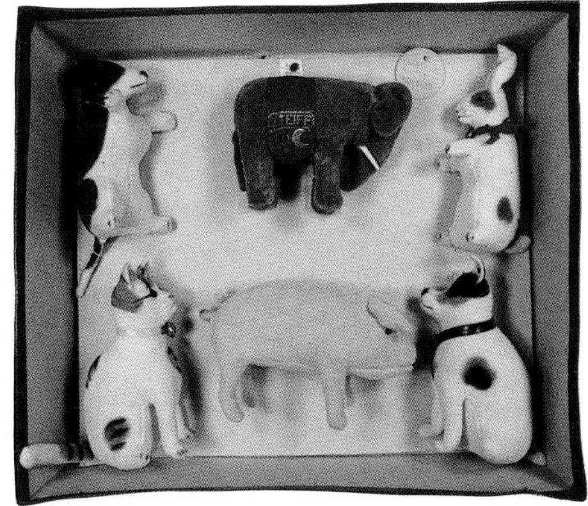

Illus. 38: *Selection of animals from 1900.*

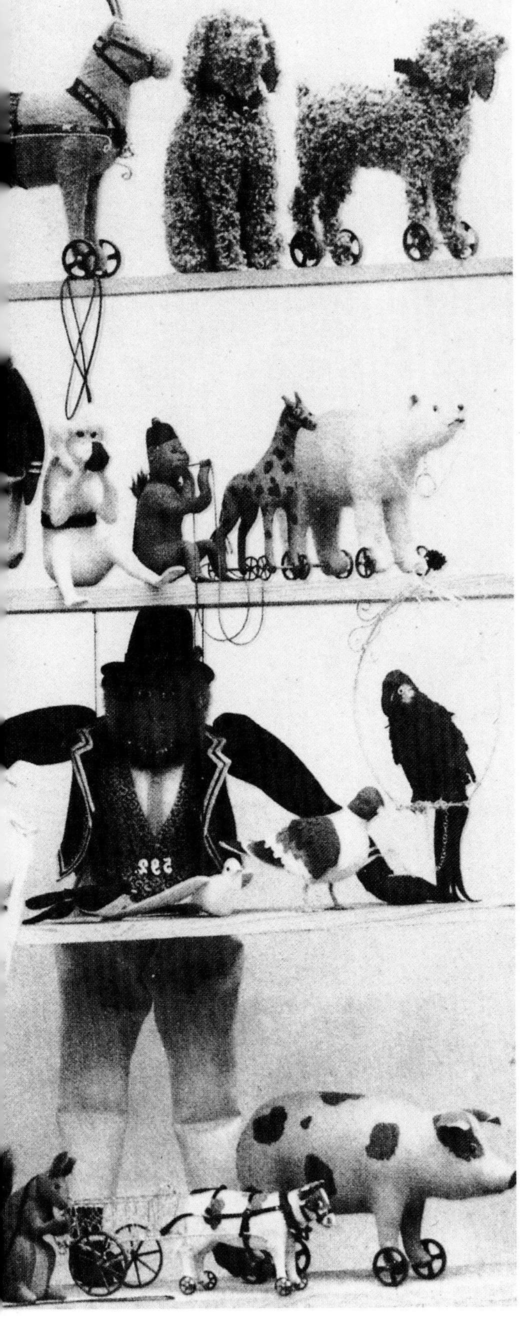

the buildings of the 20th Century. And yet these buildings may be viewed as an almost anonymous avant-garde prototype for the masterpieces of famous architects like Adolf Loos, Walter Gropius and Mies van der Rohe."

Certainly the first designs and sketches for these highly original buildings were the work of Richard Steiff. He wanted to create ideal working conditions with an abundance of light, and so he designed a factory complex that was as ageless in its time as it is today! Buildings that were not only ultra-modern, but practical as well. The blue-prints of the first building were sketched by hand and the construction was carried out by "Eisenwerk Muenchen AG., previously Kiessling-C. Moradelli" (Munich Iron-Works).

The Steiff family watched intently as the building went up – after all, the nephews of the enterprising Margarete Steiff, were also the sons of the building contractor, Fritz Steiff!

Therefore, it is hardly surprising to find that the next new building at the Steiff plant was designed by Hugo Steiff, and in 1905, although he was still a student of mechanical engineering at the School of Engineering in Mannheim, the new factory complex was put into his sole charge. This was a practical decision intended to keep costs minimal and to encourage him to complete future projects independently. He completed the task using day-workers and a few carpenters.

The first glass building, the East Wing, was completed in 1903 and is 1,080 square meters. (Today the company's archives and the Steiff Museum can be found in this building.) In 1905 the West Wing was added. This was another glass building with a huge area of work space, some 6,840 square meters. Margarete Steiff informed her customers proudly, "... the new factory buildings and boiler house incorporate approximately 9,000 square meters of unbelievably light and airy space. They were built ▶

Illus. 39: *Company seal.*

Illus. 40: *Stencil drawing of the "elephant" trademark used on transport cases.*

Illus. 41: *A "Snow-Elephant" made by Hugo and Ernst Steiff in 1898. A thoughtful surprise for aunt Margarete.*

Illus. 42: *Sketches of a design for an elephant on a velociped (tricycle), circa 1897.*

43

Illus. 43: *Margarete Steiff (right) at her desk. She is holding a felt cat (rattle) in her left hand.*

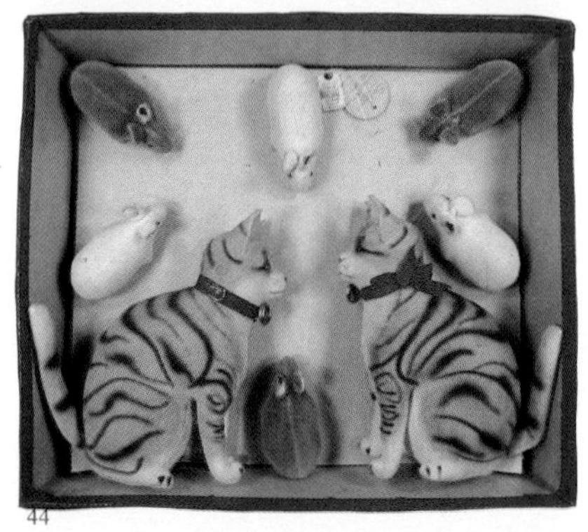

44

45

Illus. 44 + 45: *Boxed set of felt animals, circa 1900.*

46

Illus. 46: *Velvet cat, a rattle from 1899. As early as 1892 Steiff offered felt cats as pincushions, balls, or simply for room decoration. The cats were given glass eyes on request naturally at an extra charge!*

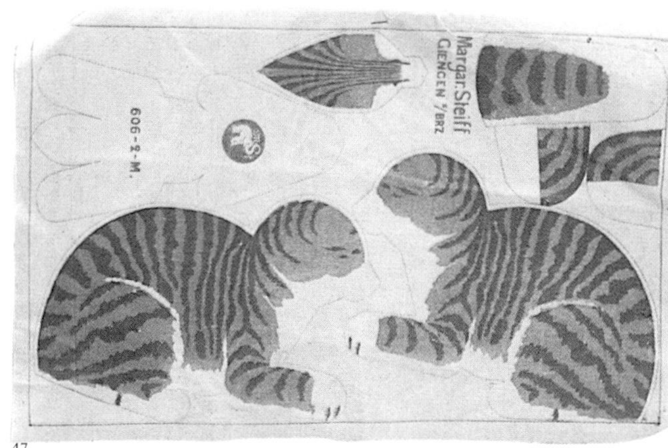

47

Illus. 47: *Cloth printed with the design No.DRGM 115 108, cat (rattle).*

from our own blue-prints at exceptionally low cost. They have double walls of sheet glass, steam heating, the latest arc-lighting and twenty-five telephones." A further expansion took place in 1908 when the North Wing, with an area of 6,120 square meters, was built. In 1910 the carpentry shop (1,080 sq. meters) and several additional rooms were added onto the North Wing.

During these years Margarete Steiff did not leave anything to chance. She watched over both production and quality and she continuously set out to win new customers. The demand for Steiff products was so unexpectedly high that she had to steadily increase the number of persons she employed.

On comparing the growth of production in the years leading up to the turn of the century, it soon becomes obvious that an organized program was first used from about 1890 onwards. All the animals which were made during this period were first made up as samples by Margarete Steiff herself, before being adopted into the Steiff program. By sewing all the samples herself she was aware of the weaknesses which could arise during production and was able to look out for these weaknesses in the finished articles which were brought in by the home-workers. Margarete Steiff was extremely fussy and many items had to be remade.

The secret of the toys from Giengen lay in their material – the felt. The little town of Giengen was the home of the "United Felt Factory", and Magarete Steiff was related to the factory owner! No wonder she changed her "Felt Mail-Order Company" into the "Felt Toy Company".

Margarete Steiff placed particular emphasis on the quality of the material she used as a filling for her toys. At first she chose to use lambswool, and later, in 1890, she began using fine wood-shavings (excelsior). The company proudly stated in their early catalogs that the filling in their products was: "light, ▸

1902-1903

Felt-Toys

Felt-, Plush-, Velvet-, Skin-, Wool- and Stuff-Animals.

For children only the best is good enough! True to this principle, I am now sending out my 7th Illustrated Price List.

The greatly extended patronage which my business continues to receive, especially during the past year, together with

Increasing export sales, and the demand generally for further numbers of every kind of animals, prompt me to enlarge my business and to very materially increase and improve my stuffed toy animals, both as regards artistic and technical execution. My new catalogue now contains again

Many novelties.

As to the indestructible character, durability, originality and popularity of my goods, I have received a large number of testimonials from my customers, a fact speaking sufficiently for itself. I therefore only here briefly describe the

Registered constructions of the animals.

The stuff-covering consists of best quality felt, plush or velvet, especially manufactured for the purpose, and as far as possible protected against moths.

The stuffing is light, soft and pure (no sawdust, animal hair, &c.).

The strong metal frame serves to hold the form, and to import the astonishing bearing-strength to the larger animals.

The light weight in proportion to the high value involves only small duty and low charges for transport.

My trade-mark »M. St. Elefant« should be particularly noted, in order to guard against worthless imitations, such as have been put upon the market of late.

Leading Felt Toy Manufactory.

48

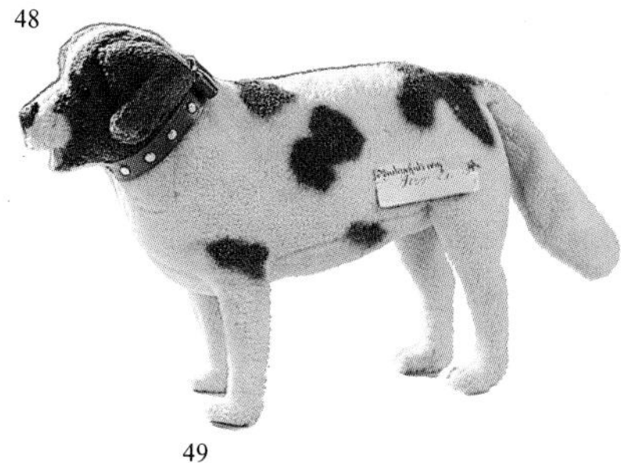

49

50

Illus. 48: *Title page of the 1902/1903 Steiff-catalog.*

Illus. 49: *St. Bernard (Catalog Description: "Bern 28") with a sealing-wax nose. The dog is wearing a collar which is trimmed with elephant buttons (patent 1904), 11in. tall.*

Illus. 50: *Velvet cow ("Ox-14") with elephant button, circa 1904, 5in.*

***Illus. 51**: Velvet skittles sets were available as early as 1892. Many different animals were offered, either as single sets or in groups. The king was characterized by a colorful head-dress. One bowling ball was included in each set. For the European market 9 skittles comprised a set, whereas the sets intended for America had 10 skittles.*

Prior to 1900 Margarete Steiff used several materials to make her animals: Felt – which was easy to work with; to cut, to stamp, and to emboss. The strong felt cloth was produced by a machine using a complicated crushing procedure to adapt wool, thread or hair. The high quality felt which Margarete Steiff worked with was shorn and the excess wood-shavings were pressed out and discharged by a mechanical cloth-making apparatus. The felt was then finely painted with individual spots and stripes in order to simulate fur, or skin. Plush – a velvet like material, with longer hair than actual velvet, was woven from silk, cotton, worsted, jute and angora silk. High quality animal plush was woven from mohair. "Krimmer" – a wool weave which resembled the coat of a newborn lamb. Real fur – from several different animals,(for example, horses were covered with the skin of baby foals). Trademark: products were marked with a paper tag printed with an elephant, even before 1900.

52

53

***Illus. 52 + 53**: These velvet animals are from Steiff's production, circa 1902. Rabbit and dog in "begging" position – in other words, sitting on their hind legs, (each 5in.). Both carry a small basket on their backs, which was intended for use as a pin-cushion.*

soft and clean (no sawdust, animal hair or cork pieces)."

An account from this period explains clearly how the felt and filling material were used. The animals, which were first cut out of the felt, did not receive their final shape until they had been filled with the excelsior. When the animals had been tightly packed with the excelsior, the felt was dampened slightly, so that the material drew together and fit snugly over the filling. Through pushing and kneading the felt, and then adding a little more excelsior, the final sculpting of the animal gave the toys the designed and recognizable shape.

Good toys were quickly copied and cheaply made imitations soon arrived on the market. Margarete Steiff suffered this plagiarism herself shortly after her unexpected rise to fame, between the years 1890 and 1897. Her competition grew visibly, and in order to deal with these new problems she had to define and protect her products. It became imperative to protect the company through legal patents. Therefore, in 1898, the Steiff Company registered its first patents (DRGM = **D**eutsches **R**eichs **G**ebrauchs**m**uster) at the Royal Patent Office.

For example: 1898, DRGM 102 130 "Rocker with a covering of soft material to provide a noiseless movement." This patent was to be applied to large Ride-on Animals on Rockers, (note: similar movement to a rocking chair). The animals could be removed from the rockers and were then able to stand on all fours. A Steiff advertisement states: "Our animals have soft-covered soles, which not only protect parquet and other floor surfaces, but will safeguard your children against injury. They are tough, resistant, light and elegant. A significant invention."

A further example is the Patent No. 115 108 (1899), "Childrens' Rattle, consisting of a celluloid ball, which ▶

is encased in a soft filling and then covered with woven material, felt, or plush, in order to reduce possible danger by fire." Table-tennis balls covered in felt were another specialty item offered by the Steiff company.

It was not only important to protect the way an item was made, it was also necessary to copyright each design. One had to register each pattern at the local Court. The registration of these patterns often provides the key when trying to establish the earliest manufacturing date of old toys, since the date of registration also tends to be the date on which production started. In addition, each pattern number registered with the Court became legally binding for the particular product for which it had been registered by the company.

At first Margarete Steiff had neglected to protect the methods of production used to manufacture her felt animals. However, she soon made up for this initial lack of foresight. On June 3,1899, the local court at Heidenheim, which was responsible for the nearby town of Giengen, was asked by the Steiff company to register patterns for a number of toy animals of different materials.

The complete list follows, since this was the first Patent Registration Application made by Steiff, and thus it is significantly important to the history of the company: "To the Royal Court of Heidenheim. It is my privilege to send you, enclosed in a sealed package, 3 drawings and 23 original patterns for soft-filled toys made of cloth. I would like to apply for Patents for the enclosed graphic designs with the following fabrication numbers, for a period of three years. 207-m deer of velvet; 424-m elephant of velvet; 459-4 + 462-4m Fox Terrier of felt with brown and black patches; 468-4m Fox Terrier of velvet; 533-m + 535-m + 536-m, rabbit (lying) of painted velvet; 549-m + 55m rabbit (begging) of painted velvet; 548-m ▶

54

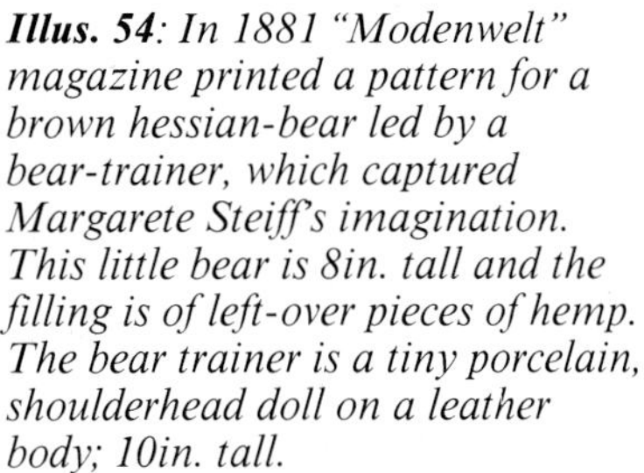

Illus. 54: *In 1881 "Modenwelt" magazine printed a pattern for a brown hessian-bear led by a bear-trainer, which captured Margarete Steiff's imagination. This little bear is 8in. tall and the filling is of left-over pieces of hemp. The bear trainer is a tiny porcelain, shoulderhead doll on a leather body; 10in. tall.*

Illus. 55: *Dancing bears at the turn of the century giving a performance in the town center of Giengen.*

Bears belong to the predatory animals. Distinguishing characteristics are their thick necks, and short, stumpy tails. Their diet consists of more vegetables than meat, and they are only found in the northern hemisphere. In ancient times in Germany, the bear was known as the king of animals. The natural habitat of the brown bear was mostly middle Europe and although today the bear is almost extinct, single animals can still be found in the Carpation Mountain. Even though the bear is a plump animal he can run very fast, climb trees, and walk on his hind legs. Bear cubs can easily be tamed by humans; they may be groomed, have inherent musical ability, and can keep in step when dancing. Bear cubs can also be taught many tricks which is why even today they can still be found in circus programs. Bear-leaders, mostly in Hungarian farmers' costume, travelled from village to village until the beginning of the 1940s in order to present their sideshows to the villagers. The bears wore muzzles and were led by a chain attached to a ring in the nose.

56

Illus. 56: *Rough sketches of designs for a dancing bear, and a bear-trainer, 1899.*

Illus. 57: Richard Steiff designed these animals between 1897 and 1899 for advertising purposes. The bear is 4ft. 10in. tall. An elephant, a monkey-doll and a life-sized stork, carrying a baby-in-a-diaper in its beak, were also made at this time.

rabbit head of painted velvet; 555-1 elephant on tricycle; 581-5 dancing bear; 591-e monkey as Hussar; 591-f monkey as Infantryman; 591-g monkey as Coachman; 591-i monkey as Cuban; 605-2m + 606-2m cat (lying) of painted velvet; 606-m cat (sitting) of painted velvet; 643-1 bird; 715-1 Nansen (the explorer) with Polar Bear; 716-1 Bear-handler with brown bear; 1241 frog; 461-a 2m Dachshund."

Recognition and success were Margarete Steiff's rewards for the energy, perseverance and diligence which she had shown during these years. She brought a wealth of ideas to her work and her indefatigable spirit was nurtured by the close-knit relationship which she shared with her family; most especially her brother Fritz, and his sons. These young men with their enterprising ideas and youthful unconcern helped to steer the small company to world renown.

Richard Steiff was the driving force on this road to fame. He applied himself diligently to the extension of the Steiff program. He was responsible for numerous new designs at the turn of the century. His sketches of the animals at Stuttgart Zoo were the basis of many new creations.

In one of the many note-books Paul Steiff filled about these early years, he remarked: "Richard Steiff designed the animal patterns between 1897 and 1899." Brother Paul, with his technical know-how, was at Richard's side, to help transform the sketches and ideas into practical patterns.

Richard Steiff's first designs were sewn by Margarete Steiff herself, or by her closest employees. As the animals grew in size, they were given wooden frames to ensure stability. These frames were made by craftsmen in Giengen. Richard Steiff watched over the filling of the animals critically, for it was at this stage that the animals received their final true-to-life shape. ▶

Paul Steiff notes: "Sometimes, he (Richard) was forced to take over the filling of an animal himself, to make sure that it received the lifelike form he desired." A local photographer, Schuster, was responsible for taking the photographs of the finished animals which Richard Steiff had designed. One of these photographic "documents" shows a large bear, approximately 5 feet tall, in the center of a group of animals. The bear was designed by Richard Steiff before the turn of this century!

The animals offered in the 16 page catalog of "The First Felt-Toy Company in Germany" dated 1902/03 could be compared to the variety of species offered by a large Zoo! Several breeds of dogs, cats, elephants, giraffes, donkeys, cows, camels, sheep, lions, pigs, storks, goats, zebras, and of course, the bears which would later help the company to worldwide renown. All the animals were available with or without wheels.

It is important to note that as early as 1892 "soft-filled bears for small children" were already being offered in two sizes, 5 and 8in., and several colors: white, gray, brown, and black plush. The 8in. bear also had a growler. Unfortunately, these bears are not illustrated, but later catalogs show several bears which are comparable: a pull-along bear on metal wheels, standing on all fours, and also a bear on two legs, representing a dancing-bear with chain and stick.

In 1899 the Polar Bear and Brown Bear were offered in the Steiff program: "Pat. No. 576, and 576-1, Ride-on bear of plush on metal frame with pull-along chain and weight-load capacity over one hundredweight. No. 581-0 Bear standing on hind legs, fixed on wooden base with movable wheels; very realistic!" Continued: "Pull-along bear on revolving wooden disc. Latest addition (No. 581-1); No. 581-5, Bear on conical wooden base (Roly)." A bear-trainer with a ▶

Illus. 58: *Richard Steiff's sketch pad.*

Illus. 59: *Otto Steiff with contemporary bears, circa 1900.*

Illus. 60: *Catalog photograph, 1900. Bears on hind legs "Roly Poly" toys; bears on brushes, which danced when the toy was rolled along; bears on wooden platforms – with wheels; Bears on discs which revolved on a pole when the toy was pushed or pulled.*

Illus. 61: *Left – "Roly Poly" bear of brown burlap – in worn condition, 8in., circa 1896. Right: – Bristle-bear in burlap, elephant tag, 8in. (Pat. 1899).*

Illus. 62: *"Roly Poly" bear, 1898 onwards, with printed Steiff button, 1905, 13in.*

61

62

dancing bear was also offered in this early catalog.

1902 and 1903 were important years in the story of the toy factory. The animals were given movable joints! There is no hint or record anywhere as to who was responsible for the idea of these movable joints. One can only guess at the identity of the person or persons. One theory is that a wholesaler, a salesman, or even a member of the family, chanced to remark: "Why don't you make the animals' arms and legs move?" Another theory is that the "Doll-Boom" which had broken out in the nearby Thueringia district provided the necessary stimulus, since in order for a manufacturer to remain competitive, his dolls had to have movable joints.

It was Richard Steiff who tried out various methods to provide the animals with the desired flexibility. Not all animals were suitable for his experiments; only those which could be said to have similar movements to humans – (i.e. walking on two legs). For this the monkey and the bear were most suitable. The basis of these trial attempts seems to have been the sketches which Richard Steiff made at the Stuttgart Zoo and at the Hagenbeckschen Animal Circus during his student years. In his sketch pad he "immortalized" a family of bears. These drawings helped him to achieve true-to-life positions for the prototypes of his first plush animals. A whole series of animals with movable joints was available at the end of 1902; among these were a jointed monkey (Monkey 60 PB) and a jointed bear (Bear 55 PB).

Thus we know that "Bear 55 PB" and "Monkey 60 PB" were not single items! They belonged to a series of jointed toys which included both animals and dolls. The number 55 after the word "Bear" indicates the size (55 cm = 21.5in.). The "P" stands for plush, and the "B" for "beweglich" (which means jointed). The jointing on these early animals was very primitively achieved – were simply attached to the body by string.

At the beginning of 1903 a large container of sample toys, the latest in the program of the Giengen toy factory, was sent to a showroom in New York which was being run at that time by Paul Steiff. He had been sent there in order to promote the sale of Steiff toys in the United States.

Paul Steiff, a methodical archivist, listed in his journal exactly which animals had been included in this particular shipment. The S. S. Hannover, a ship of the North American Lloyd Line, transported five wooden crates across the ocean and these arrived in New York in mid-February 1903. Paul Steiff made a long, detailed list of the contents of Crate No. 3945 – at the end of which we find "Bear 55 PB". A handwritten note adds that one of these bears cost 4 Marks, a dozen cost 48 Marks, and therefore, the three dozen of this first shipment were worth a total of 144 Marks.

Paul Steiff was now responsible for promoting these toys of his aunt's – especially the bears. Yet no-one was really interested in them. The latest jointed toys from the little German toy factory were too expensive for the Americans. Paul Steiff returned to Germany a few months later, extremely disheartened. He had achieved nothing, and his report notes: ". . . and even our newest addition, the Plush Bear, appears to have been too large, too heavy and too hard to appeal as a child's toy. It was severely criticized and did not sell."

As Richard Steiff pointed out later to a journalist, even his aunt Margarete was not convinced of the appeal of the droll little Bear. He said: "Gretel Steiff did not place too much hope on the success of the Bear because of its high price."

In March 1903, at the Spring fair in Leipzig, the Steiff bear "Bear 55 PB" was shown in Germany for the ▶

	Spiz 28 siz	1	16,50	16,	50
	" 43	1/2	48.–	24	.–
	Has 17 siz M	1/12	9,60	.–	80
	Blumen Nad sort 3		4,50	13	50
	Bär 55 PB	1/12	48.–	4	
Kiste No 3944	277 69		M.	626	32
Kist	8.80 286,49	./. 10%		62	62
Kiste N. 3945	626,32		M.	563,	70

63

64

MARGARETE STEIFF ⁂ GIENGEN-BRENZ

Erste Filzspielwaren-Fabrik Deutschlands.

Neuheiten 1903-04.

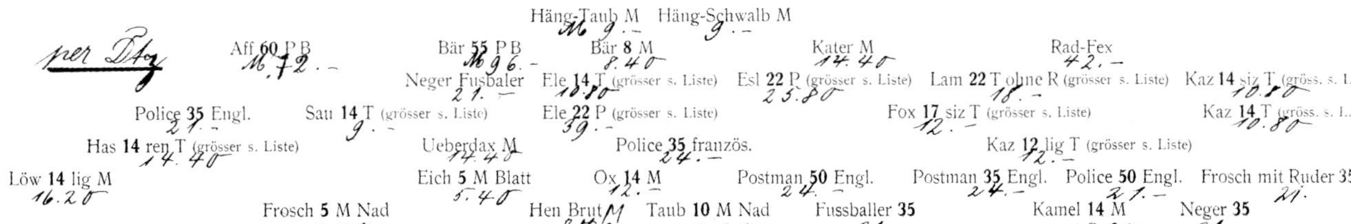

65

***Illus. 63**: A page torn out of the diary which Paul Steiff wrote during his stay in New York, 1902/1903. He was sent to establish the Steiff subsidiary in the United States. With meticulous accuracy he wrote down precisely which samples had arrived from Giengen. Thus we learn that as early as February/March 1903 the first jointed Steiff bear (Bear 55 PB), was already being offered to retail toy stores in New York.*

***Illus. 64**: Hermann Berg travelled regularly throughout Europe from 1896 onwards, as the Chief Buyer for the Toy Department of the George Borgfeldt & Co. Department Store, New York.*

***Illus. 65**: The latest novelties at the Leipzig Spring Fair, 1903. An absolute sensation: animals with swivel joints were presented for the first time. This photograph is the only document in existence which features the first Steiff bear. Explanation of text: P = Plush, PB = Plush, beweglich (Plush, jointed); T = Trikot stoff (stockinet material); M = Samt (velvet). The hand-written sales prices are for one dozen of each item.*

first time. However, here too, it was not a great success. Richard Steiff showed the bear to numerous buyers, but they all shrugged their shoulders regretfully. No-one wanted his bears.

At the end of the Fair, as the Steiff brothers were nailing their wooden crates closed, a buyer, Hermann Berg, from the Geo. Borgfeldt & Co. company (New York), chanced to come along. Steiff's official history recalls this memorable moment, which would later determine the success of the bear, thus: "He (Hermann Berg) was grumpy and complained that he had not found one really new item at the whole fair. He was looking for a nice, soft, cuddly new toy. Could they perhaps design something for him? Richard Steiff simply walked over to one of the half-open crates and pulled out a bear."

Hermann Berg was captivated and immediately ordered 3,000 of these bears. Whether he was ever able to sell the bears (and where) remains an undisclosed secret! On both sides of the ocean these first prototype bears seem to have disappeared and not one of them has ever been found and identified as a Steiff bear. "Bear 55 PB" is also missing from the otherwise complete Steiff Museum. It would be very difficult to recognise one of these first bears as a Steiff product. The only record available is a rather blurred catalog photograph which gives the impression of a dark, plump shape. It is probable that these early bears did not even have the Button-in-Ear, which would have helped with identification.

On July 13,1903, the pattern for the jointed bear was registered at the Court in Heidenheim. Some of the first bears which were made were sent to a showroom in Berlin, where they were available to anyone who wished to buy them. The owner of a large Berlin toy store, E. W. Matthes, recalled those early years and the "Bear Boom" in a trade journal dated 1925. He recounted this story of a business associate:

"How reserved, even faint-hearted, the members of our (toy) industry were, is illustrated by the following ▶

***Illus. 66**: Catalog photograph from 1908.*

***Illus. 67 + 69**: A view of the light, airy rooms at the Steiff Toy Factory (1903/1904) where the products were packed and stored, ready for shipment.*

story," he said. "I shall repeat here a story which was told by the owner of one of the leading Berlin toy stores at a conference for the industry. This toy-store owner was offered Steiff's first plush bears at 6 Marks each by a Berlin Warehouse. He decided to buy 4 bears. Once out in the street he hesitated, and thinking that perhaps the risk was too great – he returned to the warehouse and cancelled 2 of the 4 bears which he had ordered. As he walked down Leipzig Street he looked into my shop window and saw an improvised cage with ten of these lovely bears inside. He said to himself, 'Heavens, ten bears in the window! How many more inside?' He decided to go ahead with his original order for 4 bears after all."

Richard Steiff went to great pains to improve the bear "55 PB". His design became smaller and less plump, and the joints were improved. The bear was now made in light colored mohair plush. The shape of the new bear was not as true-to-life as the original "Bear 55 PB", but the jointed movement was greatly improved. On March 5,1904, this new model was registered as "Bär 35 PB".

***Illus.** 68: Advertisement and catalog photograph from 1906/1908.*

That same year Margarete Steiff sent her nephew Franz to the World's Fair in St. Louis. "Would the little bear be a success?" she worried. Her fears turned out to be groundless. Franz Steiff returned from the United States with his order-book full. The bear had achieved the desired breakthrough – and Margarete and Richard Steiff were awarded Gold Medals as a reward for their industry and effort. The company was also awarded the prestigious Grand Prix Award. At the end of the year the Steiff company could boast a proud total of 12,000 bears sold.

By now Steiff were determined to find a way to set themselves apart from their competitors. How were they to do this? The only way would be to ensure that their products were instantly and easily recognizable. Until 1900 an elephant with an "S" shaped trunk (for M. Steiff) was used as the business logo for the company. This ▸ 34

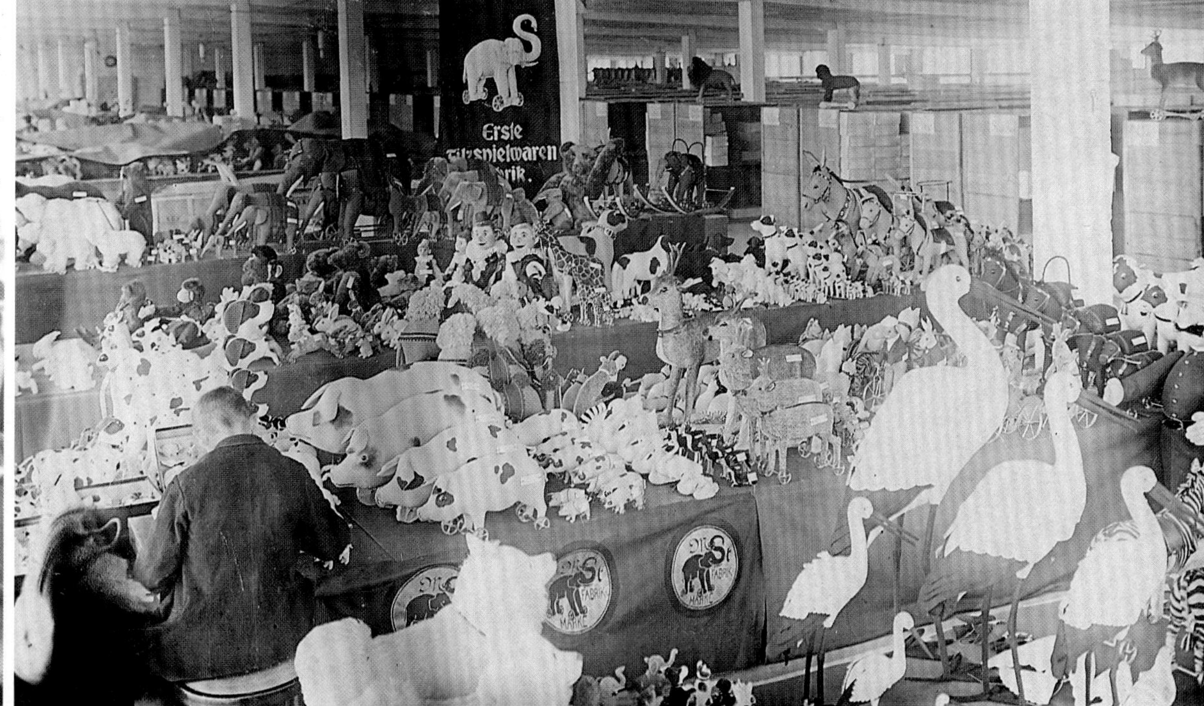

eft: Otto Steiff checking a packing list.

70

71

73

74

75

76

***Illus. 70-77**: The two earliest bears in the extensive Steiff archives are shown here in a "Bear hug". They were featured in advertisements circa 1905, and offered under the name "Bärle", (**Illus. 77**). The bear on the right is the model "35 PB", (= 35cm sitting, 50cm full length), which had its premier at the Leipzig Spring Fair in March 1904. His particular characteristics: twine thread-jointing through cardboard discs, shoebutton eyes, sealing-wax nose, excelsior filling. Weight 28oz. (ideal weight 33oz.). This bear is the revised model and successor of the first bear, "55 PB", which was made in dark brown plush. On the Left: Bear "28 PB"(= 11in. sitting, 16in. full length), which in turn is a further revision of "35 PB" and first saw the light of the "Bear world" in 1904/1905. His particular characteristic is the horizontal seam across his head – from ear to ear. The head was stuffed from the top and then the seam was handsewn. Shoe-button eyes, sealing-wax nose, 19oz. (Ideal weight 18oz.). The X-Ray shows clearly the metal rods used for jointing (Patent No. DRGM 255 036, June 18, 1905 = "axis or rod having the distinct advantage of adhering securely to moving objects"). These detailed photographs (**Illus. 73-76**) show the numerous poses which were possible for bear "28 PB" to assume. – A further example of "28 PB" from 1905 **(Illus. 71)** actually has the "elephant button" in his left ear **(Illus. 70)**. His characteristics: 11in. sitting height, 16in. full length, 17oz. (18oz. ideal weight), shoe-button eyes, remains of sealing-wax nose, metal-rod jointing, horizontal seam from ear to ear. – This metal-rod jointing has not only been found in bears but has also been seen in elephants and dolls, and was also used for other Steiff articles with movable joints.*

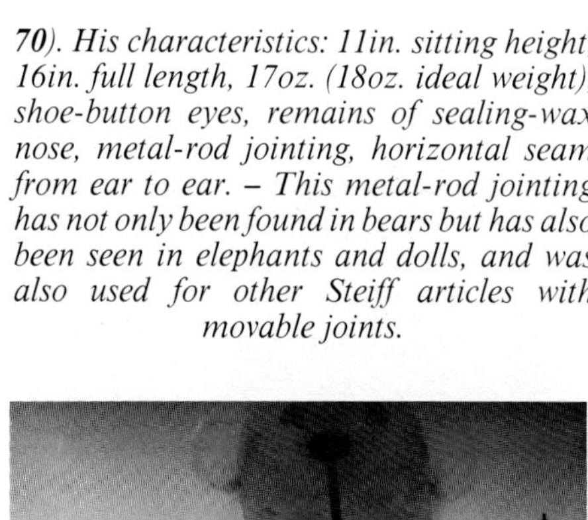

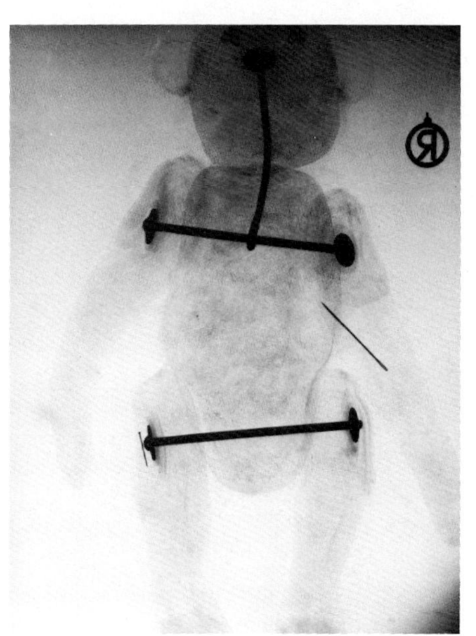

72

77

elephant was also printed onto small cardboard labels and fastened onto the body or clothing of the animals and dolls. But these labels were easily torn and lost, and then one could not be certain whether the item was from the Steiff company.

Franz Steiff, searching for a more permanent means of identification, finally hit upon the "Button-in-Ear" idea. At first the toys were issued with a small blank button inserted into the left ear – but these blank buttons were quickly substituted for a button embossed with the elephant. This button-in-ear was so easily recognized that it quickly came to be associated with Steiff products.

Margarete Steiff states in a newsletter to her customers: "Trademark – (Elephant with "S" shaped trunk). As of November 1, 1904, I shall identify each article without exception, with a small nickel-plated button in the left ear. Our logo is stamped on these buttons and is legally protected."

However, the German Patent Office was of a different opinion. They insisted that a "Button" in the ear could not be legally protected by a patent. Steiff found it very hard to accept this decision. The company attorney in Berlin, Herr Zeisig, offered advice which found a way around the problem. He suggested that they apply for a patent on the words "Button-in-Ear" rather than on the button itself. This was accepted by the Patent Office. The trademark "Button-in-Ear" was registered on Dec. 20, 1904 in the U.S.A. The Patent was legally confirmed in writing on May 13, 1905. The "Button-in-Ear" was on its way!

An archivist reporting Steiff's 50th Jubilee states: "It was certainly a wonderful idea to give each Steiff animal a button in the ear. And with single-minded promotion, it has been possible to have our trademark associated in the minds of the public, with childrens' toys of the finest quality."

Illus. 78: *"Bärle" (PAB 35 = 14in. sitting, 20in. full length) soft filled, shoe-button eyes, sealing-wax nose, circa 1905.*

Illus. 79: *Advertisement, 1905.*

Illus. 80: *Original drawing of a bear for a Steiff advertisement.*

This remains true, even today; only a manufacturer with confidence in the quality of his products could allow himself such an easily identifiable trademark.

Even the trade magazines were approving. The "Directory for the Toy, Fancy-Goods and Haberdashery Industry" reported in an article on the Steiff Company: "There will probably never be any faulty item found with this trademark. This shows clearly just how critically the owner (Margarete Steiff) watches over the work in her large factory and just what pains she is prepared to take in order to secure her products in the favor of the public."

In Giengen, however, the jointed animals were still causing headaches! Further experiments were undertaken. The jointed arms and legs had to be improved upon. The heavy thread which went from the outside of the limbs through to the body soon proved impractical. After being played with for just a short time, the thread became loose and the arms and legs hung slackly on the body. A similar method of attaching the joints using wire instead of thread proved to be too dangerous; children could cut themselves on the ends of the wires which were visible on the outside of the arms and legs.

On December 6, 1904, the solution to their problem seemed closer at hand. The Margarete Steiff Co., was granted a patent (No. DRGM 242 399) for: "Toys with movable joints connected on the inside of the body by double wires".

Although they were still using wires for attaching the limbs, they had found a less dangerous method. The ends of the wires were pushed through the joints and into the body from both sides. They were then twisted together. This twisted piece of wire was hidden inside the body, and covered by the filling material.

A second way of fixing the joints was patented on June 8, 1905. This was a firm metal rod passing through the body to the arms and ▶

legs. Steiff advertised this method thus: "... with endless possibilities for movement. Patented."

Whilst the first Steiff bear, "55 PB", was seen for the last time in the Price-List of February 1, 1904, the "Bear 35 PB" with simple "thread" jointing continued to be offered. At the end of 1904 a smaller version of this bear was added. This was the "Bear 28 PB" which was only offered for one year. This bear had the newly patented metal-rod jointing, shoe-button eyes, a long pointed snout with a nose of sealing-wax, and was marked with an elephant button in its left ear.

It is important to note that between 1904 and 1905 only these two types of bear were offered in the Steiff Program. One can identify them not only by their outward appearance but also by their weight and size (like all early bears!). The bear "28 PB" weighed 580 grams (about 25oz.) and was 16in. long. The bear "35 PB" weighed 1,050 grams (about 35oz.) and was 20in. long. A slight reduction in weight was possible because of the drying out of the excelsior.

Margarete Steiff and her nephews studied the finished bears time and time again. Surely it was possible to make the bears more appealing to children? The family group were still unhappy with the bear's appearance.

Richard Steiff designed numerous bears and finally surprised his aunt at the beginning of 1905 with a "New-look" bear, which was to become the "Teddy-bear" and cause a worldwide sensation. It was more like a "bear-doll" than a real bear; with movable joints, a less pointed, stitched nose and a rounder face.

Margarete Steiff was enthralled. On February 12, 1905 she registered the bear as Patent number "Bear 35 PAB". The bear is found in a Price-List dated August 15, 1905 under the name "Bärle" (an affectionate term used to denote something or someone dear); "Bärle" was offered in several sizes:

PAB 5317,1 10in./ 4oz.
PAB 5322,1 13in./10oz.
PAB 5328,1 16in./14 oz.
PAB 5335,1 20in./ 1lb.8oz
PAB 5343,1 23in./ 2lb.4oz.
PAB 5350,1 28in./ 3lb.
PAB 5380,1 45in./12lb.

A new system of numbering the toys can be found in this 1905 catalog which includes "Bärle". This newly adopted numerical system was easily deciphered. It also clarified the exact materials, size, movement etc. of each Steiff article. For example, if we take the number PAB 5317,1 we can read it as: "P" = plush; "A" = angeschiebt (disc jointed); "B" = beweglich (movable). If we take the number "5317": "5" = beweglich (movable); "3" = mohair; "17" = cm size (measured in sitting position); "1" after a comma originally meant extra-soft filling but after 1913 it represented the squeeze-box growler.

At this time no-one had any idea that "Bärle" was about to take the world of toys by storm! He was soft-filled, with excelsior and kapok, much lighter than his predecessor, and his arms and legs were disc-jointed, like all future generations of Steiff bears including those of the present day. This meant that the jointing was now achieved using round discs of heavy cardboard placed inside the limbs and body, and held together tightly by a metal pin. "Bärle", like the "PB" Series of bears was of high-quality mohair and was available in dark brown, light brown and white. The left ear was marked with the elephant-button, and in 1905/1906 this was replaced by the printed "Steiff" button.

A few of the bears had squeeze-box voices, as did the monkey, "60 PB". These voice boxes were of leather, with a sturdy mechanical movement which worked by pressing the backs of the animals. In 1908 an automatic growler (which worked by tilting the animal's head forward) was mentioned in the catalog.

***Illus. 81:** Advertisement, 1906.*

At Steiff a new period of development began. The program now offered over 1,000 articles. In the year 1907, 975,000 bears were made, 400 people worked at the factory and a further 1,800 home-workers were employed by Margarete Steiff. Steiff bears were being made everywhere – from Burgau in Bavaria, to Dillingen in the Donau Valley; from Neresheim in Hertsfeld to Schwäbisch Gmund in Remstal!

The demand for bears increased daily especially in the U.S.A. after 1905. Never before had a single toy created such furore! In fact, the American President Theodore Roosevelt, was largely responsible for the success of the Steiff bear. Roosevelt called "Teddy" by his friends, was an avid hunter. Through his many hunting escapades, and the stories which grew up around these hunting trips, he was the best advertisement the little plush bear could have.

The association began innocently with a cartoon in the ▸ 38

82

83

***Illus. 82-84**: After a great deal of experimenting and several improvements, Richard Steiff was finally satisfied with his prototype for the now famous "Teddy-bear". A typical characteristic of his little gray bear was the round face with the "blunted" snout and stitched nose. This design remained almost unaltered, and was produced from 1905, until 1951. Richard Steiff gave the bear in this photograph (his personal model) to his mother-in-law, Frau Dehlinger; and in 1942 she consigned them to the Steiff archives. Only two examples of the bear are known to have been made in gray plush. It is possible that this color was used for a few hand-made samples and not for an actual series. This bear is the model "5322" (= 13in.) which came out as a novelty in 1905. He has shoe button eyes, a horizontally stitched nose, and growler. In order to promote the new Steiff Teddy-bears in England Richard Steiff posed for photographs with his hand-made prototype bear and several other Steiff products (1909). This photograph was believed to have been lost; the authors "re-discovered" it among glass-negatives in the Steiff archives.*

84

85

DRAWING THE LINE IN MISSISSIPPI

86

***Illus. 86:** The famous cartoon by Clifford K. Berryman showing President Roosevelt, and in the background, the little bear-cub. Published in the "Washington Post", Nov. 1902.*

***Illus. 85:** President Roosevelt and his family in Sagamore Hill, Oyster Bay, U.S.A.. From left to right: Kermet, Archie, the President, Ethel, Mrs.Roosevelt, Quentin and Theodore jr.*

"Washington Post". In November 1902 the artist, Clifford K. Berryman, drew a caricature of "Teddy" Roosevelt on one of his hunting trips. A tiny, helpless, bear-cub was being dragged along on a leash for the President to shoot. Roosevelt naturally refused to shoot the cub, and turned away in disgust. This cartoon was so well received by the readers of the "Post" that Berryman adopted a little bear-cub for all future cartoons involving Roosevelt. (Editors note: Berryman, who went down in history as "The Teddy-bear Man" used the little bear-cub in his drawings until well into the 1930s, together with "Uncle Sam" – the personalised symbol of the U.S.A.

"Teddy" Roosevelt's increasing popularity, and the continuation of Berryman's cartoons were the best promotion the Teddy-bear could have. It is hardly surprising therefore, that the cuddly little Steiff bear, which slowly but surely captivated the American continent, was quickly renamed "Teddy's bear" – and then in 1906, "Teddy-bear". In the space of a few months the Teddy-bear became the darling of the nation and President Roosevelt's name was to be associated with the Teddy-bear forever after.

The Americans adopted the Teddy-bear as a mascot which openly declared their love and respect for their President. Roosevelt was born in 1858, and after studying in Germany he returned home to go into politics. He began as Police Superintendent, was later elected governor of New York, and after MacKinley was assassinated in 1901, he became President of the United States of America.

Roosevelt was from one of the most respected families in America. The "Berliner Illustrirte Zeitung" (Berlin Illustrated Newspaper) wrote: "More than any other person, he represents the modern American; with all his hopes and aspirations, his ideals and his feelings. He is a firebrand and a calculating statesman at the same time. A hero of both the sword and the pen, he knows how to impose his own personality on each situation he faces and each office he is given." The newspaper went on to compare him to the German Kaiser, Wilhelm II, and remarked that these two great men could exchange places at any time because of the obvious similarity of their temperaments.

Roosevelt had America at his feet and as a result, "Teddy-bear mania" swept through the country. In 1911 the Leipzig "Illustrated News" noted in a review: "Children throughout the whole of the United States have taken the plush Teddy-bear into their hearts and incorporated him in their dreams, ladies carry him gently in their arms, and men are taking him into their clubrooms." ▶

The Teddy-bear became a cult figure and a fetish at the same time. He was a fashion accessory for ladies, companion on motoring journeys, and even accompanied his owners on shopping trips. On such expeditions Teddy had to be suitably "dressed", so it was not long before he had outfits to match each occasion. He was even seen with jewels as the U.S. magazine "Playthings" reported in an article in 1906.

A similar success was soon seen in Germany. Here, too, the Teddy won more and more admirers – both young and old. The German Magazine "Handarbeit" relates: "In the drawing-rooms of artists and intellectuals the Teddy-bear can be found sitting on the sofa or next to the desk; actors and actresses are unable to perform if Teddy is not nearby. A famous opera singer forgot her Teddy when she drove to the Opera House one evening and her chauffeur had to return to the house immediately, to collect the forgotten bear. The start of the Opera was delayed as the singer insisted she would only begin her performance after her Teddy-bear had arrived."

There are many stories of supposed meetings between Theodore Roosevelt and the Teddy-bear, there are even those publicized by the Steiff company themselves – for the purpose of advertising.

One story relates that President Roosevelt's daughter used Teddy-bears to decorate the table at her wedding reception in the White House; another tells of a party for the President arranged by hunting colleagues, again using teddy-bears as decoration. Neither of these stories has any documented proof, either in the archives at the White House or at the Theodore Roosevelt Museum. These stories were surely the clever idea of Herr Vallendor, Publicity Chief of the Steiff company at that time. He circulated the stories when none of the people involved were around to contradict them.

Only one story of an "actual meeting" between the President and the Steiff Teddy-bear can be corroborated. In 1910 Roosevelt returned to Washington from a safari in Africa, and held a reception for those people who had accompanied him. Each guest found a little Steiff Teddy-bear at his place as a small token of thanks.

After the Roosevelt era, William H. Taft became the new U.S. President in 1909. He was a minion of Roosevelt's and the newspapers featured him in cartoons as Roosevelt's Teddy-bear puppet. Taft, eager to get rid of his Teddy-bear image, decided to distance himself from the ex-President. The pair became extremely hostile towards one another.

However, the American press were not keen to relinquish their popular Presidential mascot, so when Taft provided them with an opportunity to replace the Roosevelt Teddy-bear they responded quickly. At a dinner party which was held in Taft's honor in Atlanta, Georgia, one item on the menu was "Opossum aux patates" (Opossum with sweet potatoes). Taft was so fond of this dish that he praised it unequivocally and the press clutched thankfully at this straw. "Billy Possum" was born.

Steiff followed the media's lead and in 1909 they registered a pattern for an Opossum. "Billy Possum" was made for five years, until 1914, but he could not compete with the success of the Teddy-bear. 10,028 Opossums were sold the first year, but in the following four years only a few hundred were sold yearly. "Billy Possum's" short success could not match the Teddy-bear's popularity.

Back to the Teddy-bear. Had the Steiff company originally designed the Teddy-bear solely to conquer the American market? (For it was certainly thanks to the Berryman cartoons that the bear became popular almost overnight in the U.S..) The question must be answered in the negative. No! The ▶

87

Illus. 87: Caricature from the "Daily Dispatch" of November 1908. William Taft, newly elected U.S. President, protegee of his predecessor, "Teddy" Roosevelt; was shown as the "Teddy-bear's" successor. In this sketch he is featured with the American "national hero", Uncle Sam. The words, "For Uncle Sam – A present from Teddy" are clearly visible on the box in the foreground. This newspaper clipping carries a hand-written remark by someone at Steiff: "Onkel Sam bitte als Neuheit machen" ("Please make Uncle Sam as a novelty"). Illus. 88: The "Onkel Sam" doll was registered in 1904. It had a velvet face, and felt body (blue torso, red, white and blue striped pants) and wore a gray hat with blue band. The doll was 20in. tall. Illus. 89: Cartoon from the British magazine Punch, March 1909, after U.S. President Taft had severed connections with Roosevelt. Punch: Taft proves his independence – by breaking away from "Teddy" (bear) Roosevelt.

88

HIS INDEPENDENCE DAY.

89

birth of the Teddy-bear in far-away Giengen was purely coincidence.
"The stars were favorable" remarked one Steiff worker in a handwritten note. The Teddy-bear had needed a two year development period (from 1903 until 1905) to perfect his final appearance. He evolved without outside influence. No-one, neither Teddy-designer Richard Steiff, nor namesake and godfather, Theodore Roosevelt, could possibly have imagined that the soft-filled bear of 1905 would achieve the popularity which is his today: "There is only one Teddy-bear, which has been equally loved by each new generation – the Steiff bear."
Naturally there are others who claim to have been the first on the market with a Teddy-bear. They claim that the Steiff bear is a plagiarism. They have never been able to, nor will they be able to find any credible proof for these claims. They use transparently obvious imitations of the Steiff advertising slogans. In the world of commerce these people, who ride on the crest of each new wave and prefer to jump on the bandwagon rather than attempt a more individual approach, are held in contempt by the majority. They are always around when someone else has achieved success – most of them are motivated by greed and envy.
As early as 1908, Steiff felt the need to inform customers of their copyrights. A newsletter sent to all customers read: "For the Leipzig Exhibition you will receive a new Price-List with information on all Steiff cloth animals (including the Original Teddy-bear Series) at new reduced prices. These jointed bears, which have become world famous ▶

90

91

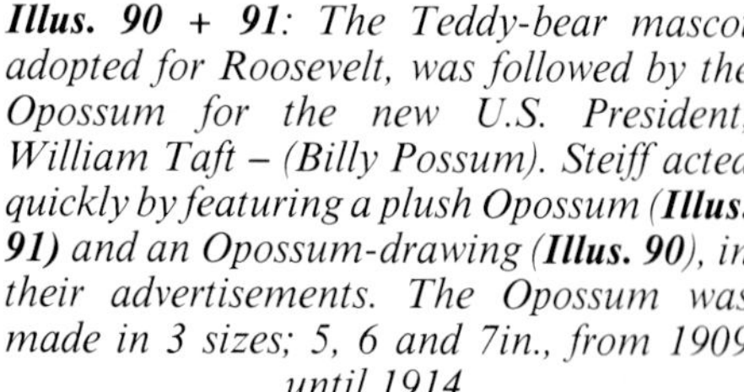

*Illus. 90 + 91: The Teddy-bear mascot adopted for Roosevelt, was followed by the Opossum for the new U.S. President, William Taft – (Billy Possum). Steiff acted quickly by featuring a plush Opossum (**Illus. 91)** and an Opossum-drawing (**Illus. 90**), in their advertisements. The Opossum was made in 3 sizes; 5, 6 and 7in., from 1909 until 1914.*

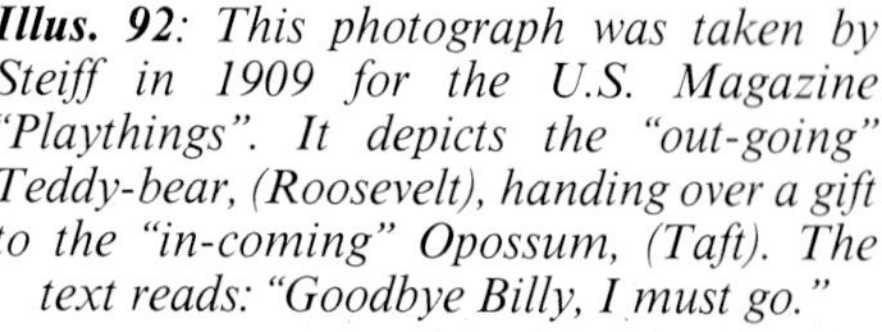

***Illus. 92**: This photograph was taken by Steiff in 1909 for the U.S. Magazine "Playthings". It depicts the "out-going" Teddy-bear, (Roosevelt), handing over a gift to the "in-coming" Opossum, (Taft). The text reads: "Goodbye Billy, I must go."*

93

94

"I beg to announce", he said with a bow,
"America is my country now;
My service is here, at her command,
Though I dearly love my fatherland."

"If it please you all, and my hostess fair,
I would like to speak", said the German Bear.
"I'm glad the good Queen Isabel
Sold the jewels she loved so well,
That sent Columbus across the sea;
I'm glad that Washington made you free."

***Illus. 93-95**: Teddy-bear "fever" in America. In 1907, "Mr. Cinnamon-Bear", one of the first Teddy-bear books to be published, was written by Sara Tawney-Lefferts. Her book was based on the cinnamon colored Steiff bears made for the U.S. market. The story told in this little book centers around a little cinnamon bear which is presented to other dolls and children at a special tea-party given by a little girl named Dorothy Vandervare. The highlight of the book (for Steiff) is a reference to Margarete Steiff.*

95

Sarah Tawney-Lefferts "Mr. Cinnamon-Bear":

"Then they sent three cheers across the sea,
To a little old lady in Germany
Who started the Bears on their Career,
Who fashioned them first and sent them here;
And three cheers more for their hostess fair –
For little Miss Dorothy Vandevare."

96

Illus. 96: *This advertisement published in the "Wegweiser" (Pathfinder) on February 10, 1906, by the Heinr. Silberstein Co., Berlin, led to a legal conflict between Silberstein and the Margarete Steiff Toy Company, Giengen.*

under the name Teddy-bears, are made from our own unique design. The pattern did not come from America, neither did the idea!"

Almost from the beginning the toy industry has existed on copies and reproductions. Neither the Patent, nor the copyright, nor the registered pattern were respected among competitors in the toy industry. Hundreds of court cases in the last 130 years of the toy industry's history are proof of this. Whenever a company was responsible for bringing a successful article onto the market they could expect cheaper copies to appear soon afterwards.

This is precisely what happened to the Steiff company with the Teddy-bear. Competition sprang up everywhere in 1905; especially in the Sonneberg/Neustadt region, in Nuremberg, and in Berlin. The American buyers had to pay a great deal of money for Steiff toys – for quality has always had its price! Therefore it is hardly surprising to learn that resourceful buyers were soon travelling to Sonneberg and Neustadt with Steiff Teddy-bears under their arms. They searched out small family businesses and placed orders for hundreds of thousands of Teddy-bear copies. In Neustadt two factories were started up at this time simply to produce the excelsior used for filling the Teddy-bear copies!

In America the demand for Teddy-bears was immediately recognized, and the profitable possibilities easily calculated. The first American Teddy-bears were produced sometime between 1906 and 1907. The problem of achieving the same high standard of quality as the Germans was dealt with discreetly. The American advertisements read: "Exact replicas" or "Exactly like the Imported Version". The American, "Ideal Novelty Co.," advertised in "Playthings" magazine in 1908: "Why send to Europe for your animals when you can buy them here for half the price? Our bear is an exact reproduction of the foreign model. Made of the finest plush. . ." What this advertisement failed to state was that the plush and the voice boxes were imported from Germany!

Margarete Steiff tried to protect her company. She wanted to distance herself from the bothersome plagiarists of the industry – the copycat professionals.

She turned to the retailers and pointed out in her advertisements that all animals and dolls which left the Steiff factory would carry the "Button-in-Ear" trademark.

"Those people familiar with my products will not mistake these cheaper, low quality articles, for mine. If the bears recommended above have been copied, I ask that my honored customers provide me with evidence. Only articles which carry our 'Button-in-Ear' trade-mark are truly long-lasting and artistically attractive toys."

The "Leipzig Illustrated News"

97

Illus. 97 + 98: *Original Steiff photograph (**Illus. 97**). An illustration from Heinrich Silberstein's catalog, Berlin, (**Illus. 98**). Silberstein registered a Patent in 1906 for a "bear with velvet paws, limbs jointed to the body by a double-split pin." Thus the entry: "Ges. Geschützt" (Legal Patent) under the bears.*

98

wrote: "For the toy industry's agents in New York, the old Württemberg town of Giengen on-the-Brenz soon came to represent the hub of the industry and so it happened that in 1907 approximately one million dollars were transferred from the U.S. to Giengen. This was quite apart from the huge sums which were sent to other towns in Germany as payment for copies of the original toys."

Margarete Steiff decided to set an example. She was particulary aggravated by the Heinrich Silberstein Company, Naunynstrasse 39, Berlin, who were blatantly unashamed both in their imitation of Steiff toys and in their advertising. In the trade magazine, "Wegweiser" they unscrupulously laid claim to their "unbreakable toy animals". Their advertisement featured a dog, a rabbit and a jointed bear. In a letter dated February 14, 1906, Margarete Steiff wrote to her attorney, Herr Zeisig, in Berlin: "It is worth doing something about this case. It is patently obvious . . . I do not want to let this pass without going to Court, for I want this to be taken as a warning by other offenders."

She also wrote to the Silberstein Company: "I wish to warn you against any future infringement of the copyright laws . . . and ask that you immediately stop production of the items mentioned." Further more she asked the newspapers to refuse any advertising text relating to these items. At first Silberstein refused to acknowledge the existence of a copyright protecting the Steiff bears, but he had to concede defeat when he received copies of the pattern numbers registered at the Court at Heidenheim.

What had Margarete Steiff thus achieved? Unfortunately, not much. The advertising of imitation toys was brought to a halt but the production of these copies carried on. Everywhere!

Steiff had now reached the pinnacle of success and they were hardly able to fulfill all the orders which they received, both from home and abroad. The year was 1907 – America was hit by a severe economic depression. The "Bear Industry" was not spared the effects of this recession. The results appeared to be catastrophic; the numerous orders for bears which had been completed and were stored ready for shipment, were cancelled immediately by the American buyers. The huge quantities of mohair which the Steiff company had ordered had to be collected and paid for. "One had to be vigilant and enterprising in order to withstand this setback."

***Illus. 99**: From the catalog of the Wilhelm Strunz Mechanical, Felt and Cloth Toy Company, Nuremberg, 1904.*

Although this economic slump was relatively short-lived it affected everyone; and the sudden paucity within the market aggravated the competitive situation still further. It was hardly surprising that the relationship among manufacturers became even more aggressive in the fight to secure a place on the market and to maintain a reasonable income.

Many of Steiff's competitors tried to think up imaginative ways of usurping the Button-in-Ear trademark. For example, on March 21, 1908, the toy manufacturer Deuerlein of Nuremberg, received a letter from Herr Bertelsmann of the Dept. of Trademarks, Royal Patent Office, informing him that his application for a trademark "Ring-in-Ear" had been rejected.

At the beginning of 1908 the felt toy manufacturer Wilhelm Strunz, of Nuremberg, surpassed all the other plagiarists with his blatant disregard for the copyright laws. He was not simply content to copy Steiff Teddy-bears, animals and dolls, he used an almost identical catalog photograph to advertise his products and even gave his toys a button-in-ear. Franz Steiff went to Nuremberg to represent his company. He spoke to the owners, Mr. and Mrs. Strunz and asked them to discontinue their infringements. However, nothing came of the meeting and the Strunz products continued to be marked with a six-sided metal button in the left ear to which a thin white paper tag was attached. The name of the product was printed on these tags.

Steiff dismissed all arguments out of hand: "In order to secure the tag one does not need a button; a piece of thread or a staple would serve the purpose equally well." They went on: "By simply removing the cardboard tag these toys of poor quality (from the Strunz factory) could be mistaken for the respected Steiff articles." In other words, if an unscrupulous toy salesman deliberately removed a Strunz tag, he would then be able to claim he was selling the more expensive Steiff version.

Attorneys were hired, and the disagreement resulted in a preliminary hearing. Declarations were made by both parties, and statements, pages long, were written. Strunz insisted that he needed the trademark in order to distinguish his articles from those of lesser quality – sold by his competitors. Steiff remained firm:

100 ***Illus. 100**: Photograph of bears (1922) by Paul Steiff, intended to compare Steiff Bears with their American counterparts. The bears far right, middle, and far left are probably products of the "Ideal Novelty Company, Brooklyn, N.Y..".*

"We have all product copyrights for the 'Button-in-Ear' trademark."

After months of arguing backwards and forwards the parties reached an agreement on October 28, 1908. Strunz was allowed to attach his paper tag in the left ear; however, he was ordered to secure the tag with a staple. A sample of a plush ear, complete with staple and tag was filed with the papers.

Strunz himself soon lost interest in this compromise since it was of little value without the button-in-ear. He used a different method to outsmart the Steiff company; from 1910 onwards all his Teddy bears were marked with the word "Präsident" (President).

Steiff could not compete. The terms "Teddy" and "Teddy-bear" could not be legally protected as the German Patent Office had already rejected their earlier application for this copyright. An incomprehensible decision as far as Steiff was concerned, for it meant that each of their competitors could sell their products as a "Teddy-bear".

Steiff, however, left no stone unturned in their efforts to get around the problem – they were even prepared to circumvent the law if necessary. They wanted to develop a growler which would sound like the word "Teddy" when the bellows were operated. Their patent attorney Zeisig, in Berlin, wrote to inform them, on November 7, 1907, that: "the voice as such" could not be patented. This attempt ended unsuccessfully, just as Steiff's effort to patent a "Kaiserhasen" (Kaiser Rabbit) was rejected.

Nevertheless, the company in Giengen was quick to learn. Strunz had no sooner abandoned his idea of using a stapled tag in the left ear, when Steiff decided to adopt the idea themselves. From this time on all Steiff products were marked with a small tag in the left ear, fixed of course, with the patented "Button-in-Ear". These tags were of hard-wearing cloth and were printed with the name, product number and symbol of the item. This system is still used today.

The Bing Company in Nuremberg was probably the largest toy manufacturer in the world at this time and now they also ▸ 55

101 ***Illus. 101**: Advertising 1906/07.*

102

›F IM OHR

Spielwarenfabrik Margarete Steiff, G. m. b. H., Giengen-Brenz (Württemberg).
Erfinder und Fabrikanten des weltberühmten „Teddy-Bären“.
Überall zu haben. Schutzmarke: Knopf im Ohr. Katalog No. 20 gratis. Kein direkter Versand an Private.

M OHR“ aus Glanzplüsch, weiss, hell- und dunkelbraun. Kopf und Glieder drehbar. In Grössen von 10 bis 115 cm und Preislagen von M. –.75 bis 56.–.

***Illus. 102**: Advertisement in the “Illustrirte Zeitung”, January 15, 1914.*

103

104

105

106

***Illus. 103-108**: Seymour Eaton's Teddy-bear series, "The Roosevelt Bears – Travel and Adventures" was first published in 1906. Two bears (**Illus. 106**) are featured throughout the ten chapters in the series. "Teddy B" (B = Black or Brown) and "Teddy G" (G = Grizzly or Gray). Steiff promptly produced bears which were equally well-dressed. In their 1907/1908 catalog (**Illus. 103**), a teddy in a striped sweater, marked "Teddy G" was available. – The two postcards illustrated here (**Illus. 104 + 105**) featured a complete series of "dressed" Steiff bears, which were offered under the labels: "Baru" (in felt "ruched" dress: red, white or blue); "Batro" (in sweater and striped cap); "Babad" (in knitted bathing costume, with horizontal stripes); "Baho" (in navy blue felt*

107

*pants with red suspenders); "Babo" (in boys romper); "Bagi" (in girls romper); "Basa" (in sailor suit) "Basi" (in blue felt sailor dress). A Teddy-bear named "Teddybu" in white, gold, or dark brown plush, wearing a red or blue felt vest was manufactured until well into the 1920s. – In 1907, John W. Bratton composed the "Two-Step". This instrumental dance music was an instant hit. The British songwriter, Jimmy Kennedy wrote the text for the music in 1930 – his "Teddy-bear's Picnic" has gone down in the history of the Teddy-bear. The song was recorded by Bing Crosby and came to be regarded as an "inside tip" among Teddy-bear collectors in the 70s and 80s (and a copy of the record is presented with the luxury limited edition of this book). This photograph of a "Teddy-bears' Picnic" was taken in 1912 in Steiff's own studio in Giengen, (**Illus. 107**). – This "Sailor-Teddy" (**Illus. 108**) in white mohair with brown stiched nose and shoe-button eyes, is 29in. tall and in mint condition. He has a printed Steiff button and white tag with the number "5350".*

108

109

110

111

112

***Illus. 109-116**: Soon after his "birth", the Teddy-bear was available in dark brown, white and beige. In 1909 also available in gold. Special orders by English Buyers for bears with glass eyes (1908 onwards), at an additional charge, or, black Teddy-bears, (1912/1913). Here are a variety of Teddy-bears available at this time. – **Illus. 109**: Beige bear, largest, No. "5325" (10in. sitting; 14in. standing) with glass eyes and growler; the middle sized bear, No. "5320" (8in. sitting; 12in. standing), and the smallest bear, No. "5313" (5in. sitting; 8in. standing), both with shoe-button eyes. All three bears have stitched noses. – **Illus. 110**: Dark brown bear, No. "5332, 2" (12/18in. – the ",2" indicates a growler), glass eyes, stitched nose, Steiff button and tag. – **Illus. 111**: Light gold bear, No. "3332" (12/18in.) shoebutton eyes,*

113

114

115

116

*stitched nose, Steiff button. – **Illus. 112**: This scene shows an "Animal merchant" offering the first small Steiff bears (1909); 4in. and 1910 (6in.) – **Illus. 113**: Black mohair bear with light colored felt pads, No. "5335"(14/19in.), special order for the English market (from 1912), in two designs and five sizes. (short mohair plush, "Sealskin", 1,214 bears produced; mohair – 494 bears produced). – **Illus. 115**: Black bear, No. "5228"(11/16in.) in short plush. This example from the Steiff archives has shoe button eyes and a sealing-wax nose. All other black bears found have had stitched noses and shoebutton eyes with a circle of red felt underneath. – **Illus. 115 + 116**: Bears in white mohair have always been prized. This plush veteran is No. "5332" (12in.) with glass eyes and stitched nose.*

117

120

***Illus. 117-122**: "Muzzle" bears were advertised as "novelties" in 1908 (**Illus. 117**). Made in 10 sizes in light and dark brown. – **Illus. 118**: Specially produced for the American election in 1913, were the red, white and blue Teddy-bears in the U. S. national colors. Sold under the name "Bär Dolly" (Dolly-Bear), No. "5320"(= 20/30cm, 8/12in.). This bear has the Steiff button and a white tag. (Yellow and green bears were also made). The bear's head was always white; all bears had a colored neck ruff, and were fitted with the new squeeze voice-boxes – "Hugmi". These bears were available in three sizes 10, 12 and 13in.) (1913 until 1916 = 6,015 manufactured). Altogether, a total of 6,015 were manufactured. – **Illus. 119**: Dolly-bear in training. – **Illus. 120**: A real novelty in 1907, was a 20in. bear with the No. "5335b". The bear's body was fully lined, and the front seam was left open. The bear could be closed by lacing up hooks on either side of his tummy – in much the same way as ladies boots were fastened. The "empty" tummy contained a metal hot-water tin. The Teddy "hot water bottle" was expected to be a "hot" seller. A bear for children to cuddle up to on*

118

121

*cold nights – but surprisingly there was very little interest in the bear. From 1907 until 1914, a total of only 90 bears were made. – **Illus. 121**: shaggy bear without wheels, No. 1328,01 (= 28 cm/11in. high, 01 = doubled-voice growler), long haired, white or brown mohair, extra soft filling in four sizes, 7, 9, 11, and 14in.. A very popular bear, which was in great demand. – **Illus. 122**: This photograph of a bear-leader presenting a Teddy-bear, complete with muzzle and leading-strap, to an interested doll audience (1912/1913).*

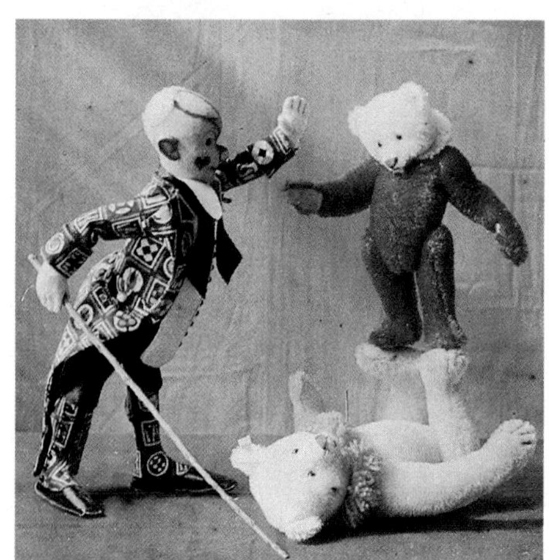

119

122

***Illus. 123**: Paul and Richard Steiff were honored to receive an award from the organizers of the World's Fair, 1904, in St. Louis/U.S.A.. They were asked to provide the decoration for the entrance to the Toy Exhibition Hall so the brothers built a triple archway, on which 24 Steiff clowns in international costume were fixed. Each clown was 39in. tall. Two police dolls in American uniform guarded the entrance; they were also 39in. tall. The photograph illustrated here is the only document which remains to tell of this extraordinary order.*

124

***Illus. 124-131**: Franz Steiff looked after the Steiff company's stand at the World's Fair, 1904, in St. Louis. Alice Roosevelt, daughter of the American president, (**Illus. 124**) visited the German Pavillion, and without doubt, she visited the Steiff display at the same time. Grand Prix Medals were awarded to the Steiff Company (**Illus. 126 + 127**) in St. Louis, and Margarete and Richard Steiff also received personal Gold Medals. At the World's Fair in Brussels, 1910, The Steiff Company shared an exhibition stand with the Maerklin Company of Goeppingen (**Illus. 128**), a joint partnership at international events, and one which lasted for many decades and is still enjoyed today. Naturally Steiff were also awarded a Grand Prix Medal in Brussels (**Illus. 129**). Documents show that in 1906, Steiff were also awarded prizes in Frankfurt and Berlin (**Illus. 130 + 131**).*

UNITED·STATES·OF·AMERICA
UNIVERSAL·EXPOSITION·SAINT·LOUIS·MDCCCCIV
COMMEMORATING·THE·ACQUISITION·OF·THE·LOUISIANA·TERRITORY
THE·INTERNATIONAL·JURY·OF·AWARDS·HAS·CONFERRED·A
GRAND·PRIZE
UPON
MARGARETE STEIFF · GIENGEN-BRENZ
TOYS AND STUFFED ANIMALS

DIRECTOR OF EXHIBITS — David R. Francis, PRESIDENT, LOUISIANA PURCHASE EXPOSITION COMPANY — CHIEF OF DEPARTMENT OF MANUFACTURES — Walter B. Stevens, SECRETARY

125

Gold Medal.

126

Grand Prize.

127

128

EXPOSITION UNIVERS…

SOUS LE HAUT PATRONAGE DE S.M. LE ROI DES BELGES

Groupe XV — Classe 100 — ALLEMAGNE

DIPLOME DE GRAND PRIX

MARGARETE STEIFF, G. M. B. H., GIENGEN (WÜRTT.)

129

AUSSTELLUNG ·KINDESWOHL·

·BERLIN SEPTEMBER 1906·

VERANSTALTET IN DER PHILHARMONIE VON DER

GESELLSCHAFT ZUR BEKÄMPFUNG DER SÄUGLINGSSTERBLICHKEIT.

WURDE

DAS DIPLOM DER silbernen MEDAILLE ZUERKANNT.

BERLIN, DEN 12. SEPTEMBER 1906.

130

Als öffentliches Zeichen der Anerkennung für

vorzügliche Leistungen

wurde bei der Preiskonkurrenz und Ausstellung des Deutsch-Oesterreichisch-Schweizerischen Fremdenverkehrsvereins in Frankfurt a. M. im Jahre 1906

der Frau Margarete Steiff in Giengen a. B.

die goldene Medaille verliehen.

Diese Verleihung wird hierdurch dokumentiert.

Frankfurt a. M., den 15. Juni 1906.

Deutsch-Oesterreichisch-Schweizerischer Fremdenverkehrsverein.

Die Prüfungscommission | Die Direktion:

Vorsitzender. | Direktor.

131

Illus. 132-137: *A glimpse inside various departments at the Steiff Toy Factory, in 1908.*

***Illus. 138**: Until shortly before her death Margarete Steiff, seen in the center on the extreme left of this photograph, continued to work at the factory, where neither the smallest mistake nor any shoddy workmanship escaped her strict control.*

wanted to share some of Steiff's success. In 1909 they decided to mark their bears with a button in the (right!) ear. A temporary injunction obtained by Margarete Steiff fore-stalled this attempt. "Fine", thought Bing, "if we can't use a button, what is to stop us using a metal sign, similar to an arrow, with a white cloth tag attached!"
Steiff refused any compromise: "The ears are our territory," was their attitude. Any idea which involved attaching trademarks to the ears met with their instant disapproval. Bing countered by fixing a "button under the arm". Steiff were once again able to successfully defend their trademark. The word "Button" remained their copyright. Bing finally gave up. In their next catalog they resigned themselves to advertising: "Bing trademark (GBN – Gebrüder Bing, Nuremberg) under the arm."
Steiff eventually gathered a wealth of similar experience with other manufacturers of plush animals and Teddy-bears. In 1914 an internal memo was issued in which all manufacturers in competition with Steiff were clearly and carefully described. Fourty-four makers of Teddy-bears, dolls and soft toys in Germany were not only listed in this memo, but also graded according to the quality of their merchandise. One had to keep an eye on the competition! The best patent attorneys in Stuttgart and Berlin were employed by Steiff, and it was their responsibility to take legal action for even the slightest infringement.
On March 3, 1893, Margarete Steiff had registered her then small and easily overlooked company at the Chamber of Commerce in Heidenheim, under the name "Felt-Toy Factory". After the unexpected boom in the so-called "Bear Years" it became necessary to change this original registration. On July 6, 1906, the company became known as the Margarete Steiff GmbH (Private limited liability Company). "The intention of the Company is to manufacture and market toys and similar articles." The company's capital stock was 420,000 Marks. The basis of this transformation was a contract which was signed on May 30, 1906. This contract stated that the factory owner, Margarete Steiff, and the three merchants, Paul, Richard and Franz-Josef Steiff were to be named as managing directors of the newly formed Steiff GmbH.
Thus armed, Steiff looked forward to the future with optimism. A new set of work rules was issued and these were supposed to ensure that the daily routine ran smoothly and efficiently. The workers were asked "to complete their assigned duties with diligence and care." They were offered daily or hourly rates, or an agreed piece-rate salary. "The week-days of the year were "to be ▶

139

counted as normal working days, with time off on Sundays, and national holidays."

The hours of work were firmly fixed. Work was to begin at 7 o'clock each morning with a break from 8.45 until 9 o'clock. The lunch-break was from 12 noon until 1 o'clock, and an afternoon break was allowed from 3.15 until 3.30 p.m.. Work finished at 6 o'clock in the evening.

On August 9, 1907, the factory was renamed: "The Margarete Steiff Toy Factory Ltd." Particular emphasis was now placed on expansion. The orders increased so quickly they could hardly be filled. The previously mentioned U.S. economic recession temporarily halted Steiff's flight to the top. The full work-force was mobilized in order to overcome this setback. The publication in honour of Steiff's 50th anniversary states eloquently: "Nevertheless the industrious human spirit always finds new ways in which to weather the storms of life, and Margarete Steiff's tightly-knit organization also withstood this crisis."

The following months were a time of consolidation. New showrooms were opened and new business connections were developed. The British market, which was the largest after the U.S. market, was besieged by a vigorous publicity campaign. Existing toys were improved upon and new products were designed and developed. Most typical of this period was the fact that the animals grew larger and larger; in fact entire herds of life-sized zebras and giraffes were manufactured.

The U.S. presidential election in 1908 provided the necessary political and economic stability; and the large-scale expansion of the factory plant in Giengen increased the production capacity.

However, fate dealt the Steiff family two unexpectedly severe blows. Franz Steiff became seriously ill; the creative energy which he had brought to his work came to an abrupt end with his early death in 1908.

On May 9, 1909, shortly before her 62nd birthday, Margarete Steiff also died. The Steiff family were temporarily immobilized and the flags in Giengen flew at halfmast. The employees also went into mourning; Margarete Steiff, the foundress of the company had closed her eyes forever. "She, the creative genius, who with her exceptional mental vigor mastered even the most difficult problems, and with her indefatigable energy and exemplary enthusiasm gave no thought to the fact that she was paralysed."

The official obituary signed by Paul and Richard Steiff was sober and short. "After a short illness, Margarete Steiff, the foundress of our toy factory, died yesterday, aged 62 years. The dearly beloved deceased started sewing her first unbreakable toys for friends and relatives almost 30 years ago. Her unceasing joy in producing these toys, her energy and the versatility of her talent, made it possible for us to develop from a small business into the important factory we are today. We intend to continue with the same company policy and hope that we shall be able to count on your continued support."

140

141

***Illus. 139**: One of Margarete Steiff's favorite pictures in the years shortly before her death was a framed print of a small girl with a Teddy-bear. The print was entitled "Delighted", copyright 1907, Gutman & Gutman, and was sold as a large-sized poster and as a postcard. In 1938, Paul Steiff, the obsessive diarist of old, noted on the back of the framed print: "Miss Margarete Steiff, foundress of the toy factory, asked her nephew, Paul Steiff for this framed print, . . .and it was displayed in her private office, in honor of the first Teddy-bear manufacturer, so that it could also be admired by the wholesale buyers (who visited). . ."*

***Illus. 140**: Margarete Steiff died a few months after this photograph was taken. The picture shows Margarete with her niece, Eva Koepff, and her small god-daughter, also named Margarete.*

***Illus. 141**: Franz Steiff, died, 1908.*

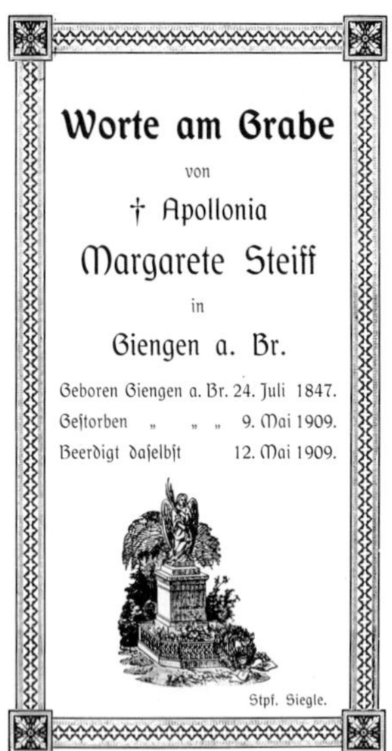

Worte am Grabe

von

† Apollonia

Margarete Steiff

in

Giengen a. Br.

Geboren Giengen a. Br. 24. Juli 1847.
Gestorben „ „ 9. Mai 1909.
Beerdigt daselbst 12. Mai 1909.

Stpf. Siegle.

***Illus. 142**: Printed funeral sermon for Margarete Steiff.*

The toy world was deeply affected. The condolence list included all the established toy manufacturers of the period. Telegrams of condolence flooded the Giengen Post Office. Eugen Maerklin and his wife, of Goeppingen: "pay our heartfelt respects." Louis Lindner & Sons, Sonneberg: "We have been deeply saddened by this unexpected news." E. W. Matthes, Berlin:

***Illus. 143**: Margarete Steiff's gravestone in the Giengen cemetery.*

". . . that I am personally affected and deeply regret the decease of . . ." Hermann Tietz, Berlin: ". . . we would not fail to to pay you our deepest respects on your sad loss." Cuno & Otto Dressel, Sonneberg: "We have always admired the exceptional enterprise, diligence and industry of the deceased and therefore we understand what her death must mean to you." Vedes, Witten: ". . . she, who enhanced the German toy industry with her ideas, who greatly assisted the reputation of German products, and who gave the youth in all the world countless hours of happiness..." And F.A.O. Schwarz, New York: "I have always felt great admiration and reverence for the deceased and I shall continue to remember her with these feelings."

Margarete Steiff was buried on May 12, 1909, and her funeral was attended by a large number of people. The eulogy at the graveside, (which may still be read in a small brochure owned by the company) honored Margarete Steiff thus: "Isn't it a wonder that such a poor, weak, fragile and helpless human being, about whom one asked anxiously in childhood: 'What is to become of her? How will she cope?' was able to take care of thousands of others in her later life? She helped numerous people through their difficulties, and not only was she the acknowledged head of her family but also the foundress and director of a world-wide company." The text continues: "You are all crying at this grave. And I say, go ahead, cry! We will not find another Gretel Steiff very quickly. The black flag is flying outside with good reason. It is as if it wants to say to us, 'Not only has the company lost its leading light, its bright and ruling spirit, it has lost much more, it has also lost its heart'."

Margarete Steiff must have realized that her death was near. On March 3, 1909, she wrote to her close friend, Adolf Glatz, and asked him to advise her with her will. On March 9, 1909, Glatz replied to this letter with some fairly detailed suggestions. He advised: "With regard to the disposal of your estate, I feel that your wishes are both necessary and correct. I would not know what to change . . . Apart from this I feel that this declaration of your wishes leaves no room for misunderstanding, so that your relatives should be happy with your decisions."

A total of eight family members were named by Margarete Steiff as direct beneficiaries of the Company. A corporation meeting was held on July 11, 1909, after the will had been read, and members decided to increase the share capital from 420,000 to 630,000 Marks. "Paul Steiff (Factory owner, Giengen) 108,000 Marks; Richard Steiff (Factory owner, Giengen) 192,000 Marks; Hugo Steiff (Factory owner, Giengen) 60,000 Marks; Otto Steiff (Factory owner,

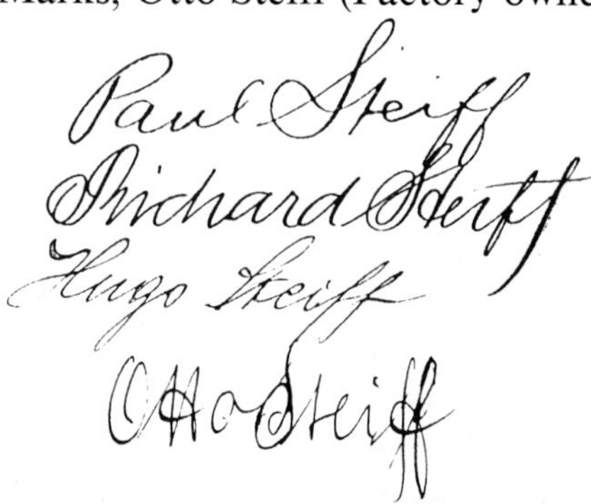

***Illus. 144**: Signatures of the four new directors of the Steiff Company, in 1909.*

Giengen) 60,000 Marks; Lina Leo (Merchant's wife, Munich) 54,000 Marks; Eva Koepff (Merchant's wife, Aalen) 54,000 Marks; Marie Baumann (Farmer's wife, Eichelsteig) 51,000 Marks and Ernst Steiff (Technician, Tomah/Wisconsin/USA) 51,000 Marks."

In order to protect the business interests of individual family members, Hugo and Otto Steiff were also appointed managing directors. They would help their brothers, Richard and Paul, to steer the family ship through all the storms in the years to come! Knowledgeable product selection, the regular appearance of new designs, and the originality of the Steiff articles, once again led the plush-animal factory to the forefront. Responsibilities were clearly divided between the company directors thus avoiding any management problems, at least in the beginning.

Richard Steiff was Steiff's creative force. Flying was both his ▸ 63

145

Up, Up and away with Roloplan . . .

151

150

149

152

148

147

146

154

155

156

153

Illus. 145-157*: Studio photograph (****Illus. 145*** *– page 56) for a Roloplan advertisement. –* ***Illus. 146****: Richard Steiff, creator of the Teddy-bear and the Roloplan. –* ***Illus. 147-152****: This series of step by step photographs shows how easily and simply the Roloplan could be assembled. –* ***Illus. 153****: A separate department was added for the production of the Roloplan. –* ***Illus. 154****: Award for the Roloplan in Frankfurt, 1909. –* ***Illus. 155****: The sleigh being pulled by a Roloplan, shows the versatility of the kite! –* ***Illus. 156****: For the extra large version of the Roloplan, an extremely sturdy clamping device was necessary. –* ***Illus. 157****: Richard Steiff with his Roloplan.*

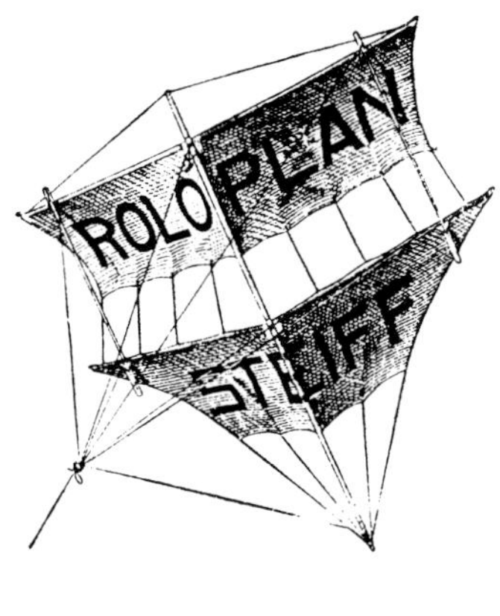

157

__Illus. 158-163__: The Roloplan had many special uses. A camera with complicated release-mechanism was attached beneath the kite (__Illus. 158)__. Naturally, one of the first aerial photographs was a view of the Steiff Toy Factory! (__Illus.159__). The power of two 3 meter Roloplans was so great that Richard Steiff allowed himself to be lifted into the air by them (__Illus. 160__). A special carrying-basket for transporting little children, was also designed (__Illus. 161__). Steiff afflicted with Roloplan fever! The bigger the kite the more comfortable the transport. The basket (__Illus. 162__) in which Richard Steiff is pictured was attached to the Roloplan by wire. He also developed small airplanes (__Illus. 163)__.

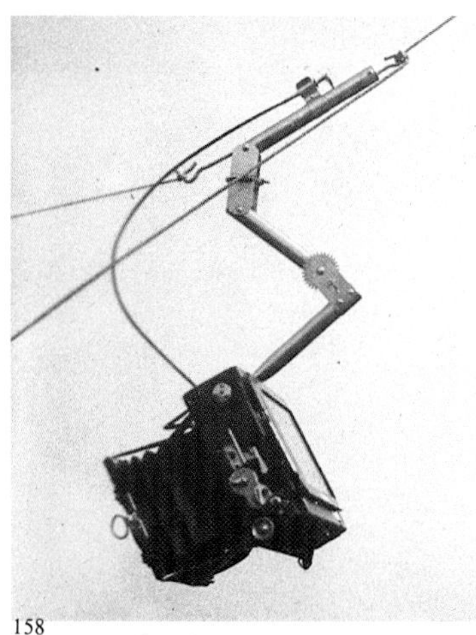

158

159

160

161

162

163

passion and his hobby. He watched the first attempts to fly a motorized airplane with astonishment and open admiration. He followed with fascination the work of Count Zeppelin, who lived in nearby Friedrichshafen on the Lake of Constance, (Bodensee). It is hardly surprising that these technical developments captured his imagination and spurred him on to developing his own designs. Flying is an age old dream of man's – and Richard Steiff achieved this dream in his own way.

He began his preliminary work in the year 1908, having spent some time carefully studying the flight of birds. His many experiments involved much calculating and work before his first attempt, a cloth kite which could be slotted together, was finished. Margarete Steiff was still alive and able to admire this new kite without a tail, which was christened "Roloplan". The new Steiff "Roloplan" created quite a sensation at meetings for hobby fliers, and went on to win many first prizes at airshows both at home and abroad. It was a huge success for the toy manufacturer from Giengen.

A photo of the Roloplan was sent to the District Court with the design, and was registered on July 3, 1909. "180/2cm long; blue/gold with curved Tonking rods, and with Tonking supports on the sides. Instead of stabilizers it is fitted with a cloth inner tube." (Tonking is a special type of bamboo rod.) On August 20, the company were accorded the trademark "Roloplan" for: "balloons, aircraft of all types, airplanes, kites, gliders, and toy kites of cloth or paper."

With this creation, Richard Steiff's motives became more clearly visible. He wanted the "Roloplan" to compete independently in the race for superiority in the air. The first efficient airplanes and the successful start of the Zeppelin provided an unexpected opportunity for the "Roloplan" to fill a void in this newly popular market. The model-kite, which Steiff sold from 1909 onwards, had two or three cloth pieces, was solidly built, and quickly assembled with bamboo rods. It could be easily dismantled in a couple of minutes. It was offered in the catalog: "for sport and play", and, "it is also used with preference and success by flight enthusiasts to measure air currents and for many other aviation purposes."

The largest "Roloplan" was 11ft. 9in. and the smallest, with two cloth pieces, measured 2ft. The pull of the kite was so strong that only a solid reel made of sheet steel was able to securely hold the string. In addition, the largest kite had to be anchored firmly in the ground. This was because the kite could develop enormous pull – depending on the force of the wind – thus allowing Richard Steiff to use his invention for several unusual purposes. The "Roloplan" was constructed in such a way that even in moderate wind it was able to reach a height of 3,250ft. ". . . and there it glides – quiet as a bird." This new wind and air toy was such a huge success that it became necessary to install a separate department and workshop at the factory to cope with the demand for the "Roloplan".

The largest models of the "Roloplan" were tested in the extensive green meadows of Giengen. Richard Steiff constructed his own harness for these experiments and allowed himself to be lifted up by the kite. He went on to design a "Steiff tripod" be used for aeriel photography, "suitable for all types of shutter cameras". By means of an attached cord, it was possible to take one shot after another. With this invention Richard Steiff became the first to use a kite for aeriel photography. Once again, he was to make contemporary history with his progressive ideas.

The science of aeriel photography was perfected as early as 1856 by the famous French photographer, Nadar. However, anyone who wanted to take photographs from the air had to be able to afford a flight in a hot-air balloon. Richard Steiff's invention replaced this time consuming and costly means of photography with a cheaper and simpler method which would be available to everyone. The tripod cost 21 Marks, a suitable "Roloplan", between 10 and 33 Marks.

Steiff presented their unusual kite to the public at every opportunity and they entered it in numerous competitions. The "Roloplan" won prize after prize. The catalog text read: "Steiff Roloplan is the clear winner among all flight competitors. Frankfurt-on-the-Main, 1909; several Roloplans were entered in competitive races and were awarded prizes. Scheveningen (Holland), 1910; – First prize for ▶

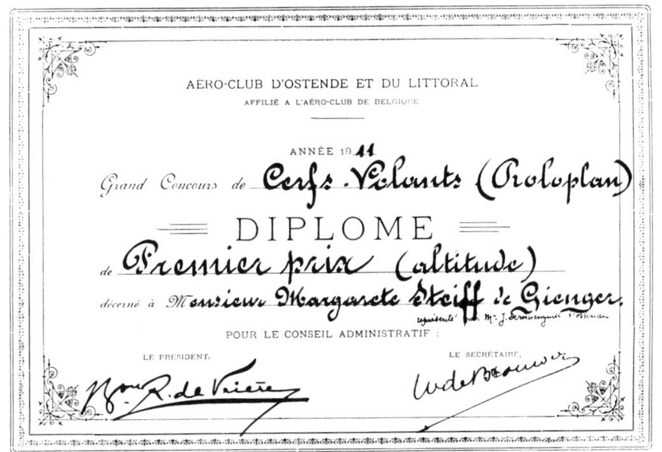

AÉRO-CLUB D'OSTENDE ET DU LITTORAL
AFFILIÉ A L'AÉRO-CLUB DE BELGIQUE

ANNÉE 1911

Grand Concours de Cerfs-Volants (Roloplan)

DIPLOME

de Premier prix (altitude)

décerné à Monsieur Margarete Steiff de Giengen

POUR LE CONSEIL ADMINISTRATIF :

LE PRÉSIDENT, LE SECRÉTAIRE,

Illus. 164: *Diploma awarded for the Roloplan in a competition in 1911, at the Aero-Club in Ostend, Belgium.*

165

166

***Illus. 165-167**: Motorization came into fashion at just the right moment for the technically minded Steiff brothers. They were the proud owners of the first motor-car in Giengen and naturally, Steiff products had to be adapted to suit these new automobiles – Paul Steiff's hour of glory. This monkey radiator cap was designed in 1912/1913 (**Illus. 165**). These two auto-figures, in original condition, ("Chimpanzees"), are 9in. and 16in. tall (**Illus. 166**). The huge variety of Steiff's "Automobile Program" is illustrated on this page from the company's archives, (**Illus. 167**). Dolls also were used as radiator caps and car mascots: Clown, Golliwog, Hunter, Farmer and Farmer's wife, the dwarves, Snik and Snak, Postillion, Max and Moritz, Munich Child and many others.*

167

***Illus. 168**: Paul Steiff proud owner of the first car in Giengen, with a large size "passenger figure".*

800m (27ft.8in.). Namur (Belgium), 1910; – Prizes for height, distance, capacity, stability, signalization and aeriel photography. Ostend (Belgium), 1911; – First prize and official diploma from the 'Aeroclub Belgique'."

The "Roloplan" was also ideal for "flying" advertisements. Many businessmen ordered the kites and had Steiff print the cloth-areas with their company names. Even the German army found use for the Roloplan. The Roloplan they used was made of light colored material, 3.60m long (11ft.8in.) with weight capacity of approximately 30kg (66lbs). This example, "of especially sturdy construction, served successfully as target-practice for many units." In other words, the German Kaiser's Artillery Units used the "Roloplan" to practise shooting at flying objects! In 1915, when the "Roloplan" was featured in a catalog with a basket attachment and a "flying" man attached by a harness, the text read: "These two photographs illustrate the weight capacity of the Steiff 'Roloplan'. However, all such attempts are dangerous and you are warned against recklessly repeating them." During the chaos of the First World War, the Steiff company used the same text and photographs to remind military officials of the many uses of the "Roloplan". Incidentally, according to Steiff's records, over 34,000 "Roloplans" were sold between 1910 and 1915!

The Steiff brothers were fascinated by technological development. They were the first family in the little town of Giengen to buy a motor-car, and this purchase soon led to the decision that their new four-wheeled toy should be given an appropriate Steiff image. Perhaps the radiator cap ought to have a mascot? This mascot would give the automobile a more personalized appearance, and it would be simple to adapt the dolls and animals already in the program for this new purpose. It was Paul Steiff who was responsible for these new creations; and he quickly found the best ways to use Steiff articles with the new automobile. He also invented some very convincing advertising slogans for the new products.

In 1913, an extra page in the catalog featured these new automobile animals and dolls. The ever popular auto-chimpanzee complete with chauffeur's cap, "prevents the splashing of hot water from the radiator". Another photograph showed the plush chimpanzee ▶

hanging head first over the radiator," . . . when the bonnet is open, or when pouring water into the radiator, it (the chimp), will protect your clothing from hot or dirty water stains". Steiff also offered a chimp with a brass steering wheel in his hands – to be used as a radiator cap.

This original series of mascots went on to include: "bear standing on radiator cap", "bear climbing up the radiator grill"; and also elephants, donkeys, pigs, kangaroos, fox-terriers and poodles which were offered as radiator mascots.

There was no limit to the number of ideas which the new automobile offered. Paul Steiff quickly realized that the head-lamps of the newly popular automobiles were especially prone to dirt and grime and it did not take him long to adapt the felt tea-cosies and coffee-pot warmers into, "automobile head-lamp covers". A rooster's head and a turkey were added to the figures already in the program.

A satisfied owner from Eisenach sent the following telegram: "Your much appreciated gift, the farmer, has accompanied us faithfully on our motoring trips. He sits on the right-hand lamp and today he prevented us from incurring serious damage when our car ran into a farmer's vehicle. Luckily, "our farmer" (lamp-cover) stuck protectively in the radiator of the other auto. Best wishes, Councillor Weber and wife."

For the colder months of the year Steiff also designed "Radiator Warmers" and "Foot Warmers". Owing to the huge variety of cars, large and small, the radiators were also of varying sizes. Therefore, Steiff offered their customers a "made-to-measure service, in felt or plush, color and size to be specified. Directions for measuring the radiators will be sent on request."

All over the world technology-freaks received Steiff's new products with enthusiasm – it seemed that anything was possible at the Steiff factory. The French toy store "Au Paradis des Enfants", owned by Monsieur E.P.Malaret sent this cable from Paris to Giengen on April 1, 1913 (no April Fools joke!): "I kindly request that you send me a prototype of a Bibendum figure as quickly as it is possible for you to have one designed and made up." Hiding behind the word "Bibendum", is the popular Michelin-tire man! This little round man, made up entirely of auto tires, has been the trademark of the Michelin Tire Company (France) since the day of his birth. He was designed by chance in 1898, as André Michelin was walking through his factory with the billboard artist Marius Rossillon. The pair walked past a huge pile of tires of varying size stacked up in a corner of the room.

"We just need to add arms and legs to turn that pile into a man," suggested André Michelin. The artist's imagination was fired by the idea, and thus it was that his first billboard depicted the little Michelin Man holding a trophy filled with nails and pieces of glass. The little man was raising his glass to a pile of tires and the words "Nunc est bibendum!" accompanied the drawing. (Translation: Now it's time for a drink – cheers!) – This billboard resulted in the little man being christened "Bibendum", which was soon shortened to "Bib". At the Steiff factory work began at once on a design for "Bib". Three weeks after the telegram had been received in Giengen the prototype had been made up and sent off to Paris. Unfortunately, the existing records do not reveal whether this prototype led to an actual order being placed. One thing is certain however, each Bibendum figure would have been marked with a "Button-in-Ear". This was one condition of delivery on which Steiff always insisted.

Steiff not only had accessories for motorists, they also catered to flight enthusiasts. The story of the pilot Wilhelm Kiessling illustrates this. Kiessling had a little Steiff pig hanging in his Ago-biplane, and a ▶

169

170

171

Illus. 169-173: *A request for a "Michelin-Man" (named "Bibendum" or "Bib") was made by French Toy Store owner E.P. Malaret. He requested two sizes, to be made in felt (**Illus. 169 + 170**). –* ***Illus. 171:*** *Trademark of the Michelin Tire Company. –* ***Illus. 172:*** *Catalog page, 1913. –* ***Illus. 173:*** *The pilot Wilhelm Kiessling (with his good-luck charm – a Steiff piglet) on his unsuccessful flight over Lake Constance (1912).*

newspaper article dated 1912 noted: "On July 1, Kiessling made his first flight in the competition for the Lake Constance trophy, but his lucky charm, a little plush pig, did not fulfill his obligations... Kiessling had to be hauled back 25 miles to the airfield! On July 3, Kiessling made his second flight for this trophy, and his lucky piglet had obviously become accustomed to the novelty of flying – for this time Kiessling completed the first round and two-thirds of the second round . . . yet the pilot still did not become discouraged. On July 4, he brought out his biplane once again, and this time the pilot and the little piglet completed the course! On Friday . . . as a result of heavy fog, the pilot lost his way on the return journey. Kiessling tried one more time to rely on the "magical power" of the little plush pig – but after one round he abandoned his attempt . . . Perhaps he will try his luck with a different charm on his next important flight!"

The short depression which the U.S.A. suffered in 1907, was felt in the Steiff Profit Report for several years afterwards. For instance, the unpaid account of the plush supplier Schulte, in Duisburg, placed a heavy burden on the company. In 1910 Steiff had to pay almost 40,000 DM in interest to the Schulte company. Someone at Steiff had miscalculated badly. Sales prices had to be dropped in order for Steiff articles to remain competitive. However, the turnover did not increase accordingly and the eventual result was a large deficit.

In 1909 costs were almost 300% higher than in the previous year. Excessive travelling allowances and expensive investments were the main cause for this increase of costs. Chief critic at Steiff was brother-in-law and shareholder Alexander Leo. He accused the Steiff brothers of being "machine-crazy". His criticism was (as was the custom at Steiff) openly stated and ▶

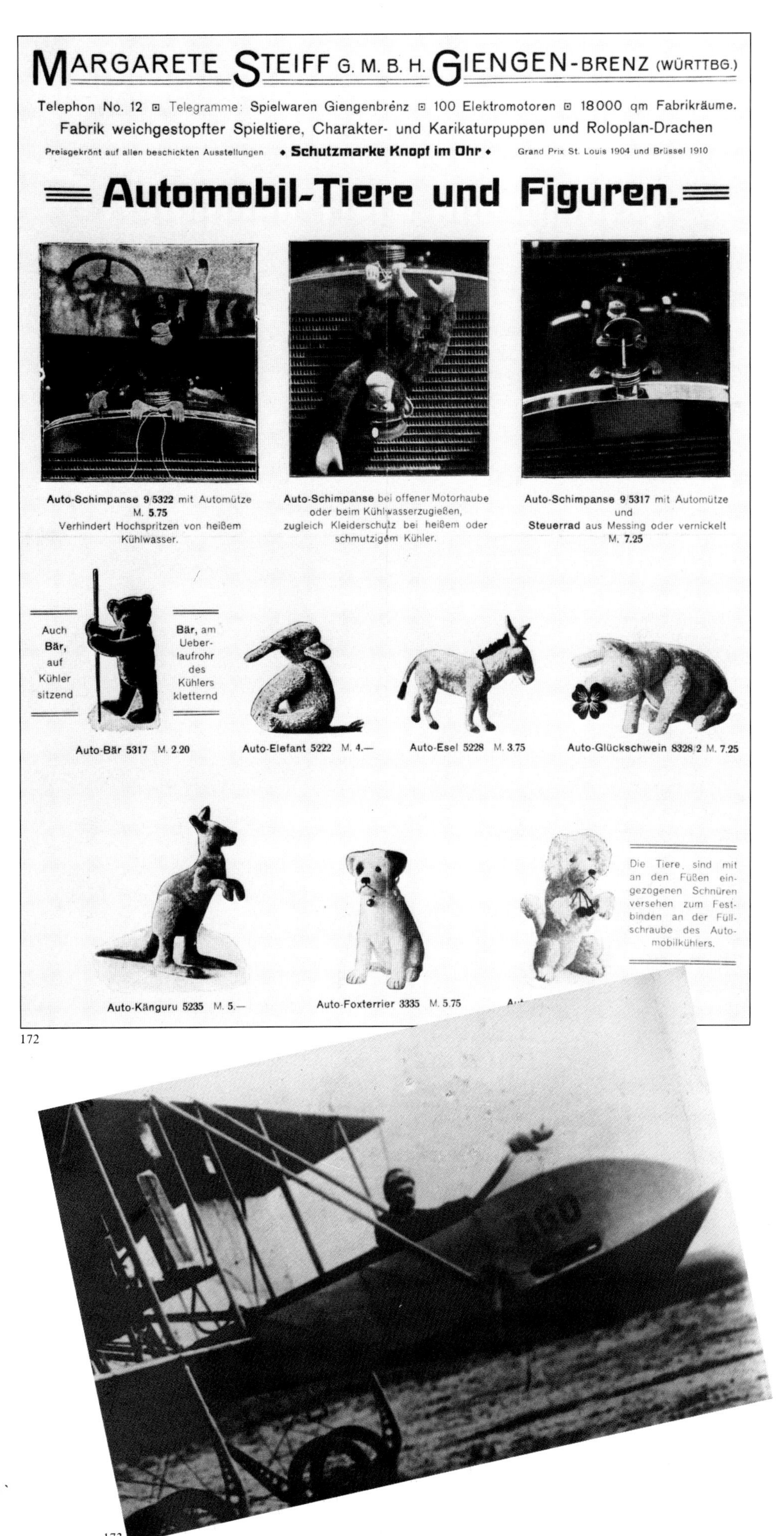

172

173

English Toy Manufacturers

DOLLS, TOYS, FANCY GOODS

AMERICAN NOVELTIES.

TRADE MARK

TELEPHONE:-
Nº 9284 CENTRAL.
TELEGRAPHIC ADDRESS:-
"TOMORROW."

HERBERT E. HUGHES.

SOLE AGENT FOR

LOUIS LINDNER & SONS, SONNEBERG. H. ROITHNER & Cº SCHWEIDNITZ.	J. J. LANDMANN, NÜRNBERG. GUSTAV NEUBRONNER, FRANKENTHAL.	MARGARETE STEIFF, GIENGEN. GEBR. MÄRKLIN & Cº GOPPINGEN.

9, LONG LANE, London, E.C. 19

174

discussed – an example of the liberal and constructive attitude adopted within the family. Leo accused: "Your love of all mechanical things has led you into purchasing more machines than was necessary. You have furnished the carpentry shop with wood-working machines which are so expensive that you are certainly not going to be able to produce wooden articles anywhere near as cheaply as you would have been able to buy them from specialist factories."
Another criticism was: "You can't call this simply a welding department any longer, since even some middle-sized factories are not as well equipped as this is!" Leo's remarks were especially critical of the "Do-it-yourself" technical hobbies of the Steiff brothers,

175

***Illus. 174-176**: Letterhead of Steiff's English representative – Herbert E. Hughes. **Illus. 175**: Herbert E. Hughes. **Illus. 176**: Delivery note from the London store, Harrods, 1908. Here, too, one can see an example of the special orders which Steiff often produced for favored customers. For example, on this delivery note: "Lord Fauntleroy" or "Boy Doll with sweater", both 29in. tall.*

"... which propels you all into your love of such experiments. These experiments do not simply cost a lot of money, what is worse, they cost a great deal of valuable time, since they keep you away from the day-to-day running of the business. Do you really believe for example, that the production of a toy flying-machine could ever bring in anything near what it takes to make one? Even the kite, this discovery of Richard's, which is truly wonderful in all respects, will have to be sold in enormous quantities if it is to bring in just what it cost to produce. Three years ago you achieved almost double this turnover with only half the factory space which you have today!"
Alexander Leo concluded his sermon thus: No further building ▶

" 35	1.	Fat "	21/-	6 £43	1/2.	Clowns	32/- Dz
75	1/4.	Boy Doll w/sweater	5/- ea	100	1/6.	"	13/- each
Mi 35	1.	Mrs Captain	24/- Dz	53 15	2.	Brown Bears	15/- 17/6
Knabe 75	2 only	Lord Fauntleroy	22/- ea	5317/4.	2.	" w/muzzle	22/-
M B 28	1 Dz	H' Dumpty	24/- Dz	5322/4.	1.	" "	33/-
35	1.	"	30/-	5328/4.	1.	White & Brown w/voice & muzzle	63/- 62/6
60	3 only	Cooks	10/- ea	5335/4	1/2.	"	10/-

176

extensions; only machines which were absolutely necessary should be purchased; and a complete halt on inventions and experiments. It was important to devote more time to running the business, and most important that the brothers discuss business matters between themselves more often. Leo added: "... surely it would give you a greater feeling of satisfaction to keep up the high standard of your family business and to enjoy the profits which the ensuing stability would bring. You all earn high salaries as company directors, but at the same time it is your duty (as directors) to ensure that the other shareholders can rely on your judgement completely, in all business matters."

Was it simply a case of bad management which afflicted the company in 1908 and 1909? Had Richard and Paul Steiff really failed in their duty as directors? (For it was at them that this criticism was directed.) Or had they chosen the best possible way to recoup the losses suffered during the 1907 crisis? Was it unwise to invest their capital in order to be prepared for the assignments of the coming years? Certainly there was some truth in Alexander Leo's remarks, but the next decade would prove that the Steiff brothers had acted with great foresight. They had used the years between 1902 and 1914 to build a solid foundation for their position as market leaders in the world of soft-filled dolls and animals.

The numerous overseas agents who represented the company in all parts of the world contributed to the superior image which Steiff enjoyed. It is especially important to mention at this point the branches in London and New York, which acted as supporting pillars for the headquarters in Giengen. Steiff had enjoyed a particularly close business relationship with London from as early as 1895. Buyers from London had placed regular orders at the Leipzig Fair and also bought directly from the factory in Giengen. Margarete Steiff herself had signed a contract with the dynamic Herbert E. Hughes in 1899. Hughes had started his business in 1890. He was also the agent for other famous toy manufacturers, including: Louis Lindner and Sons of Sonneberg, and the Maerklin Brothers of Goeppingen.

Herbert Hughes' energetic representation resulted in an increase in turnover for the German company, and he soon took over as their sole agent. He travelled to Giengen frequently to discuss delivery dates, conditions and new items for production with Margarete Steiff personally. Hughes had numerous customers in England, including the world famous department store Harrods, several other large chain stores, and the following toy stores: Hamleys (which can still be found in Regent Street, London); C.E. Turnbull & Co.; Eisenmann & Co.; Gamages; Whyte, Ridsdale & Co.; H.E. Eckart & Co.; and Spiers & Bond.

On August 9, 1902, Edward VII acceded the British throne. He was popularly known as "Teddy" (a shortened version of Edward) and like Roosevelt, he too found himself associated with Steiff Teddy-bears. Edward VII had also taken a particular liking to a little Koala Bear in the London Zoo, and although none of these single facts had anything to do with the production or designing of the Teddy-bear, it is hardly surprising to learn that during the years of the "Bear Boom", huge quantities of Teddy-bears found their way from Giengen to England. (Incidentally, this probably explains why almost all the very early Teddy-bears, which are so highly sought by collectors today, seem to be found in England.)

Otto Steiff had a particularly close relationship with Herbert E. Hughes. He visited England on several occasions and studied both marketing and distribution procedures critically and intently. Otto Steiff also correctly assessed the company's prospects for increasing their sales capacity in England. Once it became clear that the Teddy-bear had overwhelm- ▶

***Illus.** 177: Steiff advertisement for English-speaking countries.*

Illus. 178: *An extra special greeting, and a public tribute for the Teddy-bear (1907). From "Everybody's Magazine". The whole of the front cover was devoted to the little plush hero. Clues from the artist (sketched on the sticker), reveal that this "Teddy-bear Passenger", complete with luggage, travelled on the Hamburg/America Line on August 14, on his way to the "Ridgeway Company" – the address of the magazine's publishers.*

178

ingly won the hearts of British children, and huge orders for Teddy-bears were received in Giengen, Otto Steiff returned to London; where he opened a Steiff warehouse sometime between 1908 and 1909. This ensured that Hughes's agents had access to a large variety of products at all times.

Records show that in 1908 Hughes ordered 40,000 Steiff bears for the English market alone. These bears were not only of differing quality, but also included special orders (i.e. bears with glass eyes), for which Hughes paid an extra charge.

It simply remains to be noted that the relationship between Steiff and Herbert E. Hughes continued successfully until it was disrupted by the First World War. The London Import Company, G. Greiner & Co., took over as the sole agent for Steiff products in England from 1920 onwards.

On the other side of the ocean, in the United States, the Steiff Toy Company appeared to have found an inexhaustible buyers market. Sales in the United States had grown very respectably through contacts made at the Leipzig Fair and through buyers who had visited the factory in Giengen. Margarete Steiff always welcomed the visits of these buyers for it afforded her the opportunity to exchange the latest trade-gossip and also to discuss possible improvements in the quality of her products.

In 1902 Margarete Steiff sent her nephew Paul Steiff to New York. He was to open a Steiff subsidiary to develop and organize the distribution of products within the U.S.. The official company address for a period of 18 months was: Margarete Steiff, Leading Felt Toy Manufactory – Represented by Paul Steiff, Office and Sample Room, 640 Broadway, New York. However, after only 15 months, Paul Steiff returned from the New World! He was both disappointed and frustrated at his lack of success.

Illus. 179: Original stamp with the address of the first Steiff subsidiary in the U.S.A.

He had not been able to get the wheels turning as he had hoped, and he gave up resignedly! Without the support of the huge U.S. wholesalers, who were responsible for all imported toys, and who had complete control of their industry, it was impossible for Paul Steiff to make any impact.

So, the American-Connection continued to work as always: the Teddy-bear did not change anything. In 1912 Richard Steiff travelled to the international Aero Exhibition in New York. The exhibition was held from May 9 – 18, and Richard Steiff intended to use his visit to develop an effective strategy which would help to pep up the company's sales on the American market.

Whatever Richard Steiff undertook he pursued thoroughly! He knew that in the "Land of Unlimited Opportunity," spectacular advertising methods not only paid the best dividends but would also ensure that people took notice of him, and of his products. From the sky-scraper-type building which housed the George Borgfeldt Company, Richard Steiff flew his "Roloplan" over the New York Skyline. A second kite could not be made to fly because of a manufacturing flaw, and Richard Steiff commented on the poor workmanship (on letter-paper from the New York Hotel Martinique) ". . . I think we shall have to get rid of half a dozen cutters before someone gets rid of us."

Neither did Richard Steiff get only favorable reports on his products from old Steiff customers. For instance, many complained about the voice boxes in the Steiff animals. A note sent to his brother Paul, who was in Giengen waiting to hear the results of Richard's visit, read: "If any person responsible for making the voice boxes leaves even one weight uncovered by linen, make sure you beat him till he's black and blue. At Steiners (editors note: a wholesale store), there is not one article with a functioning voice box . . . and in connection with this I found out that geese do not have voice boxes at all. There is absolutely no excuse for this."

One of his (Richard Steiff's) most important suggestions was: "We have to make display pieces, preferably simple but decorative, and nothing too heavy. Even if we take a cardboard box, cut it out to make it look like a house with windows from which our dolls can look out onto a garden where animals and dolls are playing. Here, where mountains of toys are presented haphazardly to the public, such a display would be a welcome change and far better than nothing at all." Richard Steiff continued: "We also have to display the word 'STEIFF' (not simply on the button, but also in large and elegant letters) perhaps in gold, and hang or sew it on our ▸ 100

Steiff Agents and Warehouses:

AMSTERDAM: H. Kamp & Zoon (1910)
BERLIN: G.F. Herzog & Co. (1897)
BRUSSELS: Robert Katz & Sons (1911)
BUCCAREST: J. Gottfried (pre 1911)
DÜSSELDORF: Ph. Morschheuser (1894)
FLORENCE: Giov. Pansier (1900)
HAMBURG: John Hess (1890)
LEIPZIG: (at the Exhibition from 1897)
LISBON: Pac. Rodrigues & Sons (1908)
LONDON: Herbert E. Hughes (1899)
MOSCOW: Heinrich Ditterich (1911)
NEW YORK: Geo. Borgfeldt & Co. (1913)
PARIS: Vigouroux & Gondrand (1900)
Margarete Steiff Frêres (from 1911)
SYDNEY: J.L. Lennard (1911)
VIENNA: J. Ev. Schnoetzinger (1908)

180

181

182

183 ***Illus. 180-186****: A glimpse of the Steiff warehouse in New York (***Illus. 180-182***), which was taken over by George Borgfeldt & Co. New York, on January 1,1913. –* ***Illus. 183****: Display piece in the reception area of the Geo. Borgfeldt & Co. building in New York-The Chief Buyer, Edmund Ulrich Steiner, born in Sonneberg, was made manager of the "Doll Departments" of Samstag & Hilder Bros., a New York*

184

185

186

*Department Store, in 1901. Steiner felt especially happy among the Teddy-bears in the Steiff warehouses in Giengen (**Illus. 185**). Edmund Steiner always had time to gossip with the owner of the company, Margarete Steiff (**Illus. 186**). Internal information handed down recalls that Steiner enjoyed passing on all the latest gossip and scandal from the international toy scene to the disabled old lady in Giengen.*

***Illus. 187**: Catalog photograph 1907/08: On the left, the bulldog "Tige"; Teddy-bear, and two little goats.*

***Illus. 188**: Paul Steiff (left) among the animals he designed (1904).*

It is certainly thanks to the animals, that the Steiff Company today is: "a business of world renown." Margarete Steiff began her production of toys with an elephant. This little elephant paved the way for a whole zoo! At first they were made of felt and velvet, but these materials were later replaced by a fur-like plush which encouraged cuddling and stroking. Whether they are domestic or wild animals, whether they are realistically or comically portrayed, there are so many animals, in so many different sizes in the Steiff menagerie, that it would be impossible to list them all completely. Nevertheless, on the following pages we shall do our best to illustrate and describe the many different types of animals which were made by Steiff until 1914. We shall show you the typical characteristics of these animals, point out whether they were soft-filled, or whether the filling was of a harder type. The different types of voice-boxes and the techniques used to fit them into the animals. There are Steiff animals in standing, sitting, begging and lying positions. Animals with and without wheels; as pull-along toys, with eccentric wheels, as ride-on or rocking animals, as puppets, and even as life-sized playmates. There are animals which have a unique head-movement, and animals which can somersault thanks to their clockwork mechanism. Others are fitted with music boxes. In 1903/1904 the animals were made with moveable joints; and was used to give the same principle all the other species of animals the same natural movement.

***Illus. 189**: The "stupendously" famous Teddy-bear – at work!*

Illus. 190-193: *A burst of glorious color is offered by these roosters (**Illus. 190**), beautifully handmade in felt. The roosters could stand on their own two feet, or were fixed on discs; they were made as "Roly-Poly" (tumble) animals, and also attached to eccentric wheels as pull-toys. They were produced from 1900 until well into the 1920s. – **Illus. 191**: A novelty in 1903, was this black velvet cat-later, also available in plush (5in. and 7in.). This "Tom Cat" was especially popular at Halloween time in the U.S.A., and was also in demand as a souvenir item, as "Blackie-the White House Mascot", circa 1924. The cat in the background, "Fez Kater" was first available as a tea cosey in the 1908 catalog. – **Illus. 192**: Large quantities of velvet rabbits were produced (from 1900 until 1920) as gifts for Easter-in several sizes, from 4in. to 14in. – **Illus. 193**: Red Felt Elephant (from 1909 until 1920). Also available in gray, blue or red plush.*

190

191

192

193

194

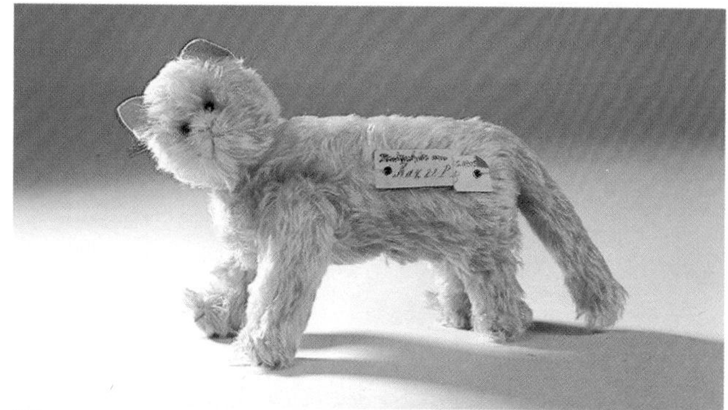

195

196

***Illus. 194-197**: Velvet Dachshund (**Illus. 194**) as pull-toy on a metal roly-poly cart (metal wheels going through from front to back), size: 5in.. This toy was also available with bears, rabbbits (in sitting or jumping position), cats, pigs, elephants and doves, (1914-1917). – **Illus. 195**: This little plush cat was offered in the program as "Kaz 22PB" (Pat.1905). The front paws are disc jointed and the back legs are attached by wire going through the body. Soft-filled, with squeaker. – **Illus. 196**: Nostalgic Christmas scene. This photograph was taken in the Steiff studio, 1912/1913. The Christmas tree is decorated with "hanging" toys (pre 1900) intended for tiny tots. Some of these toys were made as rattles. – **Illus. 197**: Pull-along ducks in felt; on metal wheels (left), or on eccentric wheels with "waddling" movement (right). The head of the duck on the right is made of velvet. Both ducks are 6in. (circa 1914).*

197

Animals on wheels – Steiff saw these as an important part of production. For this reason they used an elephant on wheels as their trademark for several years. Manufacturing procedures were constantly being improved. In 1908 the ride-on animals were fitted with an iron bar which made it possible to steer them in any direction. Life-sized bears or camels, fixed onto an iron frame on wheels were occasionally made as special orders for wealthy families. The Steiff mobile zoo was systematically enlarged in the 1890s; soon the animals were made larger and larger. The problem of attaching the metal base and wheels was solved with the help and advice of their neighbors, the Maerklin Toy Company. Steiff enjoyed a business and social relationship with the Maerklin family. The wheels and axles for animals up to 14in. were exceptionally sturdy, and were electrically welded onto the metal frames. The program in 1898 offered: large ride-on animals, animals on rockers with safety saddle both of which could be removed, "soft-filled, suitable for parquet and other floor surfaces, will not injure your children, and are exceptionally hard-wearing; nevertheless light and elegant thanks to their supple construction". Steiff was especially proud of an order which they received in 1911, from the Royal Palace in Württemburg. King Wilhelm II ordered a collection of animals in special sizes for his grand-children, the princes and princesses of Wied. Paul Steiff supervised the order and when the animals were ready to leave the factory the company photographer captured the memorable moment with his camera. – Steiff improved their animals' mobility: As of 1913 all animals on wheels could be navigated by means of a so-called "automobile" steering device, which Steiff developed with the help of the Maerklin Toy Company. One year later all animals on wheels were fundamentally improved. Instead of iron wheels, all animals were now equipped with wooden wheels which were produced by Steiff themselves. A special dry-steam plant was installed to allow the use of top quality, pure, dry wood, which Steiff obtained directly from the forests. The larger animals had wooden wheels, which ran noiselessly and were fitted with exceptionally light, anti-friction bearings. On request, these large animals could be fitted with a voice-box operated by means of a pull-string attached to a chrome-plated ring on the animal's right shoulder. In the 1920s these expensive, extravagantly produced wooden wheels were replaced by metal, disc-type, wheels.

***Illus. 198**: Advertising card, 1902. The young boy is seated on a soft-filled deer, which was made from a special design dating back to 1899.*

***Illus. 199**: This wonderful collection of Steiff animals was ordered in 1911 by King Wilhelm II of Württemberg for his grandchildren.*

200

201

Illus. 200-203: Ride-on camels in all sizes, and all designs (**Illus. 200**). These toys were permanently offered in the Steiff program in sizes ranging from 10in. to 18in. – **Illus. 201**: The stability and steadiness of the pull-along toys are being tested by Hugo Steiff in this photograph. The young boy is sitting on a ride-on animal with steering mechanism (1908) which is shown in greater detail in this photograph (**Illus. 202**). – **Illus 203**: Bears as pull-along and ride-on toys, in different sizes and designs, including a bear with movable head.

202

203

***Illus. 204**: Advertising came made for the Marshall Field & Co., Department Store, New York (circa 1908).*

***Illus. 206**: Proof of quality! The little donkey and the horse are carrying workers from the Steiff factory on their backs. Each person carries a card in his right hand, on which his weight is printed. The board above reads: "Steiff animals with normal iron framework can carry a burden of over one ton!"*

205

***Illus. 205**: This brown bear is 20in.. The rockers can be easily unscrewed so that the bear can be transformed from a rocking-toy to a pull-toy. The saddle cloth can also be taken off – (1910 onwards).*

206

207

Illus. 207-211: Jousting tournament between two Teddy-bears (***Illus. 207***). The bears are seated on two ride-on donkeys – the example in the middle has a steering mechanism (1920s). – ***Illus. 208***: The lamb on wheels was available in 13 sizes, from 3in. to 32in., with pull-string voice box. It was covered with real lambskin and was produced until the mid 1920s. – ***Illus. 209***: Painted felt ox, available from 7in. to 24in. (1900 till 1930). – ***Illus. 210 + 211***: Horse with removable saddle cloth. A pull-toy on wooden wheels, with folding hand-grip. This model was probably never put into production since it was not sturdy enough to take the "rough" handling of little boys.*

210

208

209

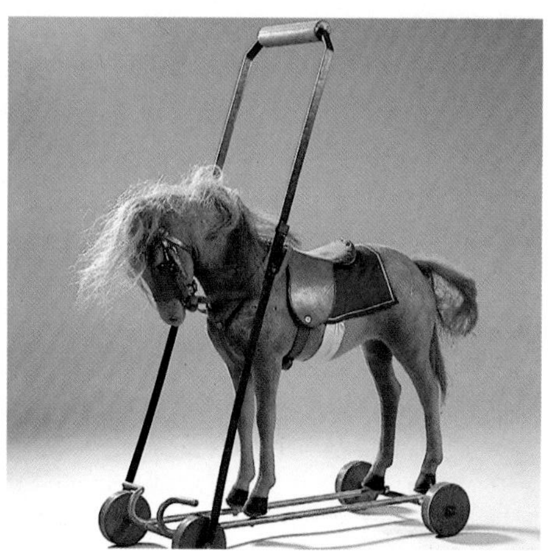

211

Monkeys greatly resemble humans in many ways: build, appearance, movement, upright gait – the more human their behaviour, the greater their appeal. During the second half of the 19th century monkeys enjoyed particular popularity. The catalog of 1892 features a monkey on a string; a monkey rider in tail-coat; and a standing monkey in costume. Later, in 1897, the Steiff production included every type of monkey imaginable: Monkey-dolls dressed as Hussars, Infantrymen, Coachmen, Cubans, Clowns, Jesters, or Gigolos in evening-dress. The workmanship on these early toys was extremely primitive – they were made of felt or plush, their limbs dangled from their bodies and their heads were sewn on. It was not until 1903 that the first animals at Steiff, the "Monkey 60 PB" and the "Bär 55 PB", were given jointed arms and legs and movable heads. The first example of the "Monkey 60 PB" has been preserved in the Steiff archives (though not, unfortunately, the "Bär 55 PB"). "Monkey 60 PB" is 24in. tall, has a felt face, felt, stiched-on ears, and shoebutton eyes. The limbs are attached to the body with strong thread and cardboard discs, and he has a voice-box. The next milestone in the development of the Steiff monkey was recorded in 1909 under the Patent No. DRGM 371 151: "Soft-filled play-figure, characterized by prominent and protuding features, i.e. eyelids, lips." The first monkey to be given these "features" was the chimpanzee, "5325" (Patented 1909). The chimp had additional bulges sewn on around the eyes and lips which gave him a particularly realistic appearance. Steiff competitor Wilhelm Strunz copied the new design immediately, but in the legal hearing which followed he had to admit to "poaching". The Steiff workshop continued to bring out new monkey-creations: the monkey as a tumbling clown; the monkey dressed in sweater and cap; the useful monkey radiator cap; the "Pantom" monkey puppet, and the mechanically operated somersaulting monkey. Steiff monkeys could pedal or bounce along on tricycles or on a four-wheeled chassis; as "Velo", or "Record" animals, or as the "Rad-Affe" (Bike-monkey!). From 1912 onwards they rode through childrens' nurseries on eccentric wheels. They were also modelled on famous monkeys from the circus and Vauderville Theater – "Monsieur et Madame", or "Lady Betty". Until 1914, Steiff sold more monkeys than any other animal in their program – except of course the Teddy-bear.

212

Illus. 212: *Steiff doll, "Anton", in the regional costume of Upper Bavaria – with his favorite monkey, and a little velvet bulldog (circa 1900)*

__Illus. 213 + 214__: This monkey is one of the earliest examples produced by Steiff circa 1892. It was manufactured in felt, in many different colors. The tip of the tail was in fur, as was the "ruff". – __Illus. 214__: Monkey clown (1902/03), in 14, 23 and 31in. sizes.

213

214

216

__Illus. 215 + 216__: "Roly Poly" monkey (__Illus. 215__) 8in. tall (circa 1898). – __Illus. 216__: Monkey "60 PB" imitating the pose of the famous "smoking monkey" in Albert Carre's circus.

215

__Illus. 217 + 218__: A rarity and a milestone at the same time: – the monkey "60 PB" from the Steiff archives. Made in 1903, he has the early "string-jointing", is 24in. tall and has a voice box. The rough plush (burlap), which resembles fur and the felt face, are his particular characteristics. The design of monkey "60 PB" was exactly the same as Bear "55 PB".

217

218

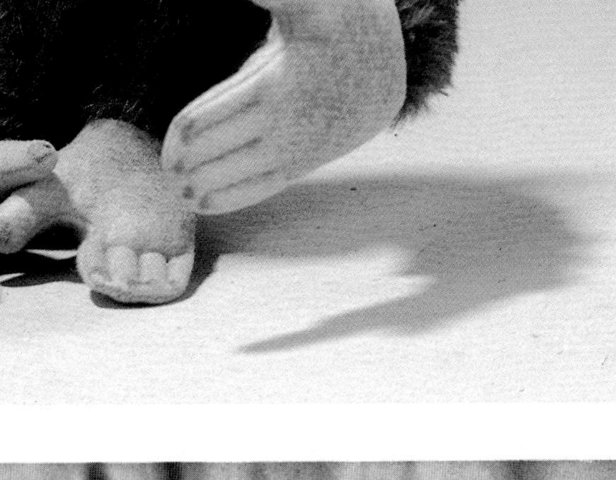

219

Illus. 219: *In 1909 the monkey was completely re-designed and now each monkey had the typical characteristics of its race. The chimpanzee, 14in., was designed in the mid 1920s.*

220

221

222

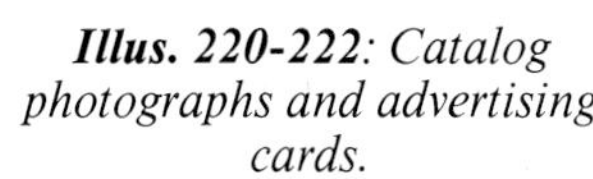

Illus. 220-222: *Catalog photographs and advertising cards.*

223

Illus. 223: *In 1912 the most popular chimps in Europe were "Monsieur et Madame X". They appeared on their bicycle in all the large variety shows. This photograph was taken at the Olympia Theatre in Paris.*

Even before 1900 Steiff had pictured several breeds of dogs in their catalogs: hunting dogs, and bulldogs, in felt or velvet, poodles in curly boucle-type material. The dogs were featured sitting, begging, lying and standing; with and without wheels. After the turn of the century the number of dog breeds was greatly increased: Great Danes, Greyhounds, or wolly little Pomeranians. In 1904 Steiff advertised: "One has to protect oneself against illegal imitations. Our new patented Pomeranians have achieved worldwide recognition within eight months." Until well into the 1920s almost every breed of dog was featured at least once in each catalog. The design of each dog was based on the actual characteristics known to be peculiar to the breed. The Dachshund was particularly popular at the turn of the century because it was the favorite dog of Kaiser Wilhelm II. Other favorites were typical German dogs like the Pomeranian and the Pug. In England on the other hand, the terrier, the pinscher, and the King Charles Spaniel were more popular. King Edward VII's favorite dog was the Pinscher "Caesar", and this breed was especially well sold as a plush toy between 1910 and 1920 – not only by Steiff but also by other toy manufacturers. The fact that the Prince of Wales, Edward Albert, had also grown attached to a dog, (the Terrier, "Gwen"), helped to boost the sales of Steiff's little plush counterparts. In the U.S.A. the Boston Terrier had the greatest commercial success. As "Tige" in the Buster Brown cartoon series, the Boston Terrier shared a great many adventures with the hero, and both boy and dog became duly famous. Generally speaking, Steiff's dog breeds were average sellers until about the time of the First World War. However, in 1920, their popularity apparently increased and they became the company's top-sellers.

224

Illus. 224: *Steiff doll portraying a dog salesman – with his commanding "Officer" and his Pinscher "Caesar", a bulldog and a fox terrier.*

225

226

227

***Illus. 225-229**: Dachshund "Dax, 1414", (**Illus. 225**), in painted velvet; the oldest sample in the Steiff archives. – **Illus. 226**: Lovable Dachshund "5317", in plush (1914). – **Illus. 227**: "Gwen", a terrier from the series "5328". "Gwen" was the favorite dog of the Prince of Wales, Edward Albert. (1911). – **Illus. 228 + 229**: The Pomeranian was the most fashionable dog at the turn of this century; which explains why the Steiff version was such a successful "seller" in 1903/1904. – **Illus. 228**: A glimpse inside the production department. **Illus. 229**: An advertising photograph.*

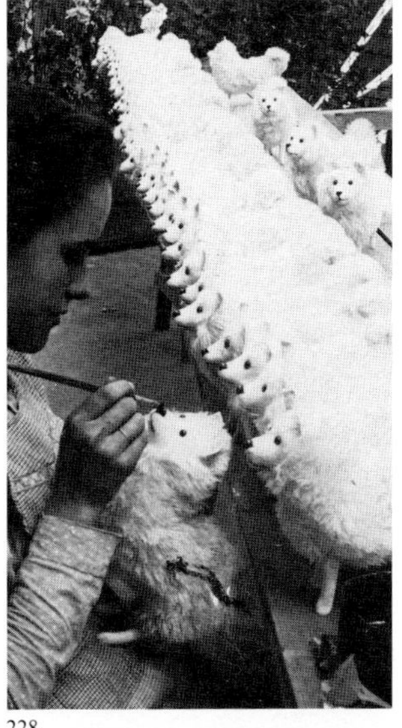

228

229

230

***Illus. 230-232**: Almost every breed of dog is represented in this scene. The photograph, which shows a "Dog Restaurant" complete with waiters, was taken for advertising purposes in 1913. – **Illus. 231 + 232**: This terrier achieved worldwide fame, and was not only produced by Steiff but by many other toy manufacturers as well. The photograph shows "Caesar", the favorite dog of the British King, Edward VII. In **Illus. 231**, "Caesar" is pictured catching a mouse, the caption reads "Naughty Caesar".*

231

232

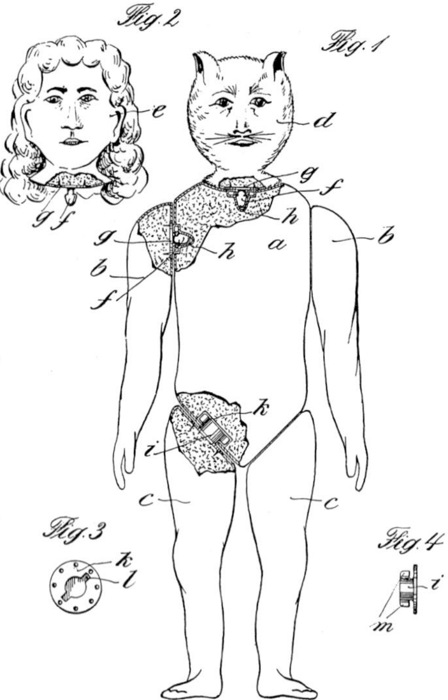

***Illus. 233**: In 1908, this Steiff patent for removable limbs was not approved ("doll with changeable limbs").*

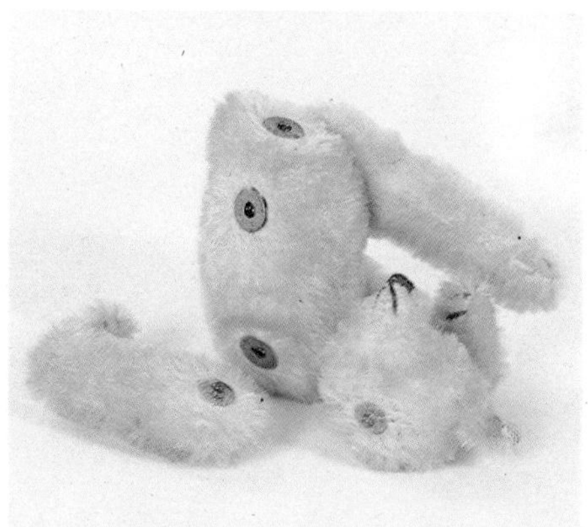

***Illus. 234**: Pieces of a small Steiff "Snap-A-part bear, 5353" (7in.), probably a factory sample.*

"Children appear to have a particular desire to pull off the limbs of their dolls during play – especially if they are jointed onto the body. And although, according to our experience, children also play happily with broken dolls, their sense of reality and beauty may suffer as a result." This paragraph, written by Steiff in 1908, was sent to the Royal Patent Office in Berlin, as an explanation of their latest design, for which they were requesting a patent: a removable fastening system for the heads, limbs and ears of dolls and animals. That is, in place of the standard disc-jointing normally used, the dolls and animals would now be fitted with tiny metal couplings (similar to the bayonet fitting on cameras), which would attach the jointed ears, limbs and head to the body. The patent was rejected, and after intensive searching, a solution was found. Steiff looked back into the past, to a discovery of Carl August Pfenning, of Barmen-Rittershausen, on August 2, 1895. Pfenning invented snap-fasteners! When Carl Pfenning registered his patent, its intended use (in his opinion), was to open and close the front fly on mens' pants. Steiff of course intended to use the snap-fastener for something completely different – they wanted removable joints for their dolls and animals! The new design was only used for the so-called "Roly Poly" figures, which were similar to the "stand up" toys except for the fact that they were made entirely of cloth. Thus it was now possible to unsnap the head and limbs of these figures and use the body as a ball. In the 1909 catalog the following "Roly Poly" figures were patented and offered as, "Toys for Tiny Tots": Dachau Farmer, Clown, Golliwog, Bear, Rabbit, Cat and Poodle. The snap-fastening method did not work quite as well for the dolls. The Steiff archives only have one example – a golliwog whose arms and legs can be unfastened. An important aid to the identification of these Steiff articles is the Patent No. DRP 88149 impressed on the snaps. This was the number of the patent granted to the inventor, Carl Pfenning.

***Illus. 235**: The patent for this "Roly Poly" Cat was registered in 1909.*

236

***Illus. 237-239**: Sample from the Steiff archives: Golliwog with removable limbs (Snap-A-part-Toy).*

237

238

239

***Illus. 240**: This wonderful "Roly Poly" Bear is 7in. tall and was produced from 1909 onwards in four sizes: 7, 8, 10 and 14in..*

***Illus. 236**: Various "Roly Poly" figures: (from the left:) Farmer Dach, Golliwog, Cowboy, Clown Clo (in felt and plush), Cat and Rabbit (1909 until 1920).*

240

241

***Illus. 241**: (from the left) Farmer Dach, Krackjack, Dolly-Bear and Roly Poly Clown enjoy themselves at a dance.*

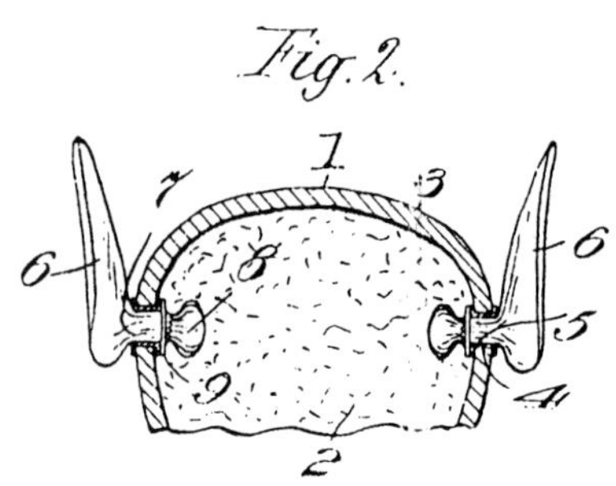

***Illus. 242**: The U.S. Patent for movable ears which was registered in September (1908).*

Steiff animals had jointed limbs and movable heads, but the ears were sewn firmly onto the heads. Real animals, of course, are different! Dogs can prick up their ears, rabbits can lay back their ears, and cats can move their ears sideways. On October 16, 1907, after a great deal of experimenting, Franz Steiff developed a system which simulated the animals' natural movement. He applied for a patent for this new design and details of the patent are available thanks to the copyright which was granted in the USA on September 8,1908 under the DRGM No. 898 018. After this patent had been approved, the animals were fitted with a turning mechanism which allowed the ears to be moved about and clicked into position. This design was copied by the Bing Toy Company of Nuremberg in 1913. Steiff wrote to Bing: "We have in our possession, a brown and white plush rabbit manufactured by your company, which has exactly the same ear-mechanism as one of our products." Bing admitted "plagiarism" immediately, and stopped production. However, this did not stop them from selling the remainder of the 500 rabbits already manufactured. This incident shows clearly, that not every article which looks like a Steiff product, or has the typical characteristics of a Steiff product, was necessarily made by Steiff! The unmistakable mark of origin for Steiff products was, and remains, the Button-in-Ear. Other methods of distinguishing a Steiff product from one of another manufacturer can only be termed unreliable. Steiff's methods of production, and even their patented mechanisms, have almost all, without exception, been copied by other manufacturers – even if only for a short period of time. Therefore, other methods of identification can only be used as a guide to the production date of an article, but certainly not to confirm the identity of its manufacturer.

243

***Illus. 243**: An original and new idea was to provide the rabbits with movable ears. On the right, a "Schlopsnies design", circa 1913, 8in. and on the left a "Holland Rabbit" with movable ears and limbs, 7in.. This rabbit was sold in great quantities as an "Easter" gift. The "Holland Hase" with movable joints in brown/white (5317).*

244

***Illus. 244**: The "Holland Hase" with movable joints in brown/white (5317), was also available in 9, 11 and 14in. (from 1910/1911).*

***Illus. 245-249**: The "Baby Bear" was intended for younger children. (**Illus. 245**). A "throw doll" with Mama voice box dressed in a colorful sewn on dress, 9in. (Patented 1910). – **Illus. 246**: Chimpanzee dressed in blue tail-coat and yellow vest, 7in. (circa 1910). – **Illus. 247**: On the left, a cat in jacket and red felt slippers (Dressed similarly to Peter Rabbit), "Kazlady" throw-doll, 9in. (both circa 1910). – **Illus. 248**: This little begging elephant was also dressed in "Peter Rabbit Style", 9in. – **Illus. 249**: "Peter Rabbit" displaying true British tradition. He was produced in painted velvet, in begging position. "Peter" wore a felt jacket and slippers, and was produced from about 1905, for the English market. A special model was available in lamb plush. Sizes: 4, 6, 9, and 14in.. (Note: Dressed animals featured here were no longer available after the First World War).*

245

246

Stories and characters created up by authors, and interpreted by illustrators have often been developed into successful products by toy manufacturers. Mickey Mouse is probably the best and most famous example of this. The Teddy-bear, however, was an exception. This extremely popular creation began as a plush toy and was already selling successfully before the first in a long series of Teddy-bear books appeared on the market. They did not simply act like humans, they were also illustrated in appropriate costumes exactly as the authors described in their stories. It was no surprise, therefore, to find other Steiff animals soon following Teddy's example and slipping into costumes and suits. A glance at the Steiff catalog of 1910/1911 reveals a whole series of dressed animals: Monkeys of all sizes in clown costumes, in stockings with sweaters and hats, or in frilled dresses; elephants – in sitting position, with jacket and slippers of felt; rabbits – in begging position, with felt jacket and slippers (from 1912 onwards – dressed as hunter); cats, in felt jacket and slippers; kitten ("Catbaby") in baby-dress, and mother cat ("Catlady") in dress and apron (size: 9in., with a voice-box); Poodle and pig – standing on hind legs – in jacket and slippers. In 1913, Puss-in-boots (13 and 20in.), and a rabbit in a dressing-gown, were added to the series. "Puss" was luxuriously kitted out. He wore a white hat with a red feather, a yellow ribbon (across his chest), red knee-high boots and carried a real sword. Puss-in-boots cost 8.75 Marks and could be provided with a "miaow" voice box at an extra charge. In 1902, a beautifully illustrated childrens' book about the adventures of "Peter Rabbit" was first published. This simple tale about a little rabbit in his blue jacket was a huge success, and brought worldwide fame to the authoress, Beatrix Potter. Beatrix Potter not only wrote and illustrated her own book, she also made a little "Peter Rabbit" doll, and registered it at a patent office in London. However, she was unable to find a manufacturer for her doll in England. News of Peter Rabbit's success and encouragement to manufacture the little rabbit reached Giengen via Steiff's London agent, Herbert Hughes.

247

248

249

250

251

Illus. 250 + 251: _Thanks to the huge variety of animals available it was possible to achieve wonderful "group" photographs. The groups were usually assembled using postcards with painted scenes as the role-models – as in the "Dog School" (**Illus. 250**) which was modelled on a postcard scene from 1906. – **Illus. 251**: Decorative scenes like these were sold or lent out to large department stores for advertising purposes._

Illus. 253: _"Cats Concert" performed by "Puss-in-boots", "Catbaby", "Catlady" and many other cats from the Steiff program._

252

Illus. 252: _An animal group, "Carnival of Animals", under the direction of an elephant! (circa 1911)._

254a

Illus. 254 + 254a: *"Puss-in-Boots" straight out of Grimm's Fairy Tales in his magnificent costume! The relevant patent for this design was registered in 1911, and this suitably attired fine specimen went into production in three sizes; 14, 17 and 20in.. Naturally he had a "miaow" voice box! However, only 1,400 examples were made, between 1912 and 1917.* ***Illus. 254a***: *In 1927 a second version of Puss-in-Boots was designed. The new model was not jointed and the boots were sewn on. 2 sizes.*

254

MARGARETE STEIFF, Gesellschaft mit beschränkter Haftung in GIENGEN a. d. BRENZ (WÜRTTEMBERG).

Spieltier mit beweglichem Kopf.

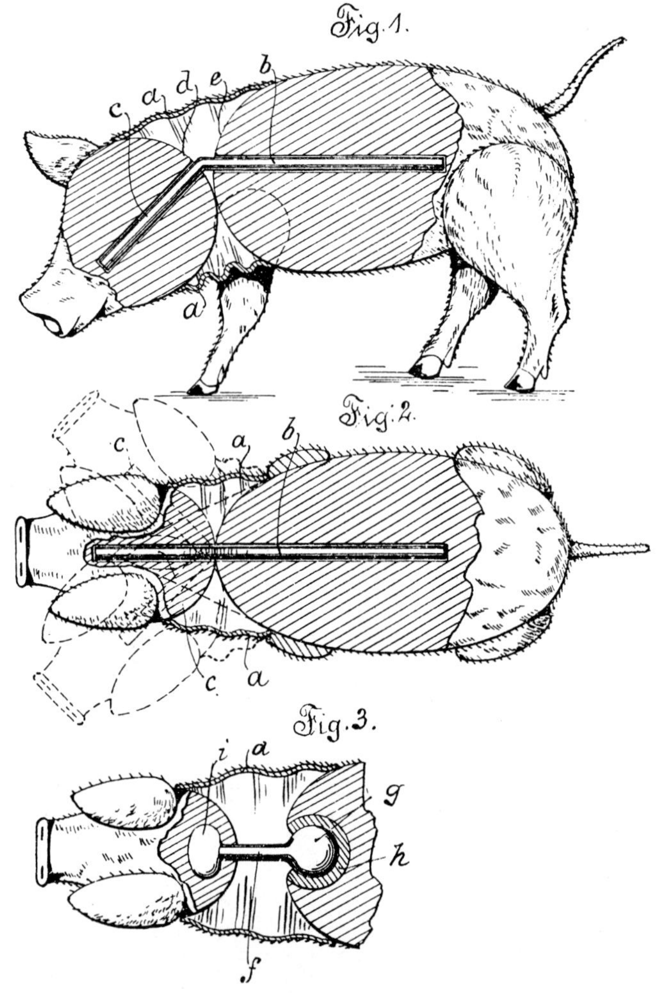

***Illus. 255**: DRP 298 992 "Toy Animal" with movable head (1908).*

"The head movement of a living animal is essentially carried out in two separate motions. Firstly by the bowing of the head from top to bottom, or right to left (or vice versa); and secondly, by turning the head around on the neck." Franz Steiff used this principle to develop a new "mechanism" for the head-movement of the Steiff animals. It was his intention to attach the heads of the animals firmly and inseparably to their bodies, yet at the same time, he wanted to be sure that their movements were as realistic as possible. His experiments proved encouraging and he succeeded in attaching a swivel jointed mechanism to the head which was then secured to the body by means of a tube running from the neck to the torso. This design was registered on May 24,1908, as, "Toy animal with movable head" and granted the patent number 208 992. The mechanism was extremely hardwearing and virtually unbreakable, unless excess force was used. This ball-jointed head mechanism was used for the following animals: Poodle (begging), pig, Polar-bear (with and without wheels), cat and opossum. The first sales figures were so promising that Steiff's competitor, Wilhelm Strunz, immediately took note. He copied the Polar-bear and its newly developed head mechanism in an absolutely unscrupulous manner. A letter concerning this matter has been retained. On October 10, 1910, Oskar Wolfsmüller, a Strunz employee who had previously worked for Steiff, wrote to the management in Giengen: "Herr Strunz knew very well that the mechanism had already been patented, since I personally informed him that this was the case." The matter was taken to court and resulted in a verdict against Strunz. This was duly reported in the daily newspapers, as well as in the trade magazines. Strunz was ordered to pay 1,500 Marks or spend six months in jail if he ever produced or marketed the Polar-bear. Steiff issued an additional warning: "We shall not hesitate to prosecute each case which infringes our legally protected rights."

***Illus. 256**: A slightly altered "Billy Possum" – the Steiff Opossum, with ball-jointed neck (Patent reg. 1909). It is highly probable that this model was never put into production.*

***Illus. 257**: A rough sketch of the successful Polar Bear.*

***Illus. 258**: This pig with ball-jointed neck was offered in four sizes: 6, 7, 9 and 11in.*

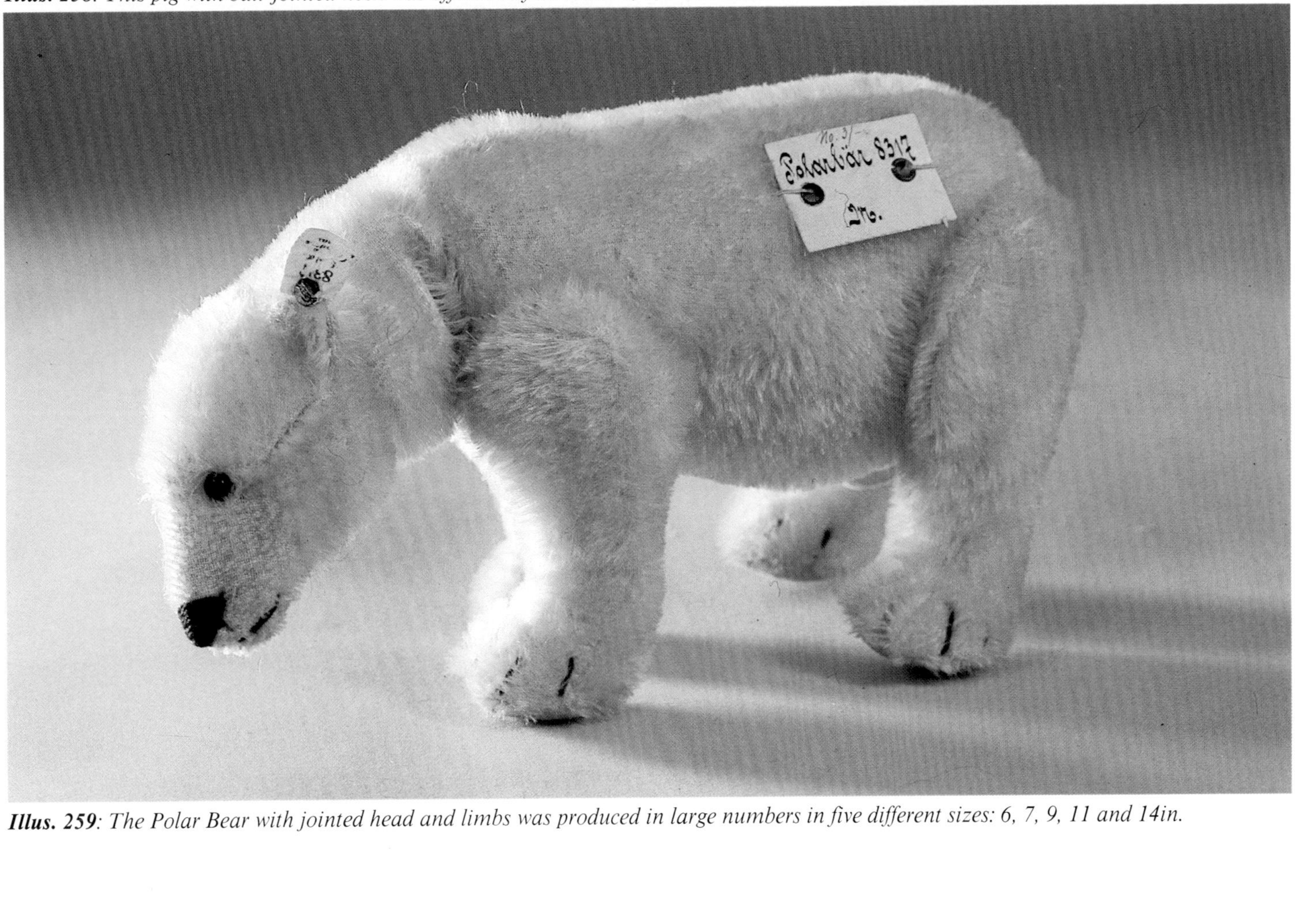

***Illus. 259**: The Polar Bear with jointed head and limbs was produced in large numbers in five different sizes: 6, 7, 9, 11 and 14in.*

260

261

Illus. 261: *"Record" Toys were on a four-wheeled chassis of metal. A pair of bellows was fitted to the rear-axle to give a sound effect. Left: Record Peter (1912), Record Struwwelpeter (1916/1917), Record August (1916/1917), and Record Felix (1926/1927).*

262

***Illus. 260**: Dolls and Animals became competent cyclists as this photograph from the 1902/03 catalog illustrates: (Available from 1899).*

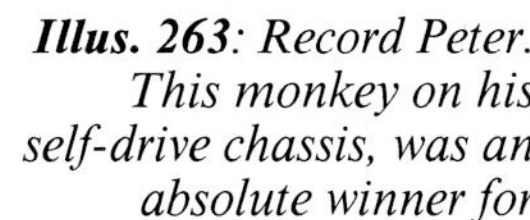

***Illus. 263**: Record Peter. This monkey on his self-drive chassis, was an absolute winner for Steiff. Some examples had the name "Steiff" printed on the wooden wheels. Numerous variations were introduced into the program: in brown without neck ruff, or in blue with colored neck ruff; in 3 sizes – 8, 10 and 14in.. The brown Record Peter was manufactured from 1912 until well into the fifties.*

In 1896 "Velocipede riding animals" – animals sitting on a metal tricycle were first featured in the Steiff catalog. The animals had their feet firmly attached to the pedals of the tricycle, and they imitated a "cycling" movement when pushed or pulled along. A rabbit, a cat, a poodle and a monkey in a felt jacket, were Steiff's first "cyclists." They were all approximately 12in. tall and their metal tricycles were almost certainly from the Maerklin Toy factory in Goeppingen. In 1899 the "Velocipede" program was extended. Patents were registered for: "Rad-Affe" (Monkey cyclist), "Rad-Dame" (Lady cyclist), "Rad-Herr" (Gentleman cyclist), "Rad-Elefant" (Elephant cyclist), and "Rad-Hase" (Rabbit cyclist). These new items were all pictured in the 1902/1903 catalog. Apparently they were not a great success, since they did not appear in the next catalog. Instead, a new toy appeared in the catalog in 1912 which worked on the same principle, but had four wheels instead of three. This little toy was registered as: "a toy with a self-propelled movement." It was granted the patent number, DRGM 528 621, and its name, "Record Peter", was also patented. "Record Peter" was a little monkey sitting on a sturdy four-wheeled chassis constructed of thin metal bars which were connected to the rear-axle by means of a metal rod. Thus, when the toy was moved backwards and forwards, it created the impression that the animal was steering himself. The advertising text for this new toy read: "Record Peter, in silky, brown, mohair plush, seated on a self-drive chassis with sturdy wooden wheels and automatic sound-box. Virtually unbreakable mechanism. Simply has to be pulled along by attached cord!" The first Record Peter was available in two sizes, 8 and 10 inches. The chimp was available in brown without a neck ruff, as well as in red, and blue, with ruff. "Record Peter" achieved record sales figures! In 1913 he was also available in blue, yellow, green, red or black with a colored neck ruff and could now be bought in three sizes – 8, 10 and 12 inches. "Record Teddy" joined the program at this time. In 1916 the program was extended still further. "Record-Puck", "Record-Struwwelpeter", "Record Radler", "Record August" and "Record Max and Moritz" joined the animals. Two years later, "Record Bäcker" (Baker) and "Record Bauer" (Farmer) were added, whilst in the twenties, "Record Felix", "Record Hase" and "Record Petsy" were also available. These toys were such a success that they were offered in the Steiff program until well into the fifties. It simply remains to be added that as a result of "Record Peter's" success, the earlier animals on tricycles became popular once again and as "Velo-figures", they enhanced Steiff's commercial success with the Record-Toys. The "Velo-figures" were animals seated on tricycles fitted with a bell. "Velo-Peter", a chimp was in Steiff catalogs until 1917. Various soldier dolls and a young boy were also produced until 1917/1918 – however, these were only available in limited quantities.

***Illus. 262**: For this advertising photograph (1914), 180 Record Peter's were arranged in a circle, in the middle of which stood a young boy holding a 39in. tall, Record Peter.*

264

***Illus. 264**: The Record program (1916/1917) included (from the left): Record Max and Record Moritz (10in.), Record Struwwelpeter (8in.), Record Puck (8in.), Record Radler (Cyclist) (8in.), and Record August (8in.).*

265

***Illus. 265**: Photographs from 1918/1919 showing the Record Infantryman, Record Farmer and the Record Baker, all of whom, however, were only sold in small numbers.*

266

***Illus. 266 + 267**: Steiff animals were also presented on tricycles (Velocipede = Velo-series). A particular favorite was Velo Peter with his bell, 11in. (1914 until 1917).*

267

***Illus. 268**: Even the world famous Teddy-bear joined the "Record"-Animals. He was manufactured from 1913 onwards in three sizes; 4, 8, and 10in..*

268

Illus. 269: *Puck the gnome, with ducks on eccentric wheels.*

October 12, 1912. Three patents were registered by Steiff on this date, at the Patent Office in Berlin: DRGM 528 622 "preparatory device for the production of spring-jointed figures with irregular movements at regular intervals"; DRGM 528 623 "eccentric wheel with counter-balance for toys" ;and DRGM 528 624 "wheels for mobile toys." The toy which was developed from these patents was brought out the same year as the latest novelty in the Steiff program. "The animals have been given a more natural movement and gait thanks to this newly developed patented method of fixing the wheels; so now, the monkey can leap, the Dachshund and the duck can waddle and the rabbit can hop. This new Steiff invention came about quite by chance. When drilling axle holes in the wooden wheels the drill was not placed exactly in the middle and the holes were then a couple of millimeters to one side. Thus, when the wheels were mounted onto the frame, instead of rolling evenly, the movement was bumpy and irregular. Steiff immediately realized that by deliberately placing the holes in an exactly measured "false" position the wheels would then produce an unusual movement. A whole series of animals was now fitted with these "eccentric" wheels: dachshund, rabbit, seal, monkey as clown, bulldog, cat, fox and duck. The advertisements read: "This waddling felt duck with brightly colored feathers is fixed onto solidly built, eccentric wooden wheels, which provide the duck with its characteristic waddle. Also fitted with a deceptively realistic "quack-quack" voice. A droll little toy."

Illus. 270*: Mother goose was attached to her goslings by wire and the eccentrically placed wheels gave the geese their characteristic waddling movement. The mother goose, on wooden wheels, pulled her children along behind her, quacking and clucking realistically thanks to a pair of bellows which provided the sound effect.*

Illus. 271*: Monkeys on "machines" with eccentric wheels. (From the left): In brown plush light gray plush wearing a Fez (circa 1930) and clown in felt (circa 1912). All 9in.*

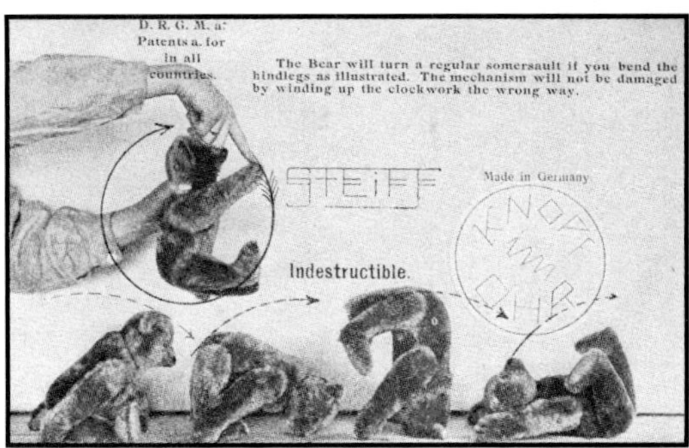

272

Illus. ***272-276:*** *Somersaults – the newest movement at the Steiff factory. In 1909 five different models were presented at the Leipzig Spring Fair.-* ***Illus. 272:*** *Bear in light brown, dark brown and white, 7, 9, 10, and 12in. (height when sitting).* – ***Illus. 237:*** *Eskimo, 9 and 10in..* – ***Illus. 274:*** *Chimpanzee, 9 and 10in..* – ***Illus. 275:*** *Elephant 7 and 9in..* – ***Illus. 276:*** *Clown, 8 and 10in..*

Illus. 277: *The Turbo Bear 1950/1951 only appeared in the program for a very short time. The bears were 5 and 6in. tall and wore a red vest and a yellow bow-tie.*

277

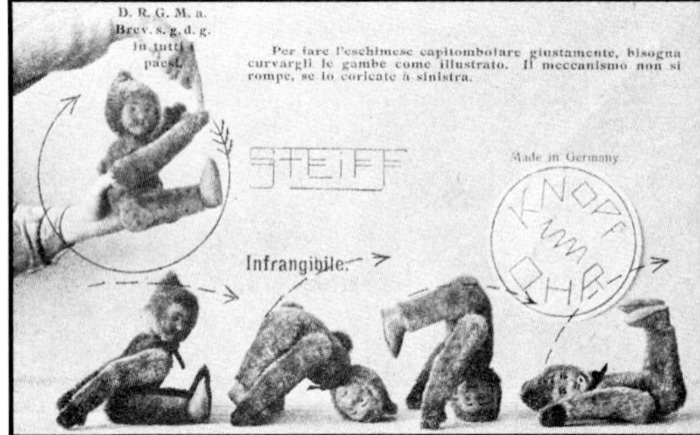

273

274

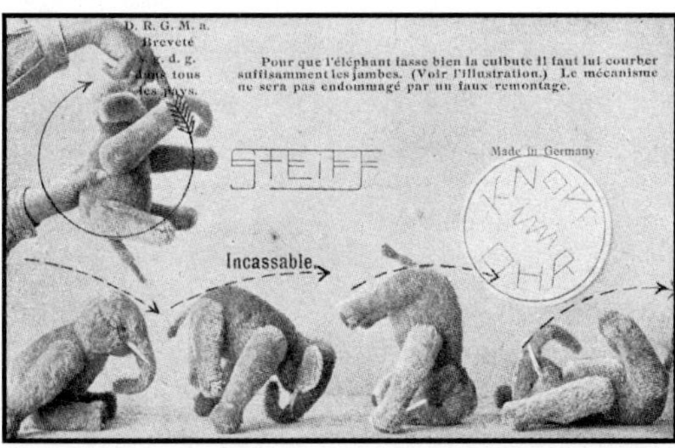

275

276

On October 12, 1908, towards the end of his long stay in England, Otto Steiff wrote an informative letter to his brothers in Giengen reviewing the market situation (for toys) in London. Enclosed in this letter was an advertisement for "a novelty from Paris" on which he remarked: ". . . comprising of a bear with clockwork mechanism. The arms (front paws) are joined by wire so that they move backwards when the mechanism is wound up, and then the bear flips over." Otto Steiff goes on to describe the clockwork mechanism in great detail, and remarks finally, "Mr. H. (note: Herbert Hughes, Steiff's sole-agent in London) now wishes to produce this article using our bear, No. 5322 . . ." The clockwork bear being sold as a novelty in London was a product of the Paris based company of Ernest Descamps. Descamps had already obtained a German patent for his bear on July 22, 1908. In addition, the Plush Toy Factory of Wilhelm Strunz had also produced and patented a similar mechanical bear. The bear had led him to introduce a whole series of mechanical animals which he offered under the name, "Barnum's Animals". Even before Otto Steiff's letter had arrived in Giengen the Steiff management had been aware of these mechanical bears, and work had already begun on this new development. Margarete Steiff decided that her nephew, Hugo Steiff, should devote himself to the new product. It would surely be possible to produce a somersaulting bear without copying the mechanism already being used by other companies. Hugo Steiff successfully developed an indestructible mechanism which was activated by using the Teddy-bear's arms as the "key". The arms could either be wound in a clockwise or an anti-clockwise direction, exactly like the Remontoir-winder which the watch-making industry had been using for a number of years. On November 14, 1908, the Steiff solution was registered as: "Mechanical toy, characterized by its clockwork arm, which is constructed of a flexible strip of iron attached to the clockwork mechanism in the body by spring couplings, and activated when the arm is wound in a clockwise direction. These couplings will be released if the arm is then wound in an anti-clockwise direction." This patent was registered in Richard Steiff's name in the U.S.A. for legal reasons. The first clockwork toys appeared in a flyer in 1909 advertising the latest Steiff novelties: Monkey, Bear, Elephant, Clown and Eskimo-doll. An example of the advertising text reads: "The monkey somersaults properly when its legs are in the air, as illustrated. The mechanism cannot be damaged by winding in the wrong direction. Unbreakable!" The monkey was available in brown mohair; the Teddy-bear in light brown, dark brown and white. The elephant and the Eskimo-doll were only available in the first catalog so they were obviously not as successful as the monkey or the bear; for which Steiff had, in the meantime, found a new use. They could be hung on a trapeze to carry out their somersaulting movements. Over 10,000 of these somersaulting animals were sold in three years; and, as always when an item proved successful, Steiff's competitors were not very far behind. A legal battle between Steiff and the Bing Toy Company of Nuremberg developed in 1911 and lasted until 1915. Bing copied the clockwork mechanism and its method of production. The case was deliberately protracted by Bing; expert opinions were brought in by both sides. Once again Steiff were able to win the case, but in the four years in which the case was dragged out, Bing were able to sell thousands of their "Mechanical Toy Animals" all over the world. Between 1950/1951, the "Turbo-bear" enjoyed renewed popularity. These 5 and 6in. bears of light colored plush, wearing red vests and yellow ribbons were only available in the Steiff program for a short time.

***Illus. 278**: This "daring young man on the flying trapeze" is an Eskimo Somersaulting Doll. (The trapeze was only available from 1909-1911).*

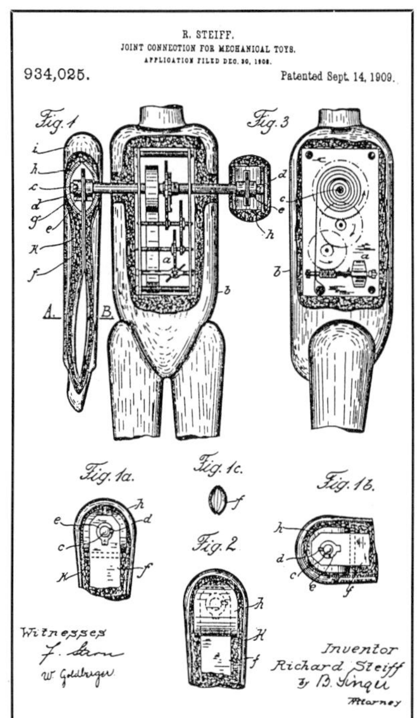

***Illus. 279**: This sketch for the U.S. Patent is the work of Richard Steiff.*

280

***Illus. 280**: The somersaulting bear (Purzel Bär) was first produced in 1909. This impressive example is in blonde plush, with glass eyes and a horizontally stitched nose. He also has the remains of the white label in his ear.*

***Illus. 281**: The somersaulting bear demonstrates all of the movements of which he is capable!*

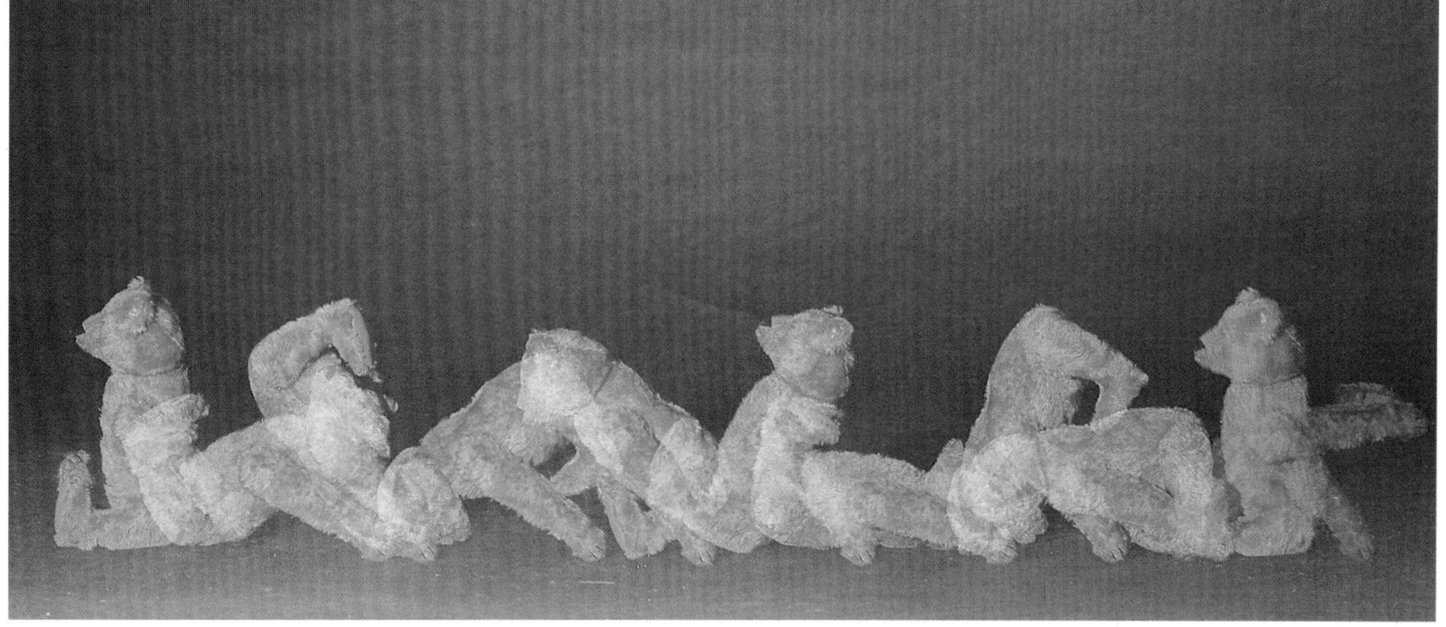

281

display. We have to make sure our name is associated with quality and we can use other fancy mottoes, like: 'Originator of the Teddy-bear'; or, 'World's Greatest Toy Factory'; or, 'I can say Mama with my new unbreakable voice box'; or, 'Look for the Button-in-Ear'!" And he noticed another trifling mistake which no-one in Giengen had apparently been aware of: Skittle sets in the United States ought to have ten pins ("Over here you only play skittles with ten pins"). Under this remark of Richard Steiff's, is a handwritten note from Paul Steiff "I already requested this in 1904, but the request was considered unneccessary!"

"On his return to Germany Richard Steiff told a journalist, "I realised immediately, that in order to get ahead in America, one had to use both elbows! Advertising is expensive over there but one has to learn to help oneself."

He gave a typical example: "In Atlantic City, on the coast, which is visited by about six million Americans every year, I discovered a toy shop in a prime situation. They were adding an extra window to the shop and I asked what it would cost to rent the window for three years, during the high-season. It wasn't too expensive at all, and so now, during the best time of the year, my products are displayed in a prime position and cannot be overlooked."

Steiff now went all out to capture the American market. Richard Steiff's suggestions were put into effect. Otto Steiff, responsible for the development of the American subsidaries, travelled to New York to discuss an arrangement (previously prepared by Richard Steiff) with George Borgfeldt & Company. A contract which guaranteed Borgfeldt sole agency rights was the basis of this arrangement. Steiff also pledged to maintain a warehouse with 50,000 Marks worth of products. Joint advertising projects, as well as the

Puppen.

Körper und Kleidung aus Filz.

Köpfe unzerbrechlich. Höhe 26 Cent.

No. 692.

No.		ℳ	₰
690	**Betzinger Bauer**	2	20
691	**Betzinger Bauerin**	3	—
692	**Betzinger Bauernpaar** in Carton	5	40
693	**Tiroler**	1	80
694	**Tirolerin**	2	60
695	**Tirolerpaar** in Carton	4	60
696	**Schwäbischer Bauer**	1	80
697	**Schwäbische Bäuerin** (Rotkäppchen)	2	60
698	**Schwäbisches Bauernpaar** in Carton	4	60
699	**Matrose**	1	80
700	**Matrosin**	2	20
701	**Matrosenpaar** in Carton	4	20
702	**Gärtner**	1	80
703	**Gärtnerin**	2	60
704	**Gärtnerpaar** mit Spaten u. Giesskanne in Carton	5	20
705	**Schäfer**	1	80
706	**Schäferin**	2	60
707	**Dame** mit Pelerinenmantel und Capote	2	60
708	**Kind** in rosa, blau, weiss, rot u. s. w.	2	60
709	**Knabe**	1	80
710	**Harlequin** mit bunten Läppchen u. Schellenkappe	1	80
711	**Wickelkind** im Tragkleid	2	60
	Carton zu einzelnen Puppen	—	10

23

***Illus. 282**: Dolls for sale in the catalogs from 1892 until 1902/1903.*

***Illus. 283**: One of the first Steiff dolls which was included in their program in 1902, as a "Grotesk Figur". This is the black footballer, 14in. tall, in black velvet, exactly as he was pictured on the "Novelty Sheet" of 1903/1904 (see page 29).*

***Illus. 284**: Advertising photograph from 1903/04. It was at this time that football (soccer) became extremely fashionable in Germany (The German Football Assoc. was founded in 1900; the first championships took place in 1903), and numerous "Footballers" appeared in the Steiff program. (From the left): A black footballer in the foreground, above him another footballer and a velvet frog holding an oar, 1902 until 1907 – in 1906 only 255 were made). Black Dude with top-hat, and Black Man in Safari Helmet, smoking a pipe. Extreme right – an English Policeman. All dolls are 14in. tall, have velvet faces and felt bodies with primitive cardboard disc-jointing.*

settlement of provisional accounts, were clearly defined in this contract. The contract was valid as of January 1, 1913, but was invalidated at the start of the First World War. It was renewed, however, at the end of the war.

A permanent display of Steiff toys was set up on the 9th floor of the huge Borgfeldt store. In February 1913 the U. S. magazine "Toys and Novelties" wrote enthusiastically: "When you get out of the elevator the first things you see are a life-sized camel and a life-sized elephant. The camel is decorated with oriental trappings and can easily carry the weight of 4 or 5 children. The elephant is strong enough to take as many children as can fit on his back. He is able to trumpet like a real elephant with the help of a voice box . . . The aisles are filled with every imaginable dog-breed; many of them are on movable wheels. In addition there are the cats, the lambs and of course, the famous, ever-popular, Teddy-bear . . .. The droll little Steiff Character Dolls are wonderfully arranged: sailors, soldiers, hotel page-boys, sportsmen, firemen, teachers, clowns with voices. . . . many of the American toy dealers are now following the successful European example and are using Steiff display pieces to promote the sales of their stock. These display pieces are made up by Steiff from their own ideas or from customers original drawings . . ."

The worldwide importance of Steiff products even before the First World War and their rapid rise to fame in a few short years, was unique even for the German economy. Appreciative reports of this success could be found in all the important newspapers and trade magazines of the day. The "Wegweiser", a trade paper for the toy industry, wrote: "This truly sensational worldwide success in such a short period of time, by a certain toy manufacturer, can hardly be bettered by any other product in our industrial society . . ." The paper continued: "There is hardly a retailer in the world who is not familiar with Steiff products . . . whilst Odol, (Editors' note: Odol is a very famous mouthwash) to pick one of the most well-known brand-names we have, is certainly not as well known, or as well used in the rest of the world as it is by us (in Germany)." What was it that had helped the "Button-in-Ear" to become so famous, so desirable and so eminent? The "Wegweiser" states: ". . . although the dolls which the Steiff company presented under their trademark were truly unique and original for the period; one could hardly make the same claim for many of their soft-filled animals. And it surely isn't just the novelty of these items which is responsible for their huge success . . ." Why there is absolutely no mention of the Teddy-bear in this article remains the closely guarded secret of its writer. However, he (or she) offered great praise for the comic and character dolls, which were made at the same time as the Teddy-bear.

It is not generally known that Steiff dolls are part of the company's tradition. The first examples could be found in catalogs as early as 1892. These dolls had unbreakable heads, and the bodies and clothes were made of felt. They were 10 inches tall and twenty-one different types of doll were made; mostly in regional costume, although there were also sailors, gardeners, shepherds, a lady, a boy, a harlequin, and a baby in swaddling clothes.

A few examples of these early dolls heads have been preserved in the Steiff archives. They have many different hairstyles, painted or glass eyes, and some of the male heads even have a moustache. It is interesting to note that these heads are stamped "unzerbrechlich" (unbreakable) and "waschbar" (washable). Records do not show ▶

283

284

***Illus. 285 + 286**: These two dolls belong to the very first series of Steiff character dolls which were made in 1903. All the dolls in this series had velvet faces. English postman in two versions – fat 14in., and thin, 20in. tall. – **Illus. 287**: An unmistakeable characteristic which should be noted: the jointing of the limbs, on both Teddy-bears and dolls, was accomplished by using heavy thread (twine).*

who was responsible for making these heads, but the distributor of these dolls was Louis Lindner & Sons, from Sonneberg. (Paul Steiff was a good friend of Emil Lindner.) The manufacturers Gebr. Haag (Haag Bros.), F.M. Schilling or Cuno & Otto Dressel all produced similar types of heads at their factories and one of these companies may have been responsible for the heads used by Steiff.

The Steiff catalog of 1897 pictured a doll in uniform sitting on a horse on wheels. This was a character doll representing George Washington, and it was a popular gift at the time of his birthday, on February 22. It was also Steiff's first direct attempt at canvassing an international market.

Two years later, in 1899, the manufacture of dolls was put into force. The newest addition to the Steiff program was a doll representing Fridtjof Nansen, the North Pole explorer. This was listed in the catalog as "Nansen-Puppe" (Nansen-doll) and made of white mohair with an unbreakable head. Nansen was also offered with a polar bear, as a pull-along toy – "Nansen mit Eisbär". At the same time a "Bear-driver" with a brown "dancing-bear" was made as a counterpart. These dolls were 10 inches tall. Further additions were: Jockeys, 7 – 9in.; a Scotsman 11in.; Boer and Englishman 11 and 17in. ▶

285

286

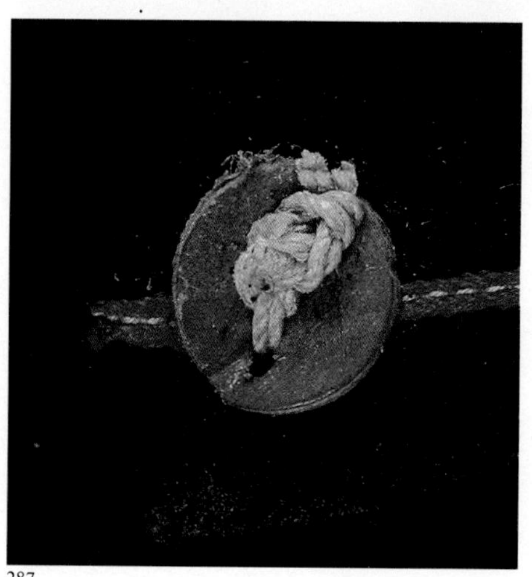

287

and Clowns made of leather in three sizes 17, 24 and 32in.. A series of "Affenpuppen" (Monkey-dolls) was also offered in this catalog. (See page 20.)

The dolls featured in the next Steiff catalog, 1902/03, revolutionized the Steiff program in particular and the doll industry in general. The "Illustrated News" described the situation thus: "To assist Gretel Steiff, who produced her early cloth toys with loving simplicity, came Richard Steiff, her nephew. With his excellent eye for detail and his artistic ability he has breezed into his aunt's amateur domain with all the enthusiasm of youth and immediately begun the search for new designs."

This sentence discloses the secret behind the success of the Steiff company: it was the creative genius of Richard Steiff which allowed the small factory from Giengen to build its international reputation. He was also responsible for "breathing new life" into the doll program. He could not "warm" to the dolls which Steiff had in their program. The faces seemed to him to be too much like the cold porcelain faces of the dolls already being produced by the other manufacturers. He tried to give the dolls new "appeal" by using felt and velvet, remodelling their faces, painting the facial details, and "fitting" them with movable joints. The results were droll, seemingly grotesque ▸

Illus. 288-290: *It was part of the Steiff tradition to continuously strive for improvement in both design and production. –* ***Illus. 288*** *shows the completed "perfected" felt version of the two English policemen; fat and thin (circa 1909). In 1913, they were produced in 16, 18 and 20in. sizes. On the other hand, the first examples of the English policemen (fat 14, and thin, 20in. –* ***Illus. 289 + 290****), which were produced at the Steiff factory in 1902, can only be described as being extremely primitive in their construction.*

288

289

290

figures, which resembled cartoon characters with their deliberately exaggerated features.

Every-day types were portrayed; "Giggerl" (Dude) – the fashion eccentric; "Rad Fax" (bicycle Fax) the fanatical cyclist; Footballers, Policemen, Soldiers and the "mean" Mother-in-Law. Like the first Teddy-bears, all the dolls had jointed limbs – at first the jointing was achieved using a thick type of string, and later by using wire. These so-called "Groteskfiguren" (grotesque figures) caused quite a stir among Steiff customers when they were patented: footballer 14in., black footballer 14in., english policeman (fat or thin) 14 and 20in., French policeman 14 and 20in., English postman 14 and 20in., black man 14in., and a frog with an oar 14in..

These first Richard Steiff dolls seem to have disappeared completely, although luckily, a few were set aside for the Steiff Archives. It is therefore possible for

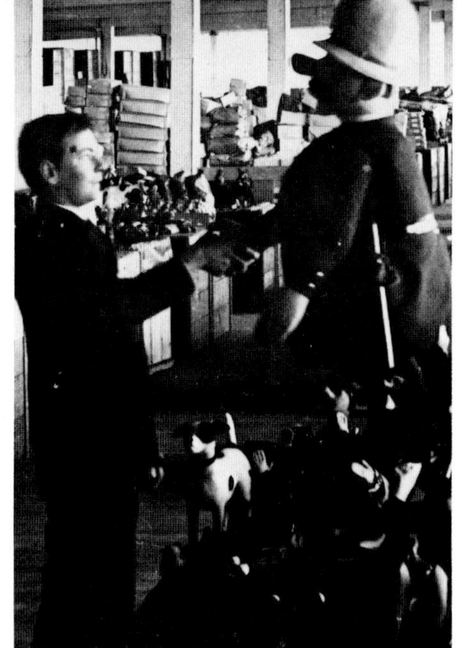

***Illus. 291**: Dolls in sizes up to 48in. were also made for advertising purposes. Each doll was thoroughly checked before shipping.*

us to describe them here in detail. A typical characteristic of these early dolls are the velvet faces which are very primitively formed. They have a center-seam, shoe-button eyes, painted features and hair, and the bodies are of velvet or felt.

In 1904, a whole series of American Cartoon Characters was produced: "Foxy Grandpa" (14in.), "Foxy Boy" (9in.), "Uncle Sam" and "Happy Hooligan". These dolls were later included in the series of dolls developed and manufactured from Richard Steiff's original designs. They were now made entirely of felt. Also included in the series were: "The Katzenjammer Kids" (a cartoon loosely adapted from Max and Moritz), "Fat Captain" (14in.), "Cook" (17in.), and "Mrs. Fatty" (14in.). A few of these characters were made in sizes up to 39in. and used to decorate the entrance to the Toy Department of the World's Fair in St. Louis in 1904.

The advertising text for the new felt dolls claimed: "One cannot imagine anything more droll than these cartoon character-dolls, which arouse an involuntary chuckle and give such pleasure thanks to their comically realistic and life-like interpretation."

Could these amusing cartoon ▶

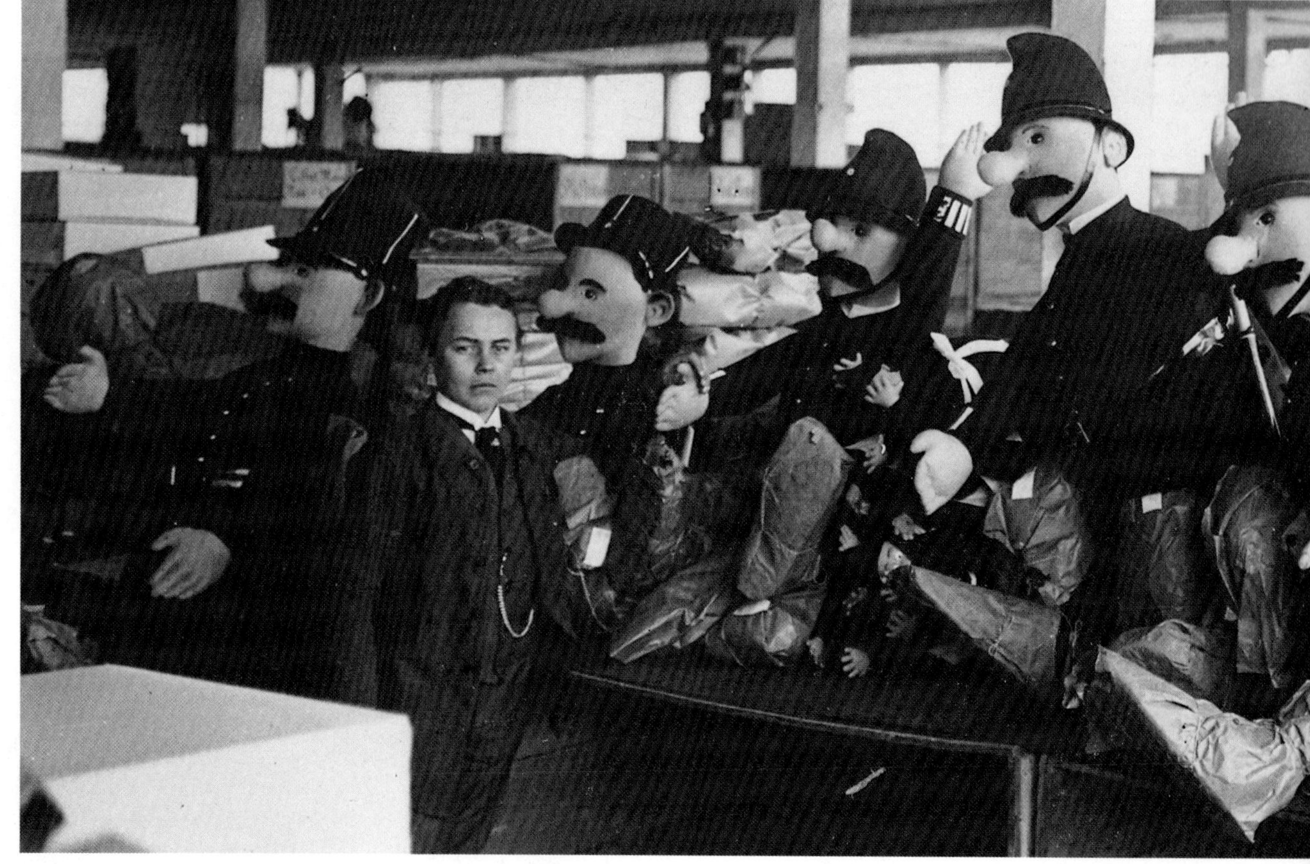

***Illus. 292**: On this packers' table in the shipping department are English policemen – ready for export.*

***Illus. 293**: American policemen soon joined the Steiff Doll Series. On the left, a policeman with a velvet face (1903), beside him – once again the fat policeman, and his thin companion – both in felt, 14 and 20in. (post 1909).*

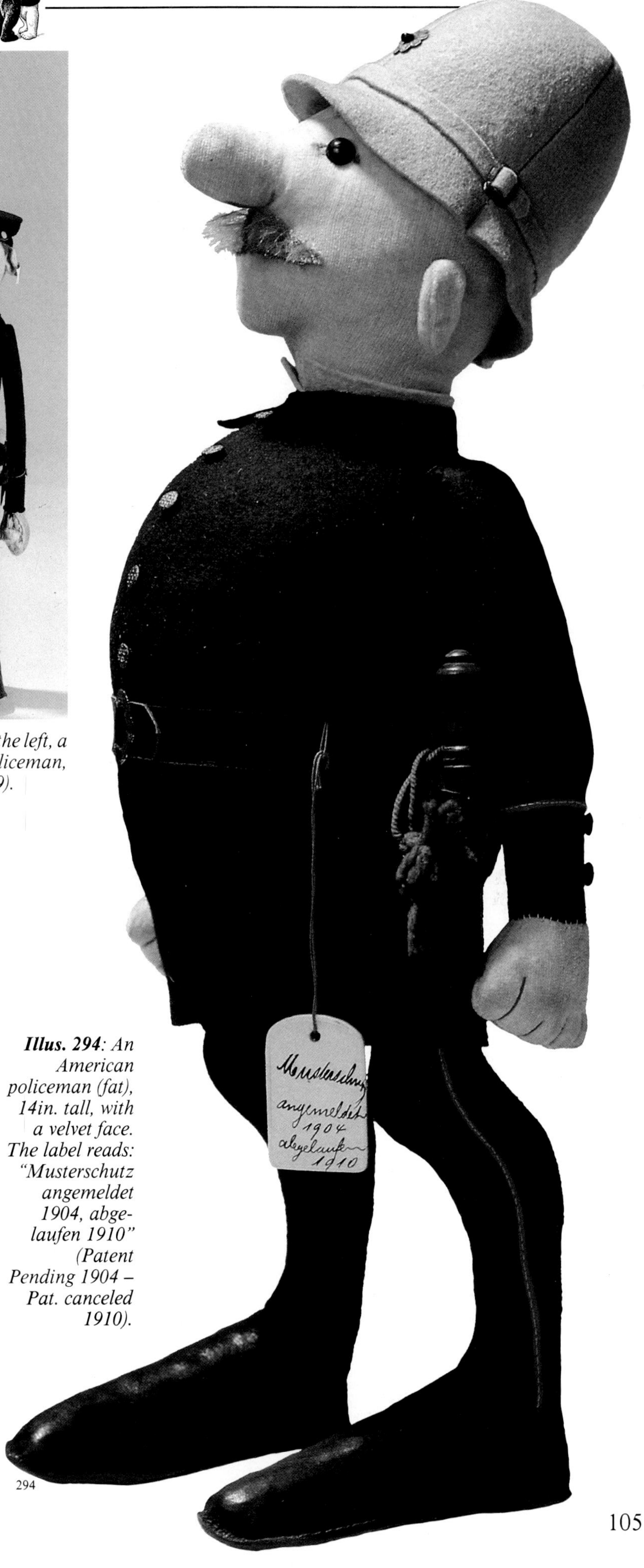

***Illus. 294**: An American policeman (fat), 14in. tall, with a velvet face. The label reads: "Musterschutz angemeldet 1904, abgelaufen 1910" (Patent Pending 1904 – Pat. canceled 1910).*

294

Illus. 295*: A glimpse inside the light and airy warehouse. Front left: Comic dolls for the American Market.*

figures create a sizeable increase in turnover? "The humor which was apparent in their (Steiff's) four-legged creations laid the foundation for future success. And so now, the toy industry has been suddenly shaken out of its boring complaisance which until now has robbed the world of dolls of its magic, and been propelled into the frivolous world of these Steiff characters which are both unbreakable and comical, and yet particularly appealing to children. The dolls are presented in every kind of costume one can imagine."

Neither did these dolls carry any of the instructive solemnity so typical of this period into the childrens' nurseries. Instead, "they encourage humor in the fantasy world of the little ones." An important factor in a time which was known as "the century of the child" according to the Illustrated News of 1911.

These comic dolls breathed new life into the toy industry and opened up a new market for Steiff. Steiff's advertising was deliberately focused on this new line in their program. Each advertisement showed a different photographic scene involving various dolls. The dolls informed matter-of-factly about quality and production: "Steiff comic dolls are unbreakble and fully jointed. The joints only assume naturalistic positions and do not creak when moved. The cloth covering over the joints is strengthened. Steiff comic dolls are neither hard nor heavy and are completely safe for children to play with. In addition, they will not lose their color or cause any staining. Steiff comic dolls are not filled with sawdust they are only stuffed with excelsior, and therefore the filling in the bodies and limbs cannot shift; thus the dolls retain their three dimensional form. Their clothing is accurate in every detail and each doll carries the "Button-in-Ear" trademark.

A second generation of dolls came into being in 1907. They were soft-filled dolls, with the childish faces of young boys and girls. These dolls were made to compete with the other more traditional manufacturers in the industry. They were produced as hard-wearing play-dolls, less vulnerable than their porcelain counterparts. They were intended to be indestructible and capable of withstanding the daily games of childhood. The prototype patented in 1908 under the name "Mausi" (little mouse), was a little different in its original conception. The head and body of the doll were of felt and the filling was of kapok. The flesh colored face was made of two halves, exactly like the other dolls. Since it was decided not to give the doll removable clothing, the body was used to represent the clothing. This was done by making a bell shaped figure which was wider at the bottom. This "bell" shape was closed off at the bottom by a piece of felt, to which the shoes of the doll were attached. After the head had been stuffed, the round glass eyes, framed by lashes, were attached with heavy thread, and finally the ears were sewn into place.

Within a few months this "Werf-puppe" (literally translated this means "throw-doll") had been transformed into a real "play" doll by the skilled hands of Richard Steiff. The face remained the same but the head was covered by a wig of long-haired plush. The arms and legs were attached by disc-jointing to the body and the whole doll was modelled to represent a toddler of approximately one to two years. Naturally only the best materials were used for these dolls and also for the large selection of underwear and dresses which were made for them.

1909 was a vital year in the history of dolls. This was the year in which the first "character" dolls came into being. These dolls were completely different from any of their predecessors and were to influence the Doll Industry for many years to come.

Whether or not the development of the Steiff dolls sparked off the huge "Puppenreform" (Doll Reform) which began at this time, remains an unposed question. The timing of this "Doll Reform" debut, and various records, indicate that this was in fact the case.

1907: First steps taken to develop a new line of dolls, at the Steiff factory.

1908: Patents registered for several "Play dolls" by Steiff.

Autumn 1908: Exhibition of Doll Artists' Dolls in Munich.

Autumn 1909: Presentation of the first "Character Dolls" by the Kämmer & Reinhardt Company, Waltershausen.

When Steiff applied for a patent on the words "Character Doll" in 1910, ▶

296

their request was rejected by the Royal Patent Office. Their competitor, Kämmer & Reinhardt, had had the same idea – a few months earlier! And their patent had already been approved when Steiff put in their application. In connection with this, a paragraph, found in the 1910/11 Steiff catalog, is worth mentioning: "Our latest line of Character Dolls represent not only the most modern, but also the best designs of our times, and they have given rise to a complete reformation within the industry."
Two important facts emerge from this sentence. Firstly the Steiff company continued to use the term "Character Dolls" until well into the 1920s and despite the fact that Kämmer & Reinhardt had been granted the patent, they did not protest Steiff's usage! Secondly, it seems clear that Steiff considered themselves to be the instigators of the huge changes within the Doll Industry. If this assertion had been untrue then certainly one of their competitors would have taken legal action against the company.
Even more interesting is the fact that in their 1922 catalog, Steiff claimed: "Character Dolls, in finest quality wool felt. (This name was in fact created by us, for our dolls – which differed from all ▸ 122

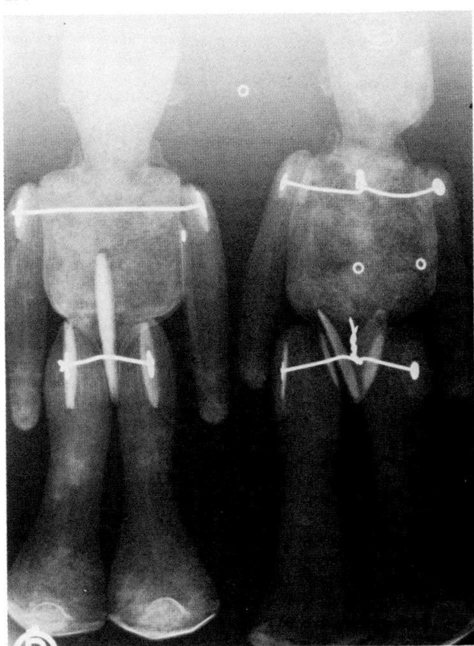

297

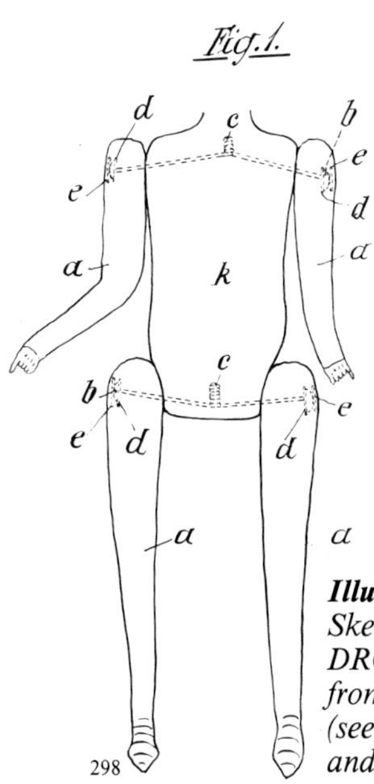

298

Illus. 296 + 297: Limbs with Metal jointing – the latest novelty! – ***Illus. 296*** *shows a sailor on the left, manufactured from the registered pattern (DRGM 255 036): "Metal rod jointing. Each joint to be fastened by a disc and small metal pin, thus allowing swivel movement." (1905); and, on the right; a sailor, DRGM 242 399; "Toy figure with jointed limbs which are attached by double wires twisted together inside the body" (1904).* ***Illus. 297*** *shows an X-Ray photograph of both dolls.*

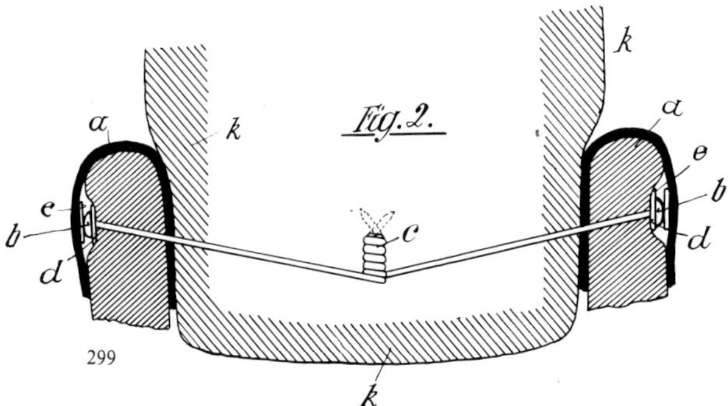

299

Illus. 298 + 299*: Sketches for DRGM 242 399 from 1904, (see* ***Illus. 296*** *and* ***297****).*

300

301

302

FOXY GRANDPA

***Illus. 300-302**: The U.S. Comic Series "Foxy Grandpa" was published for the first time in New York in 1900. The ghost-writer of these cartoons was Carl E. Schultze who worked under the pseudonym "Bunny". Schultze sketched the adventures of a grandfather and his two grandsons.*

***Illus. 303 + 305**: There are two versions of "Foxy Grandpa" in the Steiff archives. – **Illus. 305** shows the earlier design (1904) with a velvet face (14in. tall); and **Illus. 303** shows the same doll, in the felt version (available until 1914). In Germany the doll was sold simply as "Großpapa" (Grandpa), Press voice box in the hat!*

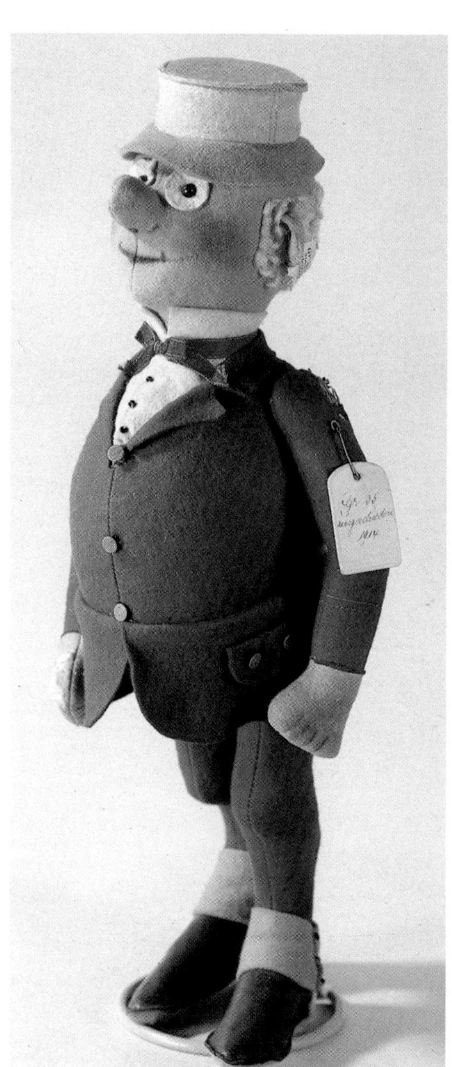

303

304

***Illus. 304**: One of the two "Foxy Boys" (9in.), with a velvet face (1904). In 1909, two "Foxy-boys" appeared in the program, (11in. tall), in velvet pants; and another young boy, "Herbert", (14in.), in a sweater. These dolls were offered as "Aviateur" (aviators) in the French catalogs.*

305

Illus. 306: *An original drawing from the U.S. Comic series "The Katzenjammer Kids", from 1905.*

307

The Katzenjammer Kids

Illus. 307: *A self-portrait by the famous Swedish artist, Carl Larsson. The painting shows Larsson with "Missis"; a doll from the Steiff program (1906).*

Illus. 308: *This photograph of a little girl holding two Steiff dolls "Fat Captain", and "Missis",was taken in the Steiff-Studio.*

308

Illus. 309: *"Missis" and "Captain" dolls, both 14in. tall.*

***Illus. 310**: The "Captain" in this advertising photograph was 39in. tall, (1908).*

***Illus. 311**: "Choosing is not easy. . .. Deciding's not always fun! Of these two super toys – How can I choose one!" Teddy-bear or ...*

310

311

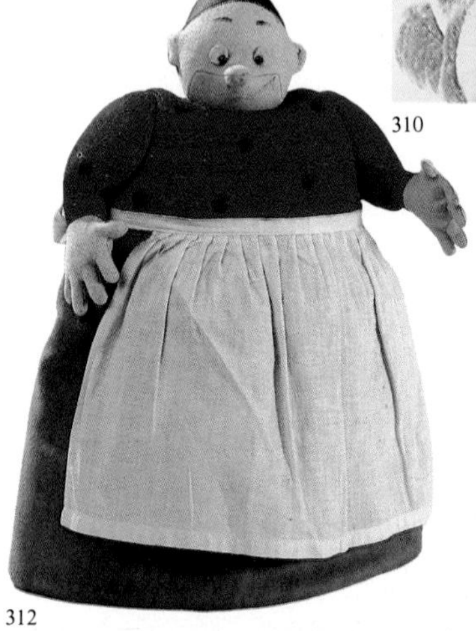

312

"The Katzenjammer Kids" were interpreted from Wilhelm Busch's picture book series, "Max and Moritz". The American newspaper mogul Hearst, hired the cartoonist Rudolph Dirks to develop the series. (Dirks was born in Germany in 1877, and emigrated to Chicago with his parents when he was seven years old). His first comic series was published in 1897 and was a huge success. The main characters were "Missis", the "Stepfather", a shipwrecked sailor- "Fat Captain", and two boys, "Hans" and "Fritz", who had absolutely no respect for anyone or anything! In their own double-dutch (a mixture of English and German) the family experienced numerous exciting adventures. Steiff produced "The Captain", and "Missis", in 1905; both dolls were 14 inches tall. A third figure from the series, "Köchin" (Cook), was 17in. tall, and was offered as a tea cosey/coffee-pot warmer.

313

***Illus. 312**: The cook, "Missis", also called "Mother-in-law". She was available as a doll, and as a tea-cosey, 17in. tall. This doll shot to fame in the space of four months as "Mother-in-law", and remained in the Steiff program until 1938.*

***Illus. 313:** "Missis" – an advertising figure for the Leipzig Fair.*

Happy Hooligan's

• • •

***Illus. 314**: The unmistakable characteristics of the cartoon figure "Happy Hooligan" are his large "stick-out" ears and red cap (with squeaker on his head).*

In 1900, Frederick Burr Opper sketched the permanently unhappy "Happy-Hooligan" a "sad smiling victim of wayward children and heartless adults", and a direct ancestor of Chaplin's, "little man." The cartoon depicted the comical Irishman with his two brothers, "Montmorency" and "Gloomy Gus", and portrayed the travels of the three tramps through England, France, Germany and Spain. Two polite Frenchmen – "Alphonse" and "Gaston", were their occasional travelling companions. This comic was virtually "tailor-made" for Steiff! Almost all of the character dolls, (Policemen, young boys, soldiers, etc.) from the Steiff program of 1902/1904 were modelled on characters from this cartoon series.

***Illus. 315**: "Happy Hooligan", 14in. tall, felt clothing.*

315

***Illus. 316**: Original 1906 cartoon: "Happy Hooligan and his dog."*

316

317

318

319

320

321

322

323

***Illus. 317**: "Comics-on-Ice" advertising! (from the left): Foxy Grandpa, Alphonse (under the sleigh), Mother Hubbard, Student, Gaston, Man-servant and Missis.*

***Illus. 318**: A velvet faced "Happy Hooligan" doll, 14in. (circa 1904/1905).*

***Illus. 319 + 321**: "Alphonse" in two variations – as a doll, and as a puppet (Pantom-Figure) on skates. (1909).*

***Illus. 320**: An original cartoon drawing of "Alphonse" and "Gaston" from the "Happy Hooligan" series.*

***Illus. 322**: "Gaston" – an early model with velvet face (circa 1904/1905).*

***Illus. 323 + 324**: Here we have two variatons of "Gaston". **Illus. 324**: as a doll, and **Illus. 323** as a puppet (Pantom Figure) on roller-skates.*

324

Illus. 325*: An original illustration from the book "Mother Hubbard and her wonderful dog" (circa 1800), a childrens classic in English-speaking countries.*

Childrens' books, like comics, have often produced classic characters. "Old Mother Hubbard" is one of the oldest story books for children and is believed to date back to about 1800 – almost 200 years! The story of "Old Mother Hubbard" and her wonderful dog was originally told in 15 sketched scenes. The dog was extremely spoiled by Mother Hubbard – for example: "She went to the barber's to buy him a wig and when she got back he was dancing a jig"; or "she went to the alehouse to buy him some beer – and when she got back the dog sat in her chair", or "she got a clean dish to get him some tripe, and when she came back, he was smoking a pipe." The dog acted in an almost human fashion and assumed the pose of a gentleman whenever Mother Hubbard returned with her gifts.

326

Illus. 326*: "Mother Hubbard" joined the Steiff doll series in 1909. She was 17in. tall, appears to have been only moderately successful, as only 1,103 dolls were sold between 1909 and 1914.*

Mother Hubbard

327

Illus. 327*: "Mother Hubbard" was unknown to German children, so the doll was sold as "Witch" – a companion to Hänsel (14in.), and Gretel (12in.), from the popular Grimms' Fairy Tale. Of this group of dolls, 850 sets were sold between 1912 and 1918.*

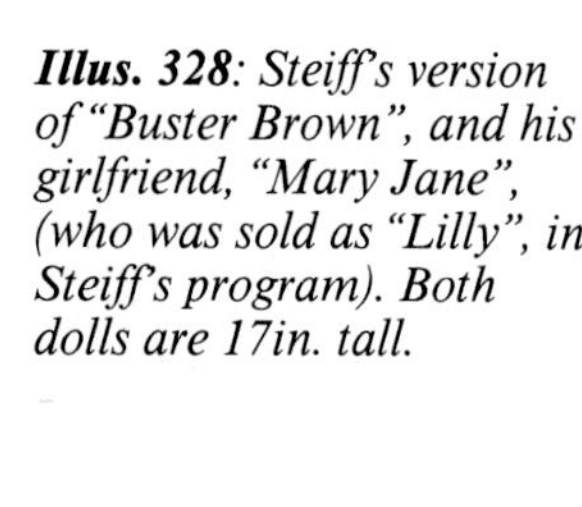

Illus. 328*: Steiff's version of "Buster Brown", and his girlfriend, "Mary Jane", (who was sold as "Lilly", in Steiff's program). Both dolls are 17in. tall.*

328

Illus. 329*: The original "Buster Brown" (cartoon character) and his dog "Tige".*

BUSTER BROWN

330

Illus. 330*: Steiff's sketch of Buster Brown's bull-terrier "Tige".*

In the early history of American comic characters, "Buster Brown" was the perfect complement to all the heroes drawn from the poorer population. "Buster Brown" came from an affluent family. He was dressed in "Little Lord Fauntleroy" suits popular for young boys of this period, and with his ferocious looking bull-terrier "Tige" he had a great many unbelievable adventures. "Buster Brown" was the creation of R.F. Outcault, who in 1906 based this comic character (as he did many of the other characters in his comic series) on his own children. With his cartoon strip "The Yellow Kid", Outcault laid the foundation for his later success. "Buster Brown" firmly established that success. This polite little hero and his wily dog played their pranks on adults and children alike. But at the end of each tale "Buster" always raised his index finger and promised to be better. . ..next time! "Buster Brown" did not typify the usual street-urchin heroes of that time. Instead he represented the tidy, well-mannered and well educated child of a good home. "Buster Brown" became so popular that he was soon being used to advertise shoes and clothing. Even a variety-show celebrated the young hero and his adventures. Toys, postcards, books, etc. became huge sellers if his name was associated with them. "Buster Brown" was never produced by Steiff under his own name. In 1908, the exclusive London Department Store, Harrods, ordered two "Lord Fauntleroy" dolls (18in.). Since Steiff apparently could not obtain the marketing rights for "Buster Brown", they used a doll already in their program (Knabe 45 – Boy 45 cm., 18in.) and adapted him for Harrods by dressing him in the "Buster Brown" look. In 1910, Steiff finally produced a Buster Brown doll under the name "Mimmo, 35". The doll was (14in.) and was dressed in a playsuit and a four cornered hat. Only 51 examples were produced and all 51 were sent to the George Borgfeldt & Co. store in New York. A variation of Buster Brown was introduced once again in the Steiff program of 1913. "Willy, 43" (17in.) a young boy dressed in a gray velvet suit. As a partner for Willy, Steiff featured "Lilly, 43" (17in.). Both dolls had the new combable wigs. "Lilly" was supposed to portray "Buster Brown's" girlfriend, "Mary-Jane". There is a single example of "Lilly" in the Steiff archives but no other records or photos of either "Willy" or "Mimmo" remain. In 1913, 27 examples of "Willy" were sold and 26 of "Lilly". In 1914 neither doll was featured in the Steiff program.

***Illus. 331-333**: Steiff Originals – "Lilly" (**Illus. 331**), and "Willy" (**Illus. 333**) with the comic characters "Buster Brown" and "Mary Jane", on whom they were modelled.*

***Illus. 334**: The Boston Bull-terrier enjoyed tremendous popularity in America and served as the model for "Tige" (Patent 1912). "Tige" had huge "googly" glass eyes and was available in three sizes; 7, 9 and 11in.. A few examples also had movable, googly-type, glass eyes (1913/1915).*

335

Mr. Twee Deedle

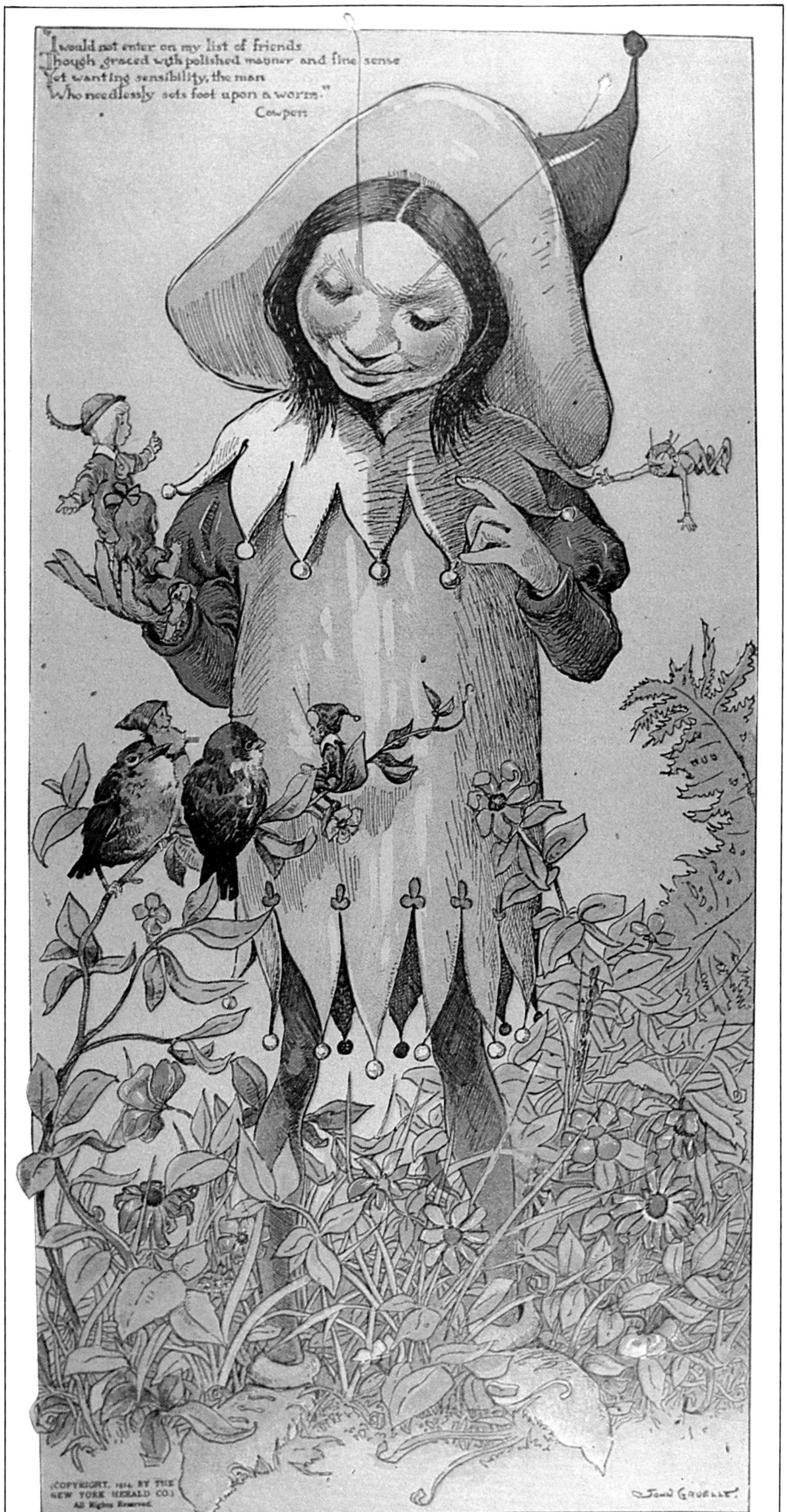

"I would not enter on my list of friends
Though graced with polished manner and fine sense
Yet wanting sensibility, the man
Who needlessly sets foot upon a worm."
Cowper

336

Fairytale adventures were experienced by "Mr. Twee Deedle", who was also created at the turn of century during the comic-character boom. His fantastic meetings in and around the world of nature provided excellent reading material for all the family. Johnny Gruelle drew this lovable character for the "New York Herald" – and what could be more obvious than for Steiff to produce this figure too?

***Illus. 335**: "Mr. Twee Deedle" in two variations, 14 and 20in. tall (1913/1915).*

***Illus. 336**: An original cartoon drawing of "Mr. Twee Deedle" from the U.S. comic.*

HUMPTY DUMPTY

Illus. 337*: Postcard featuring a little girl and her "Humpty Dumpty" doll (1910).*

"Alice in Wonderland", by the British author, Lewis Carol, was followed by a sequel "Alice Through the Looking Glass" in the year 1892. "Humpty Dumpty" played a major role in this story and soon became one of the best loved figures in the childrens' nurseries. Humpty Dumpty joined the Steiff program in 1906, and was available in three sizes; 5, 11 and 13in.. He remained in the program until the late 1920s. A few larger figures were made (20, 24 and 28in.) as display pieces. Because of copyright laws, Steiff were unable to use the name "Humpty Dumpty" in Germany, so they advertised the figure as a "man from mars". Some models were stamped "Regstd. 479 441: Made in Germany". In 1912 and 1913 Steiff also offered a plush version of Humpty Dumpty which was available on request. This version had stitched features and appears not to have been a great success since only 243 pieces were made, in the 11 and 13in. sizes.

Illus. 338*: "Humpty Dumpty" – 17in. tall.*

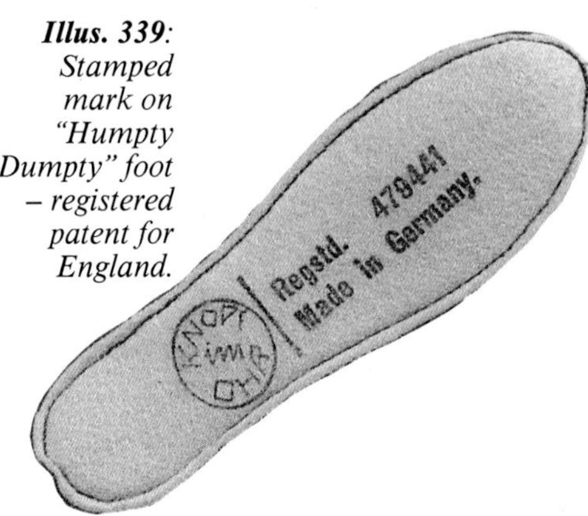

Illus. 339*: Stamped mark on "Humpty Dumpty" foot – registered patent for England.*

339

Golliwog

In 1895 a series of books by the English authoress, Florence Upton, also enjoyed unexpected popularity. The title of the first book (which was written in verse) "The Adventures of two Dutch Dolls – and a Golliwogg" gave the reader a very good idea of the contents. Unfortunately there appears to be no key in childrens' literature which would help us to discover where the golliwog got his name, or what it means. At any rate, the golly is definitely the main character in Florence Upton's books. He is always good for a surprise and amazes his friends the dolls with undreamed of adventures. Between 1895 and 1909, Florence Upton published 13 books in all. Steiff in turn made their first golliwog in 1908, and he remained in production until 1916 or 1917. The golliwog was available in a great many sizes (11, 13, 17, 20, 24, 32 and 39in.).

***Illus. 340**: Golliwog in two sizes, 14in., and 17in.. He has jointed arms and legs and a movable head.*

***Illus. 341**: Discovered in the Steiff archives: Golliwog with two admirers.*

340

341

***Illus. 342**: Postcard from 1905 showing a typical golliwog picture-book scene. The text reads: "The golliwogg is tired of dancing."*

Illus. 343: "Billiken" or "Krackjack", 12in., and also 17in. (a "special" edition, probably for advertising purposes).

KrackJack

Between 1900 and 1910 the Toy and Souvenir Industry was practically flooded with grotesque figures and lucky-charms. Probably the largest fan-club in both America and England belonged to a little grinning man, named "Billiken". There was no automobile hood without his image – and he was declared by many to be Buddha's successor. Designed by Florence Pretz and distributed by E.J. Horsman, "Billiken" went down in the history of dolls as the "God of Good Luck". In 1938, the U.S. Magazine "Playthings" wrote "...who for all the world looks as though he has beheaded a Teddy-bear and replaced it with a doll's head instead". In order to get around the copyright laws Steiff's agent in London, Herbert Hughes, registered the doll under the name "Krackjack". 7,294 examples were sold between 1909 and 1917.

Illus. 344: "Billiken" or "Krackjack", leading two elephants on wheels (1920s).

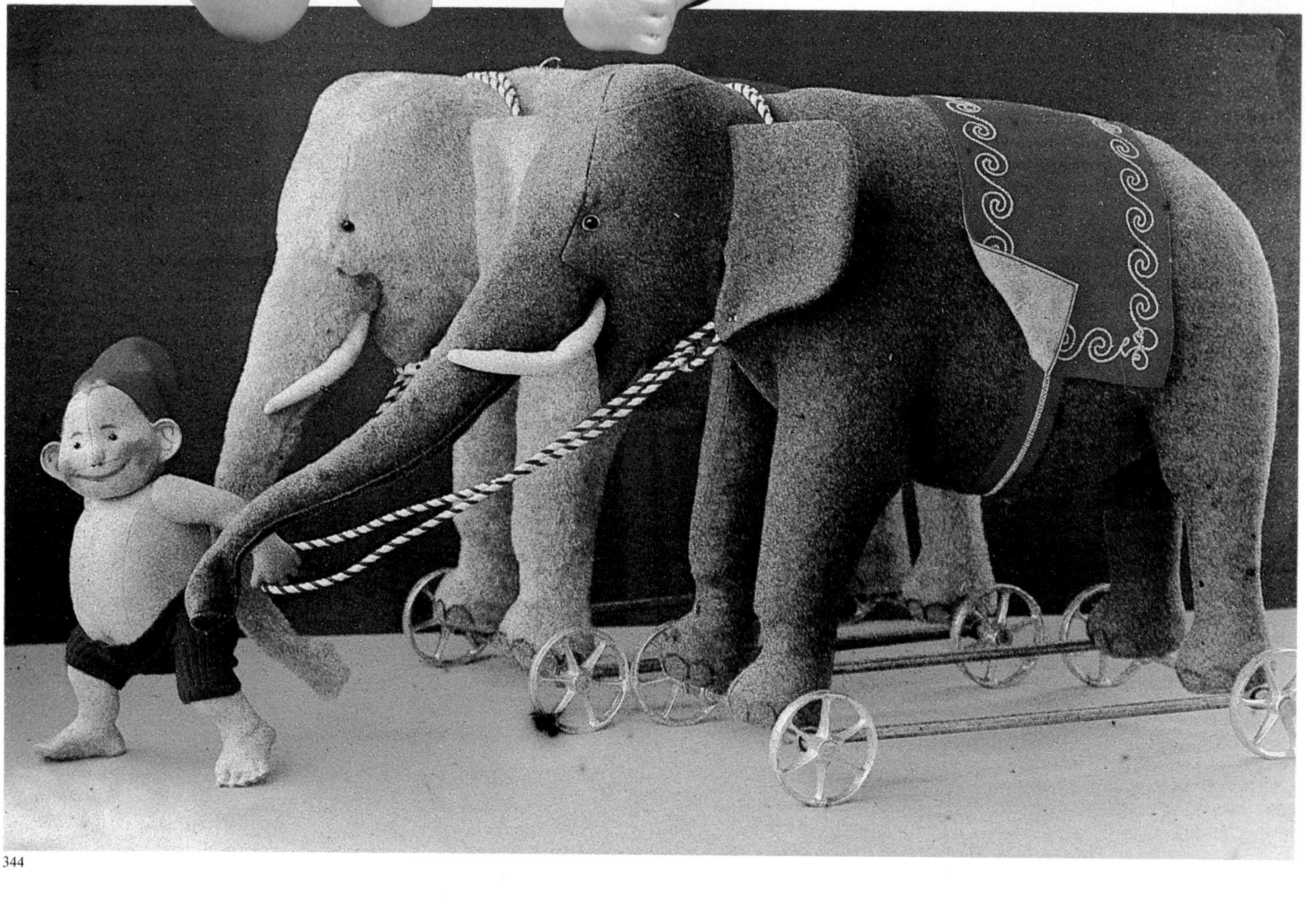

343

344

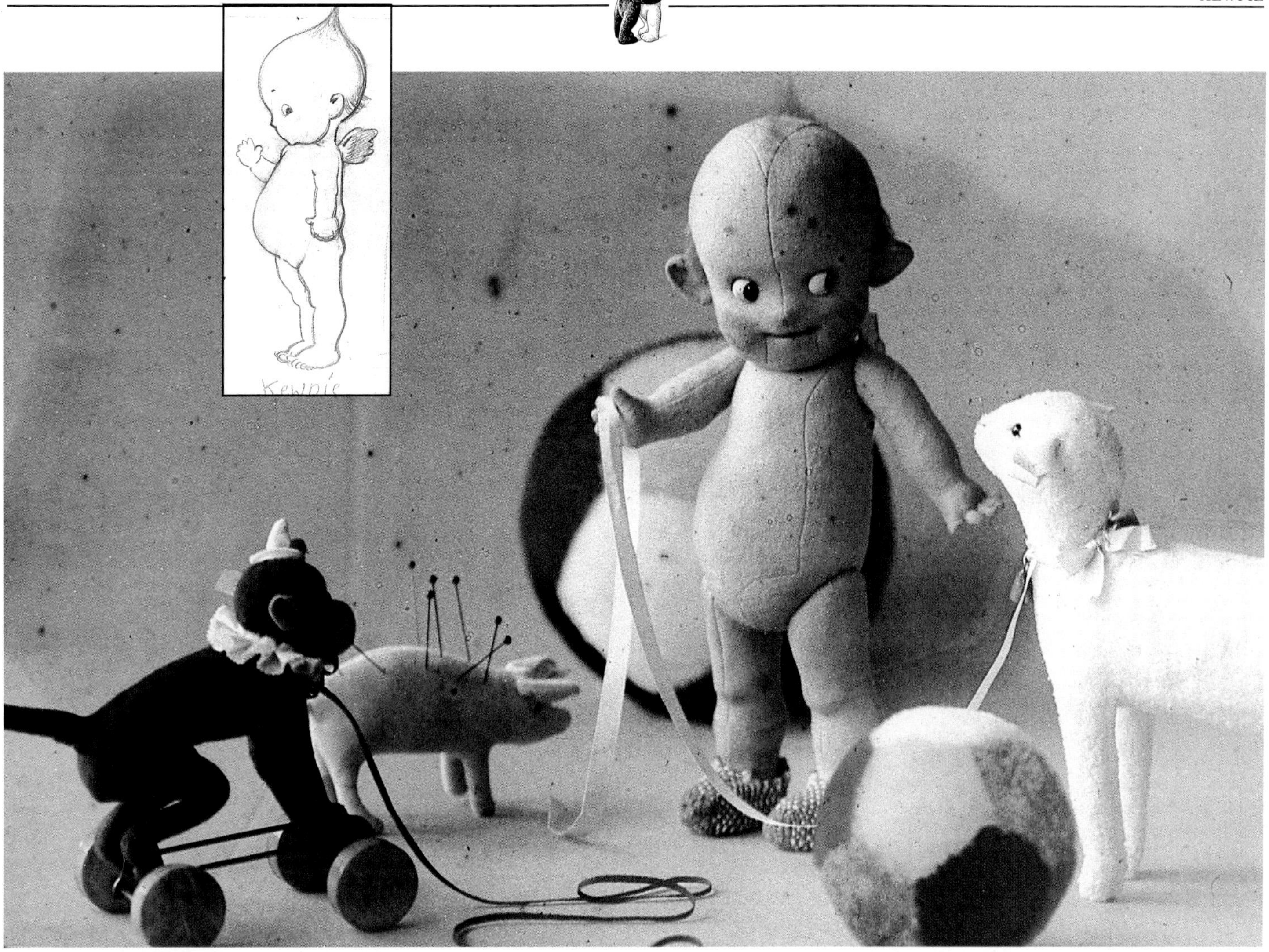

***Illus. 345**: This photograph from the Steiff studio (1913) was used as a postcard. – Top: Hand-drawn blue-print from the design department.*

Kewpie

The first Kewpie dolls were produced in 1912. The American artist, Rose O'Neil, designed these lovable creatures as illustrations for her books. The sale of the European rights was extremely complicated. Steiff, however, wanted to be part of the "Kewpie Boom" and so, in 1913, they circumvented the copyright laws by offering their "Kewpie" figure for sale under the name "Amor". An experimental design placing an "Amor" head on a "Krackjack" body, was almost immediately rejected. There are only three of these Amor figures in the Steiff archives and there are no records available to provide us with information of possible sales. Therefore it seems probable that other than the prototype figures, no further examples of "Amor" were made.

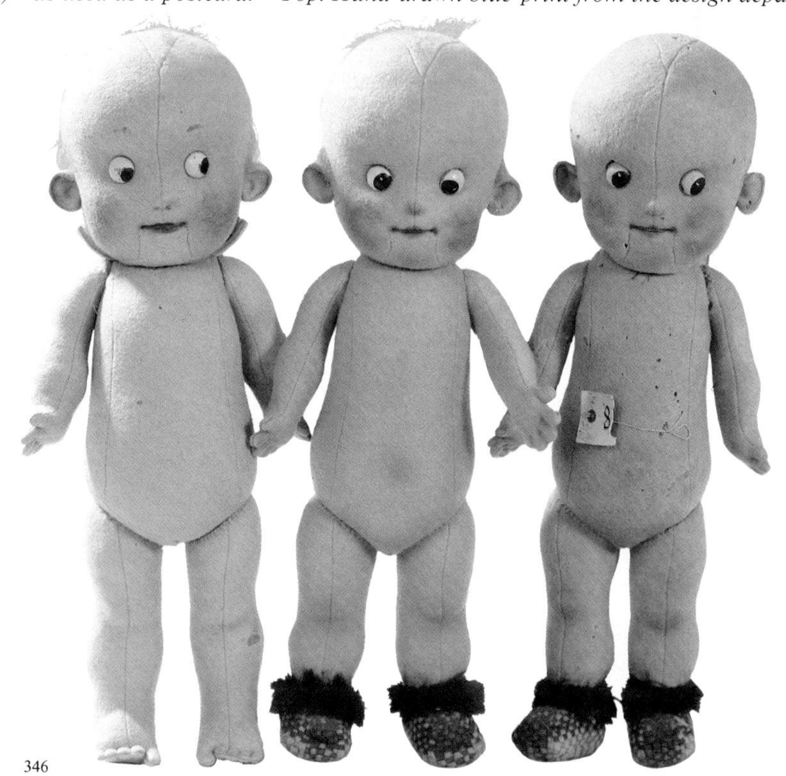

346

***Illus. 346**: The only examples of "Amor" known to exist are these three 14in. dolls from the Steiff archives, (1913).*

those other previously-produced stereotypes with their lifeless faces!) Our dolls capture the true disposition of the child thanks to their individual facial characteristics."

In other words the childish dolls produced by the Margarete Steiff Toy Factory from 1908 onwards resulted in the Doll Reform of 1909. These novel Steiff dolls provided the stimulus for The Munich Art Dolls of the period, and were also responsible for the Kämmer & Reinhardt Company's series of character dolls, which were developed using real children as models. Several other developments, including the Käthe Kruse dolls (which first came into being in 1910), may now be reassessed in view of this information.

Advertisements for the Steiff Character Dolls claimed: "Works of Art, which capture the childish temperament through their facial expression, and exceptionally realistic outfits. Unbreakable. The splendid, shining, curly hair is inserted into the scalp (not glued on) and can be brushed and combed when wet."

The years between 1903 and 1914 were fantastic years for the four Steiff brothers. Until her death in 1909 Margarete Steiff was also able to reap some of the rewards of the seeds she had sown: Creator of the Teddy-bear and driving force of the Doll Industry.

Unfortunately, she did not live long enough to witness yet another milestone which would find its place in the history of toys: Steiff were responsible for the first German movie featuring dolls.

An article which appeared in 1912 in the "Rundschau für Spielwaren" has been preserved. Under the title: "Steiff Puppen als Kinofilm – Eine neuartige Reklame" (Steiff Dolls star in a movie – a new form of advertising) the Rundschau's Berlin correspondent described his impressions of this movie in lengthy detail. Here is the first paragraph of his article:

"I recently visited a movie theatre on the Potsdamer Strasse (Potsdam Street, Berlin) and spent a long time allowing the most exciting dramas and the silliest comedies to march past my eyes; when suddenly, two droll little characters appeared up there on the silver screen. They seemed to me to be both familiar and yet totally unknown at the same time. But they only remained unknown for about one tenth of a second, and then the droll little men rolled a ball onto the screen, on which the well-known trademark of the Steiff Company, Giengen-on-the-Brenz, with the famous words 'Knopf-im-Ohr' (Button-in-Ear) was clearly visible. It was soon obvious to me that these little men were two of the famous Steiff comic dolls, the Krackjacks; and I was sure that they would simply proceed to present the latest Steiff products – the novelties and the hits – which we in the branch had already seen at the Fair. However, it was different to what I expected, completely different – and the atmosphere in the theatre was electric and attentive." The movie was called "A Dream" and it told the story of a young boy who fell asleep after playing with his Steiff soldiers. Suddenly the officer (doll) detached himself from the soldiers and went to visit his bride. Whilst there, the officer became tangled in the tablecloth and a piece of the cloth ripped off and stuck on his sword. The officer did not notice this, not even when he took the roll-call on parade."

Another scene showed a soldier secretly visiting his "one true love" – a cook. The pair were almost caught by the master and mistress of the house, but the soldier was able to hide in the pantry. That was roughly the context of the film. The author concluded: "But the Steiff Company who always seem to come up with the most up-to-date, charming and original advertisements, have successfully overcome any remaining doubts about their talent; they have produced a highly original and amusing movie which presents an interesting variety of their products in glowing colors. The movie not only brought lively ▶

347

ALBERT·SCHLOPSNIES
MÜNCHEN
KLAR-STRASSE 12
PI·PE·RO-WERKSTÄTTE FÜR FEINE GESCHENKE
KLEINKUNST · SILUETTEN UND LUXUS-PAPIERWAREN
MÜNCHEN, DEN 15 Nov 19[illegible] CONTO DEUTSCHE BANK FILIALE MÜNCHEN

***Illus. 348**: Albert Schlopsnies's letterhead, circa 1906.*

***Illus. 347**: Steiff advertisement designed by Schlopsnies.*

***Illus. 349**: A unique photographic document which until now lay "buried" in the Steiff archives: Albert Schlopsnies with his "Pantom-Doll". The "Pantom-Bear" and the "Pantom-Chimp" were produced from 1910 until 1918, in two sizes, 14in. and 16in. (only 6,268 were manufactured). Prototypes which were never put into production were: Clown, Artilleryman, Dutch girl, Alphonse and Gaston on roller-skates (see **Illus. 323**).*

350

***Illus. 350-354*: *Illus. 350*:** *Title page from Steiff Catalog, 1911. Format 5 x 12in.. This format was used until 1923, when it was replaced by a larger color-catalog.* – ***Illus. 351*:** *Advertising photograph: children with Pantom-Bear and Pantom-Monkey.* – ***Illus. 353*:** *Pantom-Bear with shoe-button eyes and horizontally stitched nose; in light brown mohair, two sizes: 14 and 16in.* – ***Illus. 354*:** *Albert Schlopsnies demonstrates the Pantom-Bear and Pantom-Artilleryman.*

351

***Illus. 352*:** *Schlopsnies adapted this photograph* **(*Illus. 351*)** *for advertising purposes.*

353

applause from the fans of these dolls, it also evoked great admiration from those people in the audience who were not familiar with Steiff's products."

A young man who had not only worked for over 15 years on promoting the Steiff image, but was also jointly responsible for the design of many of their products, may also have played an important part in the making of the movie. Unfortunately records in the archives do not reveal to what extent Albert Schlopsnies was involved in the production. Schlopsnies came from East Prussia, where he had worked for his uncle. He "scribbled drawings on every piece of paper and pleaded for a chance to study art." But to no avail! Impulsively, Schlopsnies set off on a bicycle and rode from Tilsit to Munich – a journey of over 620 miles. When he arrived, he managed to present some of his drawings to the Munich artist Franz Stuck, and Stuck immediately accepted him as a student on the strength of his obvious talent.

Albert Schlopsnies did not rely solely on his artistic talent – he also applied himself diligently to the study of Industrial Art. Some time between 1904 and 1905 he opened his own shop at Karl Strasse 12, in Munich; the "Pi-Pe-Ro Workshop for fine gifts, (Kleinkunst) silhouettes and luxury writing paper". ▸

354

One of his customers was Alexander Leo, whose brother-in-law was Richard Steiff! It was through Leo that Schlopsnies and Richard Steiff first became acquainted. At first they were simply business acquaintances. Richard Steiff went to Schlopsnies for the art materials needed at the factory and for any picture-framing which Steiff required.

It is probable that through this contact with the Toy Factory in Giengen, Albert Schlopsnies developed the interest which led him into designing his own first doll. This doll was registered at the Royal Patent Office under the number 228 275; and the copyright stated: "for use as a puppet as well as for a jointed doll intended as an article for play." His idea was that a metal skeleton should be anchored in the doll's body, and this would act as a mount to hold the puppet strings, so that the doll would have double play value. Whether the doll

355

***Illus. 355**: Circus Clowns: (From the left) – August (17in.), Clown (11in.), and Coloro (17in.).*

356

***Illus. 356**: Albert Schlopsnies setting up a display piece, "At The Circus". He was the creator of this wonderful scene in all its artistic and technical perfection.*

***Illus. 357**: Clowns of every type. These dolls were offered from as early as 1904 until 1928, in seven different sizes, ranging from 11 to 39in.. Their costumes and facial painting were adapted according to the "latest" circus fahion.*

357

for which Schlopsnies had obtained a patent was ever produced remains questionable, since the design and manufacture would have been too expensive to allow the finished doll to be at all saleable.

Richard Steiff enjoyed the company of the creative, whimsical young artist, and in 1910 he asked Schlopsnies to join the Steiff Company in Giengen. Schlopsnies did not become an employee of the factory, but remained self-employed (and continued to run his Art Shop in Munich) whilst at the same time acting as a "freelance artistic advisor" to Steiff.

However, Schlopsnies was viewed critically by the Steiff management. Richard Steiff's brothers rejected the young artist completely. Their attitude appeared to be: "Why do we need artistic advice?" It was only thanks to Richard Steiff's strong position at the factory that the working relationship between the Steiff Company and Schlopsnies was allowed to continue until 1923. Only today, when one looks back in retrospect at the work which Schlopsnies did for Steiff, is it possible to appreciate and evaluate the important part he played in Steiff's success.

Schlopsnies began his work at the Steiff factory with a design which he named aptly "Pantom-Animals" (a shortened version of Pantomime). He used this name for Steiff animals which were attached to strings, like puppets. Actually, the idea was intended to provide Steiff's products with more mobility. The puppets designed by Schlopsnies (for which he had obtained the patent) were altered in Giengen and registered under the number DRGM 428 382: "Play Dolls attached by strings."

The bodies of the animals and dolls were given a stronger skeleton-like frame since the regular Steiff articles were soft-filled and would not have been suitable for this new design. In order to function properly as puppets the limbs, body, and head, all had to be extra-strong. Each puppet was also fitted with a voice box, which was operated by a pull-string device, so that an experienced puppeteer could achieve an amazingly realistic effect.

The 1911 catalog proudly claimed: "A most original and lively toy, for young and old alike. Well built, sturdy mechanism. Pantom jumps, runs, sits, scratches, growls. Pantom can perform tricks, and may be positioned in an inexhaustible number of realistic movements and positions. Children can operate Pantom through simple hand movements and the animal will immediately assume the most comical positions." Two puppets were offered in this catalog – a monkey (10, 11, 14in.), and a bear (10, and 11in.).

The Leipzig "Ilustrirte Zeitung" carried an interview with Richard Steiff concerning the Steiff Toy Factory and its products. The newspaper quoted: "Schlopsnies's nimble fingers have been responsible for the start of a brand new chapter in Steiff's creative program. New ideas, new designs; each year brings new creations to be added to the pile of Steiff gifts already spilling over the sides of the Christmas table."

Yet not all the Steiff brothers shared this glowing opinion. Even during the First World War there were discussions as to whether Steiff needed Schlopsnies's artistic skills. As was the custom, these discussions were carried out openly. Schlopsnies's critics did not mince their words! On October 10, 1914, for instance, Hugo Steiff wrote: "From the trenches near Regnierville, North Toulon." His letter was a matter-of-fact analysis on the outcome of the war, and with regard to the "Schlopsnies Problem" he wrote: "We have to consider the ▸ 168

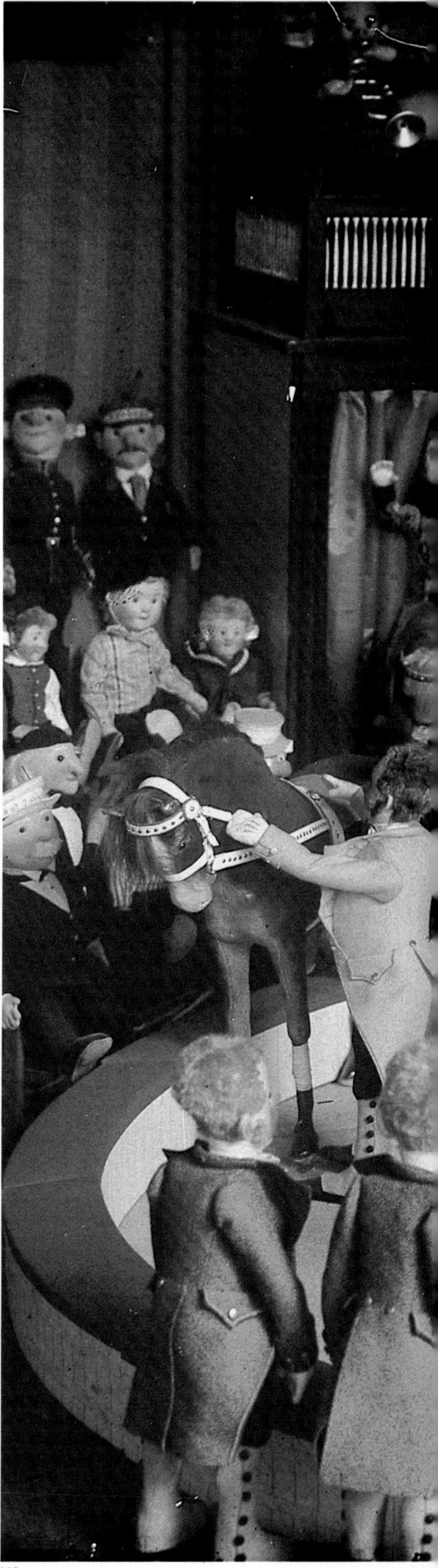

358

Illus. 358: *A circus scene designed and constructed by Albert Schlopsnies.*

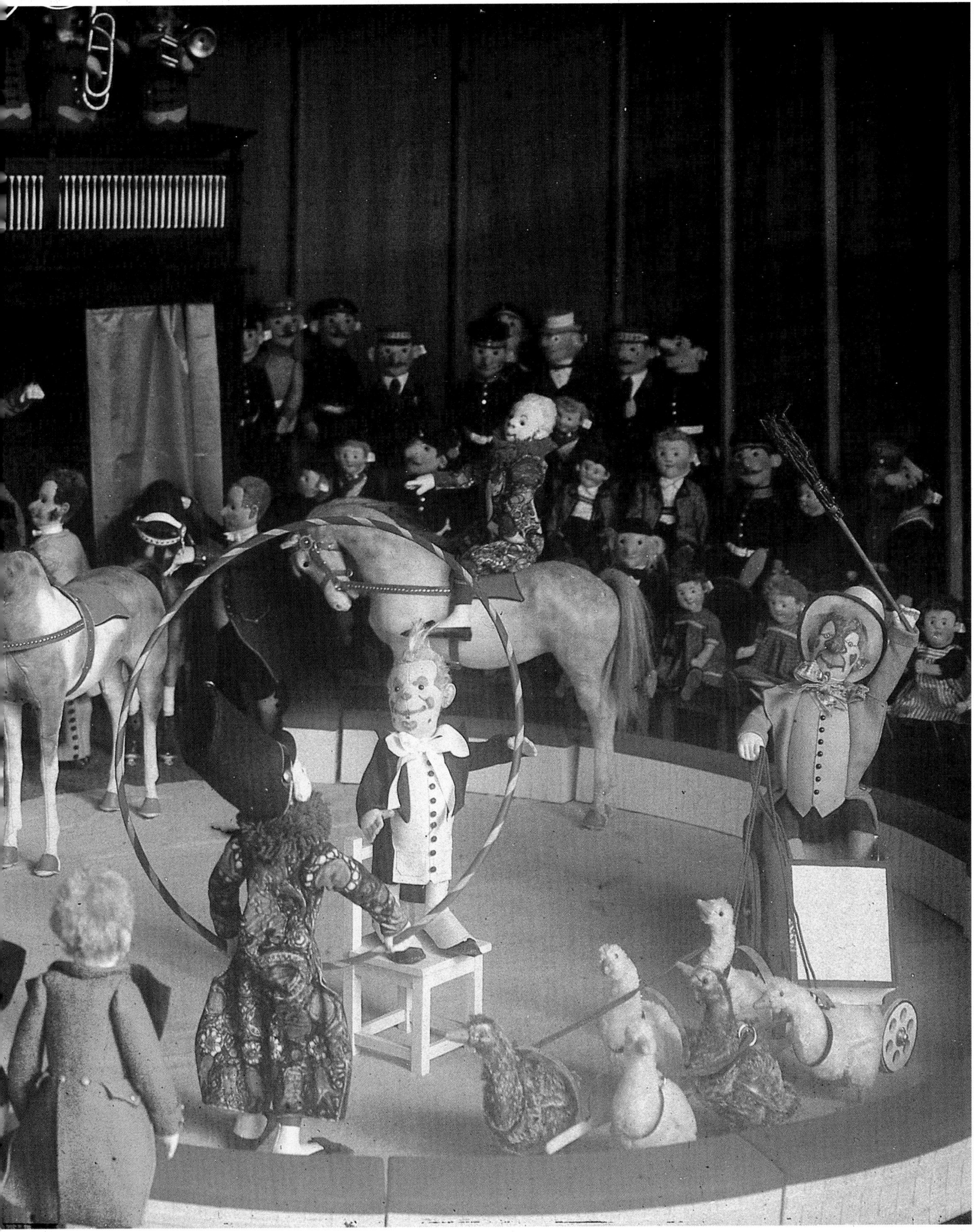

Three weeks only. At A. Wertheim, Berlin! November 1910.

CIRCUS STEIFF = Button-in-Ear.

◆ Program ◆

Admission:
All seats free.

Keep this flyer and
show it to your friends.

Concert by the two Circus Bands six hours prior to the beginning of the show.

1. **Cameldarys and Dromedels** ridden on their high humps.
2. **Six Russian horses,** captured when bolting for freedom, excelsior filled, with metal bones.
3. **Ging, Geng, Gang** "Hair raising jugglers and pig-tail non-cutters."
4. **Twelve felt elephants from Württemberg.** All ages, from the cradle to the rocking-chair.
5. **Original-Clowns, Tunix, Stuhl and Mogle** with impassive Sioux Chief, "Yellow Lederhosen".
6. **Those daring young men** – the Steel brothers, on the flying trapeze.
7. **Japanese Bamboo and Toe acrobats** with excelsior muscles.

In the intermission the circus zoo may be visited and chocolate cigars may be enjoyed.

Owing to the cold weather predicted by meteorologists, the Circus directors have decided to sell their complete show, personnel and animals to Santa Claus at the end of this last show of the season.

8. **The greatest show on earth:** Clown Goose with his roller-skating geese.
9. **Pantom monkey.** The latest novelty. Captured live and presented by the visible hand.
10. **Roaring lion group** presented by Mr. Daniel, the lion-trainer. The lions are so tame that children may ride on their backs when they are attached to a wheeled base.
11. **Clown Aduward** with his dog Caesar, with whom he went to the dogs (!) in England.
12. **Captain Cuckoo** and his juggling water-scared sea-lions.
13. **Moroccan Rifkas** – without their blood-curdling yells.
14. **Consul Peter,** the jungle's electric motor-cycle champ!

359

360

361

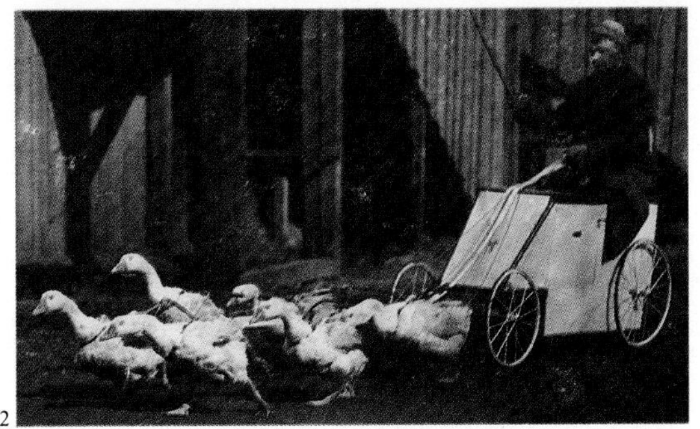

362

363

364

Illus. ***359-368****: This "Circus" display by Albert Schlopsnies caused a sensation when presented at the Wertheim Dept. Store, Berlin (1910). It had three circus-rings and visitors to the Steiff show were given a circus program – a comic adaptation of an actual program (****Illus. 359****). The Circus Sarrasani served as the model for this display, and Schlopsnies spent several days studying the actual performance (****Illus. 360 + 361****). The Japanese acrobats, elephant parade, and original performance of Clown Dellbosq, with his trained geese provided Schlopsnies with a multitude of ideas. Individual scenes such as the "Goose Carriage" were captured by Schlopsnies with his camera, and then realistically recreated (see* ***Illus. 358*** *- front left). He even signed a contract with the group of clowns, so that he could reproduce each of them individually, as dolls (****Illus. 363****). Over 30 figures were produced. Dolls 20in. and taller had movable knee-joints, which enabled them to assume true-to-life positions. Clowns (****Illus. 364-367****), Circus-aides, Ringmasters, Chinese and Japanese artists, Indians, and a circus orchestra, as well as a zoo with a velvet sea lion, horses, elephants and camels. –* ***Illus. 368****: Clear the ring for the Steiff circus!*

365

366

367

370

371

Illus. 370: Argentinian "Gaucho" and Argentinian "Tina", both 17in. (1913).

Illus. 371: Chinese plate-juggler (with power-driv mechanism).

Illus. 369: Mexican Cowboy, manufactured in 5 sizes: 16, 18, 21, 27 and 39in. (1913).

Illus. 372: Moroccan Spahis (native soldiers of N.Africa) in regimental uniform (17in.).

372

Illus. 373: Circus Hand, original photograph from 1910.

374

Illus. 374 + 375: Bamboo ladder (**Illus. 374**) – 47in. high – **Illus. 375**: "Coloro" the Clown with his trained dogs.

Illus. 376: Japanese man, 23in., (1910)

Illus. 377: "Coloro" the Clown, with bull-terrier "Tige".

377

378

379

380

Illus. 378-380: *Left (**Illus. 378**) Morrocan Spahis, without coats, 17in. (1912); right: Singhalese, 17in. (1910). – **Illus. 379**: Circus orchestra-rostrum with curtain. – **Illus. 380**: Various tribes of Indians; available in three sizes, 14, 17, and 39in.(1911).*

381

382

Illus. 381 + 382: *Black Dude (Top-hat missing), wonderful costume, 14in. (1913).*

Illus. 384: *Chinaman with a queue ("the hair-raising pigtail acrobat"), 17in. tall, (1910).*

Illus. 383: *"Caesar" the dog with walking mechanism.*

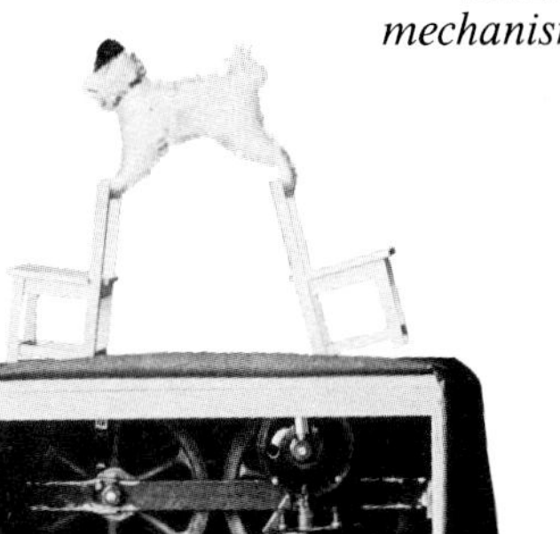

383

384

Illus. 385: *Clown "Aduward" with "Caesar".*

385

Dr. Heinrich Hoffmann's book "Shockheaded Peter" (Struwwelpeter) was one of the most popular books in the 19th century. In 1871 it had already achieved its 100th printing. Steiff were aware of Struwwelpeter as early as 1892. In their catalog of this period a felt-worked rug, the "Princess Play Rug", was featured – (the motive was also the back cover of the 1892 catalog – see Page 15). Several of the felt characters on the rug were taken from the Struwwelpeter book. They were richly worked in wool and silk and, "not only is it a soft floor covering, it is also a very appropriate and absorbing item for your dear children, and is certainly a welcome entertainment assistant for many mothers", claimed Steiff's advertisement. In 1908 Steiff made their first doll from the "Struwwelpeter" series; "Nikolas", 17in. tall. Three years later "Struwwelpeter" and the "Wild Hunter" joined "Nikolas". Struwwelpeter was available in three sizes, 11, 14 and 17in., until 1927. The Hunter was 20in.

386

Illus. 386: *Original "Struwwelpeter" (Shockheaded Peter).*

387

Illus. 387: *"Struwwelpeter" in three sizes, 11, 14, and 17in. (available until 1927).*

388

Illus. 389: "The Wild Hunter". Only three of these display pieces were manufactured.

390

Illus. 388: Original sketch from the Struwwelpeter Story Book – "Tale of the Wild Hunter".

Illus. 390: 121 examples of this magnificently equipped "Wild Hunter" were sold (1912 – 1915).

Illus. 392: Original sketch of "Nikolas" from the "Struwwelpeter" Book.

Illus. 391: "Nikolas", 17in. tall, first appeared in the program in 1908. In 1911 he was also available in 11, 14, and 20in.. "Nikolas" on the far-right has movable knee-joints.

391

392

Max and Moritz

Illus. 393: *"Max and Moritz" by Wilhelm Busch.*

Illus. 394: *"Max and Moritz" in two sizes: middle 12in. (from 1909 until 1920s), left and right 14in. (1914 until 1916/17).*

394

395

399

396

397

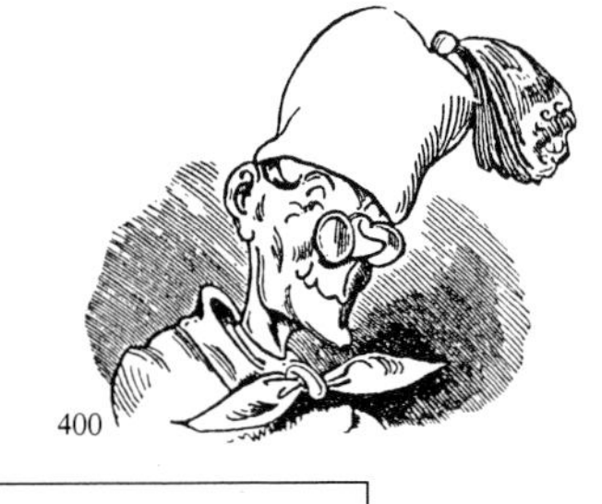
400

401

398

Max and Moritz, created by the artist and caricaturist Wilhelm Busch (1832 – 1908) sometime in 1865, were two extremely naughty boys whose sole purpose in life was to think up tricks to play on their neighbors. Steiff made their first Max and Moritz dolls in 1909. They were 30cm (12in.) tall and they remained in the Steiff program until the 1920s. Other Busch characters were later added to Steiff's program: Widow Bolte, Uncle Fritz, Teacher Lämpel, Tailor Böck and wife, Uncle and Aunt Nolte and the pious Helene (only until 1918). In 1914 Max and Moritz were re-designed. These dolls were 35cm (14in.) tall and were available until 1916/17. The work of Wilhelm Busch provided Steiff with other ideas, too: egg-cosies, a hen, a duck, and "Huckebein" the crow.

***Illus. 395-398**: Cartoon and original "Widow Bolte" and "Uncle Fritz", 17in. (from 1911).*

***Illus. 399-401**: "Tailor Böck" and his wife, 17in. (from 1911).*

402

403

404

Illus. 402 + 403: *Display piece and original sketch: "Teacher Lämpel" from the story of "Max and Moritz" (circa 1909).*

Illus. 404: *"Teacher Lämpel", 17in. (1909 until 1916/17), also made in 20in. size.*

Illus. 405: *Schoolgirl with satchel, 11in. Body of rough cotton, World War I production.*

Illus. 406 + 408: *The Village school (**Illus. 406**), a display piece by Steiff. – **Illus. 408**: "Teacher Lämpel", the role-model and "founder" of the Village School.*

Illus. 407: *Advertisement: "The Village school" with "Max and Moritz".*

405

406

407

408

"Good children in pursuit of knowledge apply themselves at school or college. . ." This quotation from Wilhelm Busch's "Max and Moritz" was responsible for a small series of display pieces based on the theme "School". The most famous is the village school, in two designs: 4 x 29 x 29in. with nine dolls as pupils (11in.) and their teacher; the second display was (65 x 50 x 40in.) with 13 pupils (11in.) and teacher. All school-furniture and accessories could be ordered from Steiff. In 1910 Steiff sold 45 complete school displays.

409

Illus. 409: *The first advertisements for the school. Pupils have drawn a Zeppelin on the blackboard.*

Illus. 410: *Postcard from 1913, titled "The Secret". A group of Steiff schoolchildren.*

410

Illus. 411: *The French Village School.*

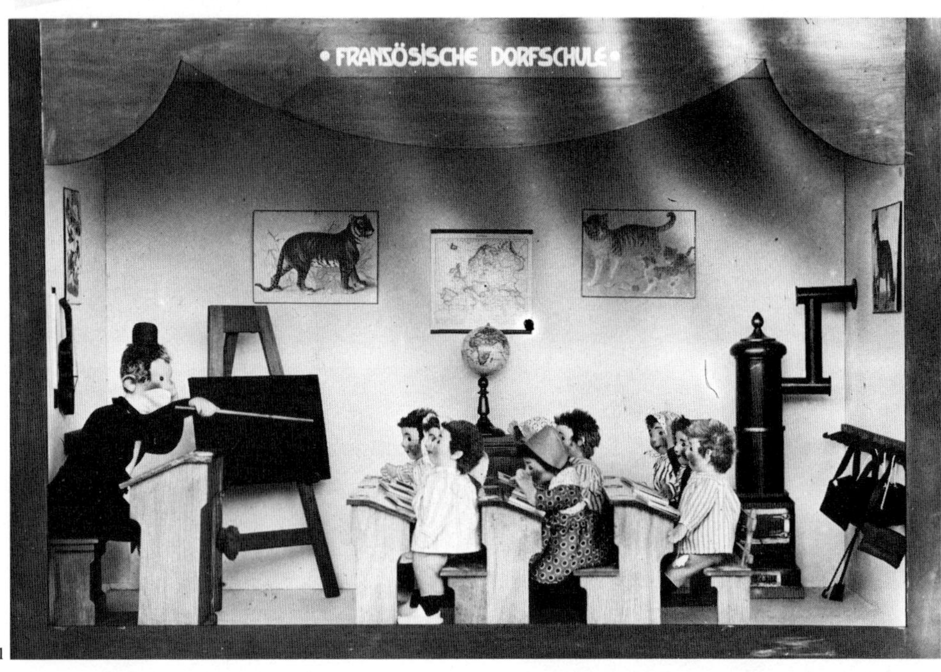

411

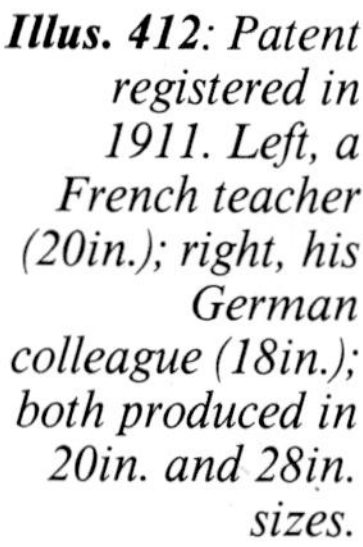

Illus. 412: *Patent registered in 1911. Left, a French teacher (20in.); right, his German colleague (18in.); both produced in 20in. and 28in. sizes.*

412

Illus. 413: *Two black schoolboys, 14in., for the American Village School (1911).*

Illus. 414: *The American Village School with teacher and black schoolchildren.*

413

414

Illus. 415: As early as 1895, Steiff had a doll with a Polar-bear in their program – representing Roald Amundsen, the Norwegian Polar explorer.

Illus. 416: The U.S. explorer Peary as a doll, 17in. (1909). Only 263 examples sold.

In 1909, the American explorer, Robert E. Peary was famous all over the world. In competition with the explorer F.A. Cook, Peary was the first person to reach the North Pole. This expedition led to a new series of dolls by Steiff: Eskimo dolls. Peary's little daughter, Marie Anighito also served as the model for the "Snow-babies"; tiny, comical little dolls whose cheeky faces were all that was visible under their white fur snowsuits.

Illus. 421: The Eskimo doll in reclining position is from a display piece (22in.). The Samojeden are 14in., (also in 30in. size), jackets and legwear removable.

Illus. 422 + 423: Design sketch (**Illus. 422**). The Eskimo doll (**Illus. 423**) was available in 11, 14, and 17in., white or black. From 1908 until 1919.

416

Illus. 417: "Peary" in arctic fur snowsuit.

Illus. 418: Steiff sketch.

418

420

Illus. 419 + 420: Original sketch by F.A. Cook, with Steiff sketch. 14 dolls were made, but an example has not been retained.

421

422

423

Illus. 424: *"Uncle Zeppelin", 14in. size.*

***Illus. 425 + 426**: Display piece, "Flight of the Zeppelin" (1912) showing last preparations before final "take-off" of an airship.*

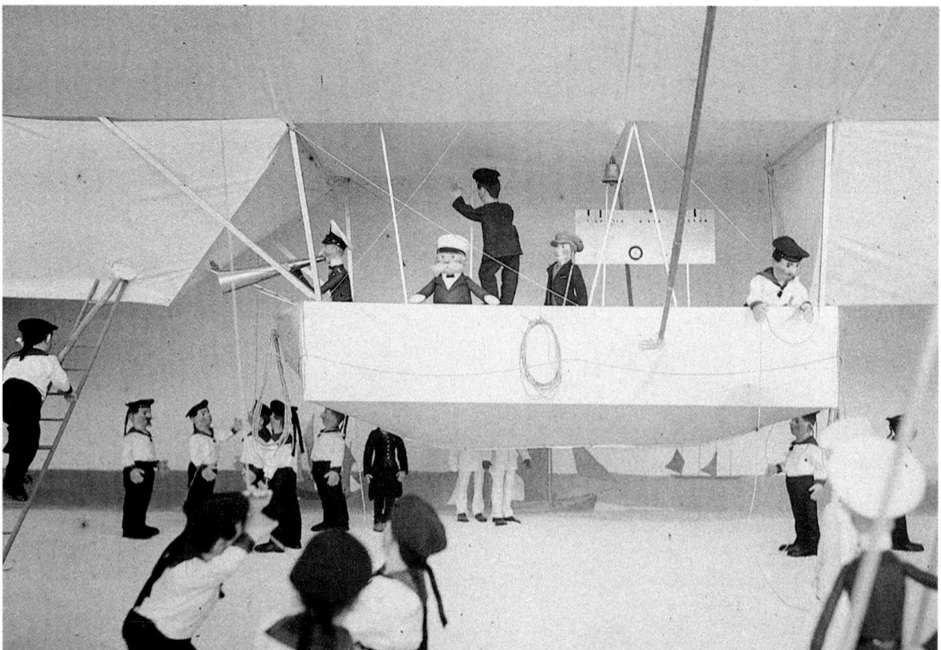

425

426

Zeppelin – a magical word at the turn of this century. The word was adopted from the name of Graf Ferdinand von Zeppelin, who was born in 1838 in Constance. After years of military service and diplomatic duty, Graf Zeppelin devoted his time to the construction of an airship which was later given his name. In 1898 he formed a shareholding company to further the development of the motorized airship, and on July 2, 1900 his first airship was launched. Zeppelin experimented with several designs until the airship LZ4 was destroyed by an explosion in 1908. Zeppelin's money had run out. A fund-raising enterprise throughout the nation captured the imagination of the public and achieved a total of six million marks. The Zeppelin Airship Construction Company was founded in Friedrichshafen on Lake Constance where the company built airships until the late 1930s. Margarete Steiff was fascinated by her first glimpse of an airship, and wrote to her nephew, Otto, on August 25, 1908: "Your brother Hugo also saw the balloon make its last ascent (note: the LZ4) . . .and now they are trying to raise 2 million in gold for further experiments." The toy manufacturer, like many others, decided to use Graf Zeppelin's popularity to further her own products. An "Uncle Zeppelin" doll was developed, and Steiff tried to patent the name. On August 29, 1903, patent attorney Zeisig wrote from Berlin: "I advise, that before you offer the doll for sale in the shops, you register it at the Petty Court. . .the Patent Office informed me that the product name "Onkel Zeppelin" can be legally rejected by Graf Zeppelin, since you are obviously making use of his name . . .perhaps it might be a good idea if you contact Graf Zeppelin personally for permission to use his name." Although, the Graf refused to give his permission; Steiff persisted with their doll, and the name (1908 until 1913 = 5,301 "Onkel Zeppelin" dolls made).

***Illus. 427**: An old photograph of "Uncle Zeppelin" from the Steiff studio.*

427

***Illus. 429**: Postcard view of a Zeppelin over Lake Constance (Bodensee).*

***Illus. 428**: Graf Zeppelin.*

429

430

431

432

433

***Illus. 430-440**: Farmers' wives (**Illus. 430**) in various costumes (1908-1910) – **Illus. 431**: Steiff advert.: "Porter, Porter", Gentleman and elegant lady (Fanny, Sidonie, Beatrice) – 1912 until 1914, available in various outfits of felt, silk or muslin. – **Illus. 432**: Display piece "The Market" (1912/13). – **Illus. 433**: Baker, Cobbler and Butcher, all 14in. (1911). – **Illus. 434**: Student, 17in. – **Illus. 435**: Several farmer dolls (1908-1910). – **Illus. 436**: Shepherd with pipe and cloak (1913) and sheep in several sizes (1930). – **Illus. 437**: Display piece "At the Linde", a students' bar in Old Heidelberg (1912/13). – **Illus. 438**: Advertising Photo: "The Santa Claus sensation!" from a design by Schlopsnies. – **Illus. 439**: Male and female dolls (from the left) Student, 17in.; Lady, 20in.; Lady pink/white dress, 20in.; Lady in lilac costume, 18in.; Sportsman, 20in. – **Illus. 440**: Caroline, the maid, 17in. (1911).*

434

435

436

437

38

439

440

***Illus. 441**: This Noah's Ark was Steiff's most successful display piece (1913/14) and was on view at numerous exhibitions.*

In 1911, when Richard Steiff persuaded the young artist Albert Schlopsnies to join the company in Giengen to produce display pieces, no-one had any idea that a new milestone had been reached in the Steiff success story. Display pieces – these were original scenes of day-to-day life which were created using Steiff dolls and animals. These displays were ordered by large department stores to decorate their windows; they were shown at Exhibitions and Trade Fairs, and became a tradition which has continued right up until the present day. The first modest display-piece was featured at the Bavarian Trade Exhibition in Munich in 1910. "The Childrens Ring" adapted from Ludwig Thoma. Schlopsnies touch is easily recognised in this display from 1912, the "Great Fire in Dingharting", which drew huge crowds. Steiff displayed 220 doll types: students, circus people, ladies, soldiers, firemen, occupational dolls, citizens etc.. Many of these dolls were prototypes, and only a few were produced as a series. However, any doll could be made up as a special order. The ideas for these window displays came from Albert Schlopsnies or Richard Steiff. Occasionally they used a certain Herr Goldmann to paint the backgrounds. Many of the display pieces featured in the old photographs in this book were sold to interested Toy Stores. Just how well they were received by the public is illustrated in this description of the Bavarian Trade Exhibition, Munich in 1912. "In the center of the toy display is the collection of the Steiff company. The main scene shows the village firemen putting out a huge fire; saving people and possessions. The whole scene is alive with activity. Individual firemen, their stance, every action is so typical; copied realistically from life. The facial details, the wonderful uniforms and the humorous yet natural expressions, present such an enjoyable picture that one is filled with praise for the creators of this original and entertaining colletion . . . This display piece was the main attraction at the exhibition, and on certain days the crowds around it were so huge that security men had to be employed to ensure that things remained safe and orderly." A Berlin daily newspaper reporting on the Berlin Exhibition "The Child" in 1913, wrote: "The main attraction is the 'Fire in Zipfelhausen', a show-piece of Steiff's artistic toys. The whole group evokes a feeling of humor and sunny cheerfulness . . .." The "Noah's Ark" display at the "Sanitary Fair" in Stuttgart in 1914 was even mechanised! All the animals from Steiff's zoo were fixed onto the moving planks of the boat. Flexibility – herein lay the secret of wonderful combinations for the toys of the future. Right until the present day, numerous show-pieces have been created in Giengen – to be admired by young and old all over the world. Display pieces – another well-kept secret for Steiff's enduring popularity.

442

443

Ausstellung für Volkstümliche Weihnachtskunst zu Chemnitz

Fa. Margarete Steiff
Giengen a. Br.

beteiligte sich an der von der
Allgemeinen Zeitung, Chemnitz
veranstalteten Sonder-Abteilung

Puppen-Ausstellung

und wurde von der unten verzeichneten Preis-Jury der Ausstellerin diese

Ehrenurkunde

in Anerkennung der Betätigung künstlerischen Geschmackes zuerkannt.

CHEMNITZ, den 14. Dezember 1911.

DIE PREIS-JURY:

Frau Generalleutnant v. Laffert, Exzellenz	Privatmann Bielenberg
„ Oberbürgermeister Dr. Sturm	Oberbaurat Prof. Gottschaldt
Fräulein Friedrich	Prof. Lossow-Dresden
„ Pfaff	Hofrat Prof. Seyffert-Dresden
„ Schrag	Dr. med. Streubel
	Dr. med. Thiele.

Allgemeine Zeitung, Verlag.

444

445

*Illus. 442-447: Store-sign featuring Steiff's products, Carl Schäffer, Toy Shop, Osnabrück. – **Illus. 443**: A glimpse inside the Doll Department at the Steiff factory. – **Illus. 444**: An award from the Doll Exhibition in Chemnitz, 1911. – **Illus. 445**: A shop-window model for a Stuttgart store. **Illus. 446**: A "special order" for Steiff, from a company in Breslau. – **Illus. 447**: An advertising figure for "Nigrin" shoe-polish.*

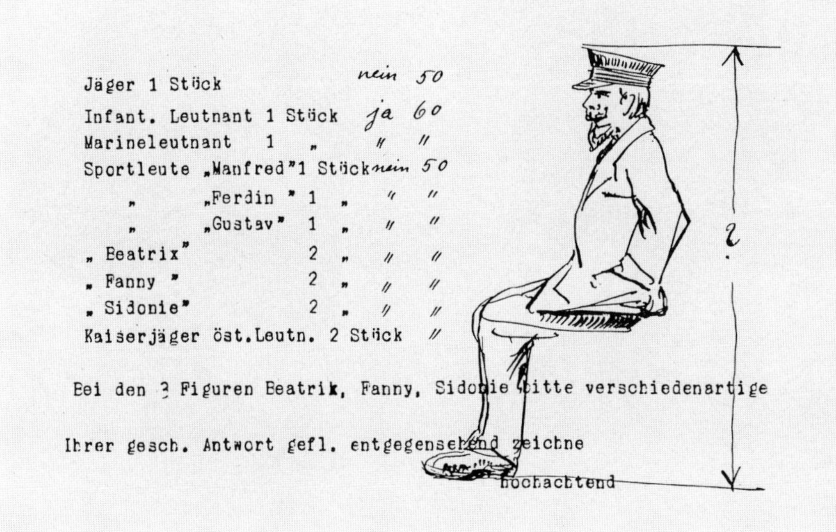

Jäger 1 Stück nein 50
Infant. Leutnant 1 Stück ja 60
Marineleutnant 1 „ " "
Sportleute „Manfred" 1 Stück nein 50
„ „Ferdin" 1 „ " "
„ „Gustav" 1 „ " "
„ Beatrix" 2 „ " "
„ Fanny " 2 „ " "
„ Sidonie" 2 „ " "
Kaiserjäger öst.Leutn. 2 Stück "

Bei den 3 Figuren Beatrix, Fanny, Sidonie bitte verschiedenartige

Ihrer gesch. Antwort gefl. entgegensehend zeichne

Hochachtend

446

447

448

449

***Illus. 448-451**: Tennis, ca. 1913 (**Illus. 448**): Tennis-lady, "Bette", 17 and 20in., and Tennis-man "Eduard", 20in. "Bette" had the new combable hair and was available with a choice of headwear. A tennis racket was also available. – **Illus. 449**: Greetings (1989) from originals and replicas: Tennis-lady (left, replica) and Mr. Councillor (2nd from right, replica). **Illus. 450**: Valets were available in several uniforms, 14in. (ca. 1911) – **Illus. 451**: "Johann", the valet, 17in. and messenger-boy, 14in. A messenger-boy agency was established in Berlin in 1911.*

451

450

452

***Illus. 452**: Valet "Johann", 17in. (1911).*

453

***Illus. 453**: Two sportsmen in leisure outfits with overshoes, 20in. (1911).*

454

455

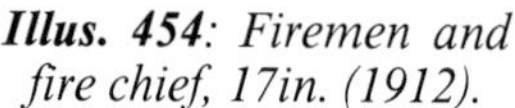

Illus. 454: *Firemen and fire chief, 17in. (1912).*

Illus. 455 + 456: *Firemen at work; with water-hose, and climbing a ladder.*

Illus. 457: *Display piece, "Inferno in Dingharting" shown at the Bavarian Trade-Fair in Munich, 1912. All the dolls were 17 and 20in. with fabulous costumes, including metal helmets and accessories. This display piece was also shown at "Gamages" in London in 1913.*

456

457

Gnomes and dwarves can be found in almost all Fairy Tales and Fables, and each nation has its own idea of what these creatures look like. In Germany they are bearded little men wearing nightcaps, who mostly live in the woods. It was no surprise therefore, that in 1910 newspapers were asking when the first dolls resembling German dwarves, would be produced. The German toy industry which catered almost exclusively to the American market was openly admonished: "German children have completely different taste, to the children in America." The highly original dolls which the British and American buyers ordered in Germany were also criticized. "Instead of these (foreign designs), it's time someone produced a German type of doll; for instance the ancient German brownies, gnomes or dwarves. One could easily imagine that a whole series of brownies would have as much success as the highly exploited Teddy-bear." Steiff paid attention and produced the dwarf "Puck", followed quickly by "Snik" and "Snak". As a travelling display piece Steiff designed "Snow White and the Seven Dwarfs". Export to the U.S. remained successful thanks to "Rip van Winkle" a literary gnome in America.

458

Illus. 458: *"Puck" made in 8, 12 and 16in. sizes. (1914 until the 1930s).*

459

Illus. 459: *"Snik" made in 9, 12, 17 and 20in. (1911 until 1930s).*

Illus. 460: *"Snak" (1911 until 1915) in 9, 12, 17 and 20in..*

Illus. 461: *Advertising photograph from the 1920s with dwarves "Snik" and "Puck", and a clown.*

460

461

462

463

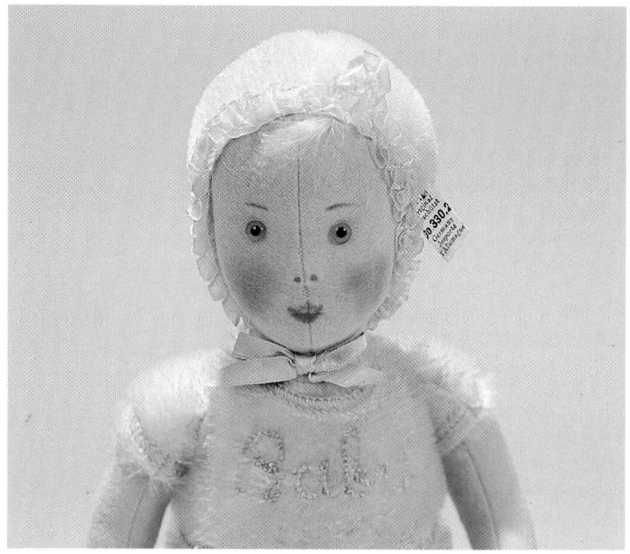

464

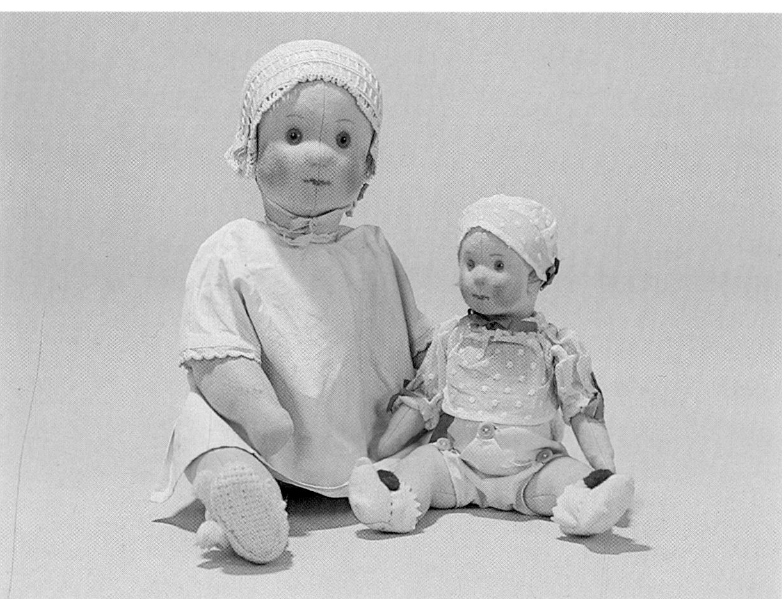

466

465

In 1907 the comical cartoon-dolls suffered competition in their own home! Richard Steiff developed a Character-doll from a simple "throw-doll", and caused a sensation in the toy world. Whereas the "throw-doll" had been simply sewn from one piece of felt, the new Character-dolls had everything children loved best: long mohair wigs to comb, disc-jointed arms and legs, and pretty clothes. A whole series was produced, and as was the custom at Steiff, the variety was huge.

467

468

***Illus. 462-469**: Throw-doll "Baby-Dolly". **Illus. 462**, the first Steiff felt character doll in red or white, with voice box and "text" as desired. – **Illus. 463-465**: "Baby-Dolly" was also available in plush from 1913 until the 1920s. – **Illus. 466**: Novelties from 1916/17: "Hemdenmatz" (11in.) and "Hosenmatz", 14in. – **Illus. 467** + **468**: "Wilma" doll (**Illus.468**) in different coats and sizes: 11, 14, 17, 20 and 24in.. – **Illus. 467**: "Wilma" with hat and collar in plush, and Teddy. – **Illus. 469**: "Kuni" and "Rudi" (14in.) in national costume of Bern, Switzerland. (1911 until 1914).*

469

470

471

472

473

474

***Illus. 470-479**: "Alfred", the Norwegian (**Illus. 470**), 17in. 1910-1914. – **Illus. 471**: "Olga" in sweater and pleated skirt, 11 and 14in. – **Illus. 472**: "Silva", the skier, with beret (from 1909), and with long, combable hair, 1911. (Photo) 11, 14, 17 and 20in. – **Illus. 473**: "Stefan" the toboganner. – **Illus. 474**: "Ruth" the toboganner, 17 and 20in. (from 1909). – **Illus. 475**: Knitting pattern for a sweater. – **Illus. 476**: Advertising photograph "Winter Fun" from the Steiff archives. – **Illus. 477**: Norwegian skier, 20in. (1913). – **Illus. 478**: Two skiers "Schifra", 16in. Their outfits were complete in every detail (1916/17). – **Illus. 479**: "Schidick" (fat) and "Schidünn" (thin), 14 and 16in. (1914 until 1928).*

475

476

477

478

479

***Illus. 480**: Footballers in various shirts, 11 and 14in. (1911).*

***Illus. 482**: American baseball player, "Baseb", with bat, ball and gloves. Available in 14, 20 and 24in. (1913-1914).*

***Illus. 483**: Catalog pictures of "Kickers" and "Baseb" – all committed to their game!*

***Illus. 481**: Soccer players "American Kickers", circa 1913. Their sweaters could be ordered in the colors of the U.S. Colleges: Yale, navy blue (marked "Y"); Harvard, burgundy (marked "H"); Princeton, orange or black (marked "P"; Columbia, light-blue (marked "C"). In three sizes: 17, 20 and 23in.. Matching football in plush was also available.*

484

***Illus. 484**: Dutch boy dolls (from the left), "Franz", "Helma", "Knut", 20in. Dutch girl dolls, 14in.. Dolls over 20in. had clogs of real wood.*

485

***Illus. 485**: Boys and girls in dutch costume (from the left). "Inge", "Jansen" and "Inge" all 14in. (1911) and "Inge" 11in. (1909).*

486

***Illus. 486**: 17in. "Alida" in national costume, also in 11, 14 and 20in. sizes.*

***Illus. 487**: Holiday on the Dutch coast. Character dolls in bathing costumes. Elegant lady in basket chair is admired by the locals (1912-1913).*

487

488

***Illus. 488**: "Anton" from Upper Bavaria, in 11, 14, 17, 20 and 24in., (1910-1920).*

490

***Illus. 490**: "Hans" the farmer from Schwaben (State in Germany), in 11, 14, 17, 20 and 24in. (1908-1920).*

492

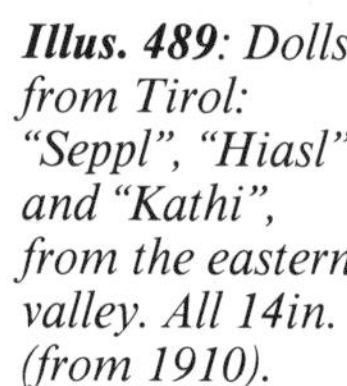

***Illus. 489**: Dolls from Tirol: "Seppl", "Hiasl" and "Kathi", from the eastern valley. All 14in. (from 1910).*

489

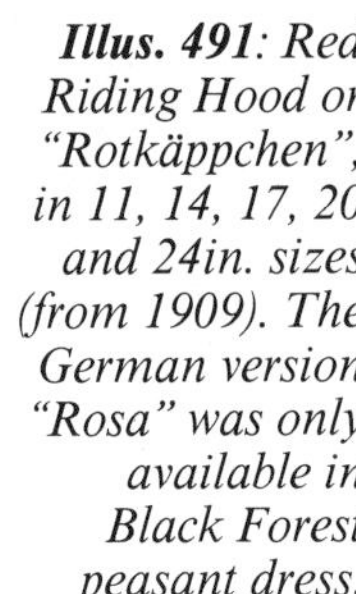

***Illus. 491**: Red Riding Hood or "Rotkäppchen", in 11, 14, 17, 20 and 24in. sizes (from 1909). The German version "Rosa" was only available in Black Forest peasant dress.*

491

Illus. ***492 + 493***: *The Tirolean Band (****Illus. 492****). From 1911 until 1915 this group was sold 42 times, with and without bandstand. The dolls were 14in., Steiff musicians were especially popular – they were sold complete with wooden instruments. Some of the dolls (wind instruments) had an extra seam across the face, to leave an opening for the mouth, to insert their instruments. In 1910/11 the display piece "Die Batzer", was shown for the first time at the Bavarian Trade-Fair. Other musical groups, included the Military Band, and Circus Orchestra (sold 75 times), a "Clown Serenade", and the most popular of all, the "Village Band" (****Illus. 493****). A country pub with landlord and wooden beer barrels could be ordered as extra decoration; 29x26x16in.. The band comprised: contra-bass (14in.), clarinet (14in.), "Trumpeter" (20in.), trombone (14in.) and violin (20in.). From 1912 until 1915, this group was sold 146 times.*

493

Illus. 494 (next page)*: This happy photograph shows the display piece "The Village Carousel", (1913).*

***Illus. 495**: A surprise at breakfast! The officer supervises, but "Max" and "Moritz" steal the gun. Display (1912/13).*

The early years at the turn of the century were "military" years throughout Europe. The call to arms, whether army, navy or air-force, was everywhere. The seriousness of military life was not to be ridiculed, yet Steiff somehow succeeded in selling large numbers of comic dolls portraying simple soldiers or higher officers. Over 120 different types of soldier doll, often in three sizes, were offered at various times in Steiff's program. Their national uniforms differed, and their comical appearance caused the public to smile. Steiff produced Germans, Austrians, Italians, Frenchmen, Turks, Moroccans, Croations, Dutchmen, Englishmen, Scotsmen, Russians, Argentinians and Americans. Dolls taller than 20in. had jointed knees! Naturally the German forces were portrayed in every uniform and rank; from Petty Officer to General in blue dress-uniform and in Fieldgray or Drill-uniform. Footwear was Steiff's speciality. Steiff buttons served as nails in the soles of boots. Minute details were adhered to in the field uniforms: Guns, helmets, swords, belts, flasks etc. As window displays the Steiff carpentry shop produced an officers mess, a parade ground, shooting targets, gym with apparatus, guard-boxes and scenes of manoeuvres. Even horses, appropriately saddled right down to the horse blanket, were not forgotten. In 1913, a Steiff customer wired his annoyance: "I am not happy with today's delivery. The items do not look at all original. The most amusing thing about these soldiers is to make their facial expressions as silly as possible." However, fun had disappeared from the toy world. For the real world was facing a crisis. Exaggerated patriotism, the increasing number of arms, drafting, war-plans and a European alliance heading towards catastrophe. World War I broke, and all humor was forgotten. The comic dolls became serious dolls; in 1915 twenty new models with friendly faces were designed. On June 12, 1915, the Berlin Toy-Export Company Hertzog, wrote to inform Steiff that an employee of the War Ministry had ordered the owner of a toy store to remove the Steiff soldier dolls from his window: "We really do not understand how these gentlemen find the time to pursue such trivial matters, for your new soldier dolls are really not caricatures any longer." Most severely criticized were a sewn-on beard and the black eyes ("rigid expression") Hertzog added: "Please send only soldiers with clean-looking faces; blue eyes and painted beards." Between 1917 and 1918 Steiff had to reduce production drastically since materials were in short supply, and soldiers were no longer desired.

***Illus. 496**: Comic Postcard, 1910.*

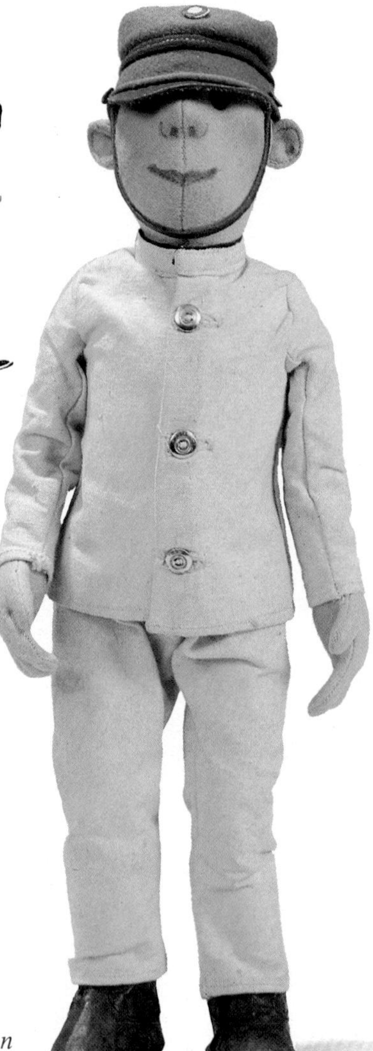

***Illus. 497**: Infantrymen in field uniform. Left in blue and right, in gray. Both with "friendly" faces of 1916/17.*

***Illus. 498**: Infantryman in drill uniform, 20in., (1912).*

***Illus. 499**: Several models of the infantryman; left, with the "new" face; sizes: 11, 14 and 17in..*

500

501

502

503

504

*Illus. 500-505: The Kaiser's Marines (**Illus. 500**). From the left: Captain, 20in.; Lieutenant 24in. and Captain, 20in., (circa 1912). – **Illus. 501**: The German Kaiser Wilhelm II, with his wife. Postcard issued for their Silver Wedding Anniversary. – **Illus. 502**: Red Cross Nurse and Ambulance-man, both 14in. Ambulance dog, "St. Bernard" (1915). – **Illus. 503**: Young heroes from 1915, 11in. tall. From the left: "Fan", "Off", "Kapi", "Gew", "Tro", "Sab" and "Fez". After the war these dolls became the farmer trio "Helmut", "Heinz" and "Hilmar". – **Illus. 504**: The patriotic flag, from Steiff's catalog (1916/17), attached to a gold-topped pole, 15 feet 11in. high. Germany and her Allies – Austria and Turkey. – **Illus. 505**: From the left: Sergeant, Chevauxleger and Major with sword and spurs on his boots (all 14in. tall).*

505

506

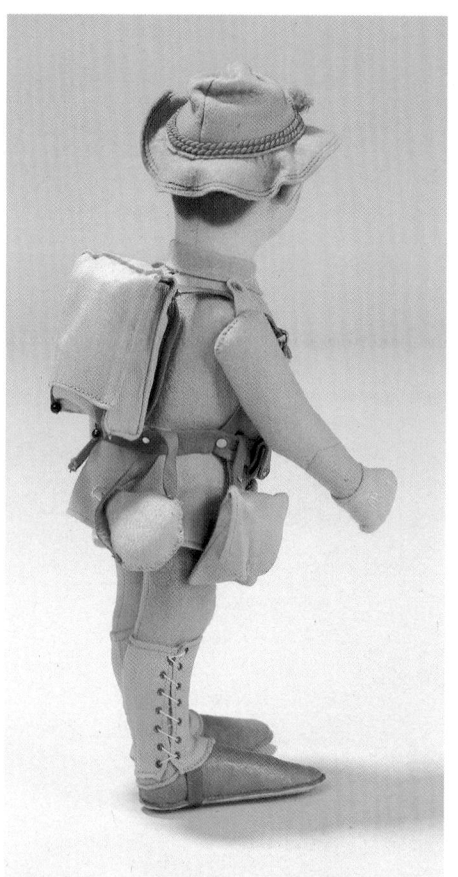

507

511

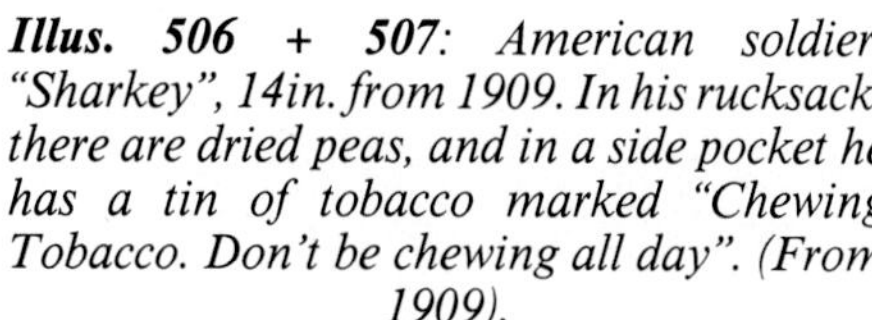

***Illus. 506 + 507**: American soldier, "Sharkey", 14in. from 1909. In his rucksack, there are dried peas, and in a side pocket he has a tin of tobacco marked "Chewing Tobacco. Don't be chewing all day". (From 1909).*

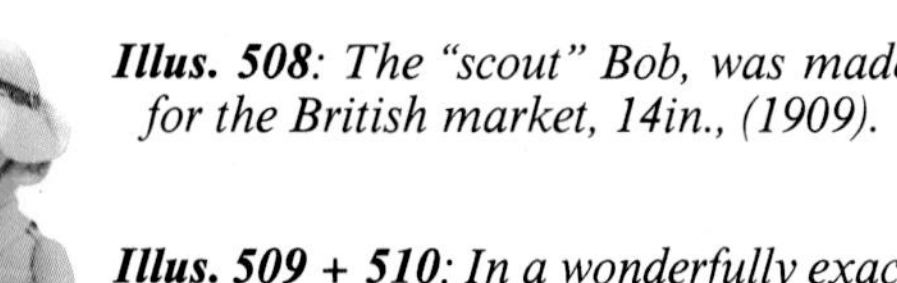

***Illus. 508**: The "scout" Bob, was made for the British market, 14in., (1909).*

***Illus. 509 + 510**: In a wonderfully exact field uniform of the Bersagliere Italian Regiment, "Bersi", 14in..*

***Illus. 511**: Front-view of Austrian infantrymen. 11 and 14in..*

***Illus. 512**: Rear view of Austrian soldiers (see **Illus. 511**).*

***Illus. 513**: English "Soe", fat and thin, 14 and 20in. (from 1904). Middle: "Tommy", (1916/17).*

***Illus. 514**: "Scott", Scottish soldier, in 14, 17, 20 and 24in. sizes, (from 1913).*

508

509

510

512

513

514

516

***Illus. 515**: Russian soldiers from the left: in blue uniform; Cossacks "Kofem" in field uniform, and "Kospa" in parade uniform; soldier in field uniform. All 14in. (1915).*

515

517

518

***Illus. 516-518**: American "Kelly" (**Illus. 516), 14in., (from 1909). – Illus. 517**: French Lieutenant, 17in. (1912). – **Illus. 518**: Italian Carabinieri (left) and Bersagliere, both 14in., (1911).*

Illus. 519: The German Crown Prince, Friedrich Wilhelm, with his wife Crown Princess Cecilie, and children, Wilhelm, Louis-Ferdinand, Hubertus, and Friedrich with a Teddy-bear. Postcard from 1914 for Cecilia-Aid. The eldest son asked for a barracks with Steiff soldiers in 1909.

state of our business at the end of this war, in order to be able to judge whether or not we can afford to run a studio for an artist – and also, whether the costs involved can be borne by the hard times we are bound to face . . . and we must, once and for all, cut down on all expenses which are not absolutely essential for our production. This decision places a heavy burden on my shoulders." He continues, "In the years to come, the company directors have to save every cent, and turn these (savings) into good, inexpensive, and sensibly produced articles. We cannot afford any new-fangled designs which we are unable to produce with the materials we have on hand. For this reason I regard the Munich Studio as being much too far away from the factory. Why should someone who consistently refuses to be part of the factory, have any right to influence our products? . . . These are my opinions written in the trenches of France during a cease-fire between friend and foe."

Copies of this letter were sent on to all the Steiff brothers in the cities where they were fulfilling their front-line duties. It was Richard Steiff who replied to Hugo Steiff's letter. On April 15, 1915, he sent out a reply with which he tried to pour oil on troubled waters: "Write and tell him (Schlopsnies) this: 'As of January 1, 1915, we request your usual services for the sum of 250 Marks per month, for the duration of this war. It is of course understood, that you cannot work for our competitors at the same time. We hope that our business does not suffer to such an extent that it becomes impossible for us to reward you and our other employees with a bonus. In the event that you come up with a particularly profitable design, we shall gladly honor your achievement with a fair share of the profits when we prepare our balance sheet at the end of the year'."

There are no records to show what Albert Schlopsnies did after the war, between 1918 and 1921. Who he worked for and how he earned his living remain undisclosed secrets! It is possible that he lived on the brink of ruin and ran up huge debts, which a letter, written by Otto Steiff at a later date, seems to imply. At any rate, in 1921, he sold his company, the "Pi Pe Ro Workshop" to the Bing group, and they renamed the business "Bing Artist Dolls and Cloth Toy Company". Bing hoped that this new purchase would enable them to uncover a few of Steiff's internal secrets through Schlopsnies himself, so that they would finally be able to usurp Steiff's leading position in the soft-toy industry. However, since Schlopsnies had never been a part of the actual production in Giengen, after a short period of collaboration, he was of no further use to Bing. Disillusioned, Schlopsnies turned his back on Nuremberg.

In 1921, Albert Schlopsnies resumed his contact with Steiff. It seems his sponsor, Richard Steiff, was still willing to support him; and in order to reinstate a working relationship, a contract was hastily drawn up for the artist. This was handwritten and signed by Richard Steiff, his brother Paul, and Albert Schlopsnies. On July 1, 1921, Schlopsnies was once again officially working for Steiff. His duty now was to "organize and oversee the whole advertising department for the Steiff Company." He was responsible for shop-window displays, posters, printed advertising, newspapers, movies, exhibitions and trade fairs. Schlopsnies was paid a fixed salary for this work and for his work as "artistic advisor" he was paid a bonus at the end of each year. Further, he committed himself to "at least 10 new designs each year for cloth animals, dolls, and wooden toys". In addition he was to provide "the two dozen designs already promised, for the 'Schlopsnies Doll' (beginning with one size, 16in.), which the Steiff Company would then manufacture".

Nevertheless, Albert Schlopsnies remained unpopular in Giengen. On October 10, 1923, Otto Steiff sent this letter to his brother Richard, who in the interim had taken up the running of the New York branch: "Is Mr. Schlopsnies still working exclusively for you, that is, for Margarete Steiff & Co. Inc.?" Richard Steiff had taken Schlopsnies to the United States so that he could help him to establish the new branch office. Otto Steiff's letter continued: "With regard to the bad debts of Mr. Schlopsnies, we have had no end of trouble with this problem and we have gradually been sickened by it . . . and therefore, we ask urgently, that he take the necessary steps to dispose of this matter for us. This should hardly be too difficult for him to manage! In spite of the fact that we have twice informed the Petty Court in Munich that Mr. Schlopsnies no longer works for us (note: for he was employed by the New York branch) we are still being continually served with writs against him."

Albert Schlopsnies did not spend too long with Richard Steiff in New York. He returned to Germany and in 1924/25 he was once again ▶

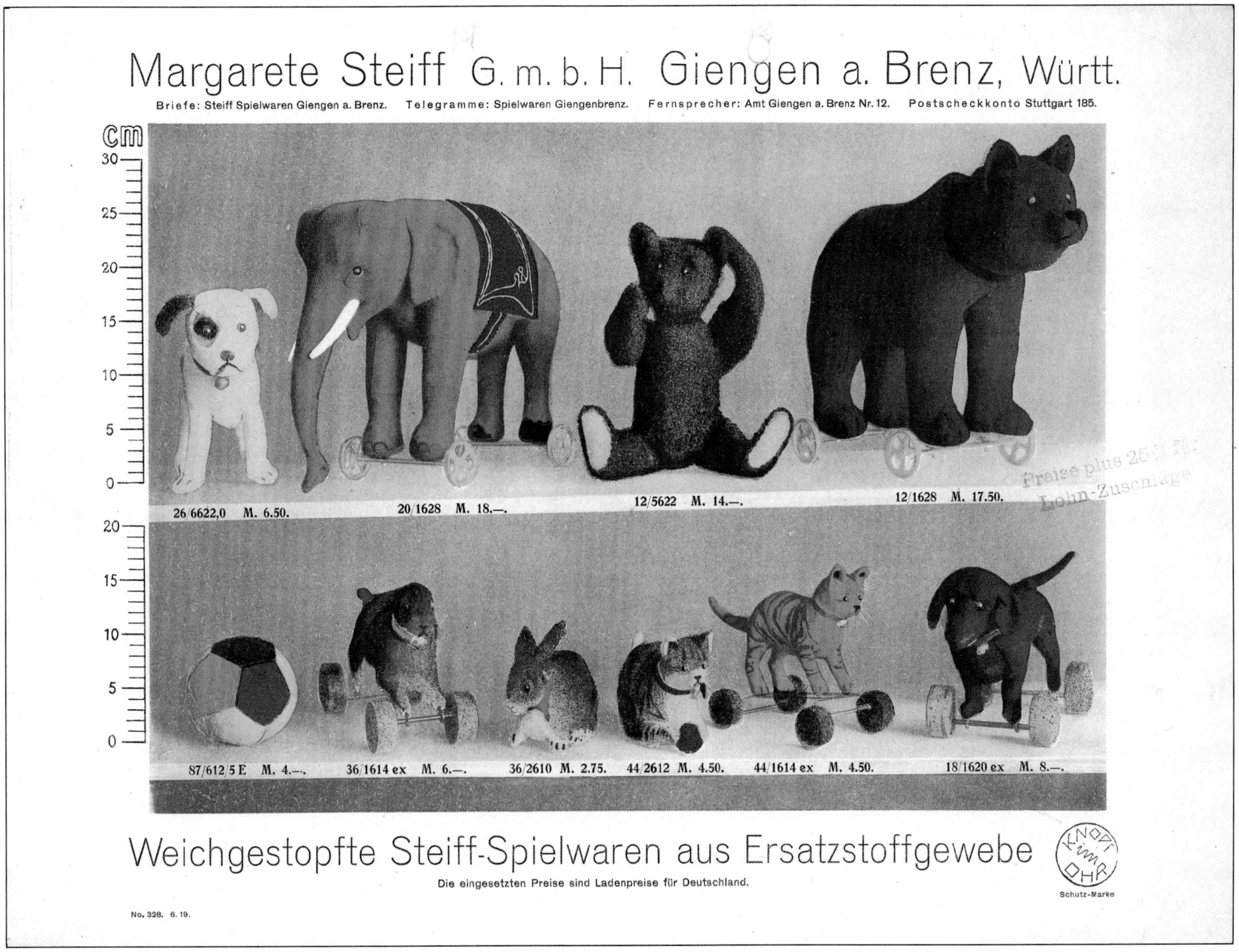
Margarete Steiff G. m. b. H. Giengen a. Brenz, Württ.
Briefe: Steiff Spielwaren Giengen a. Brenz. Telegramme: Spielwaren Giengenbrenz. Fernsprecher: Amt Giengen a. Brenz Nr. 12. Postscheckkonto Stuttgart 185.
cm
30
25
20
15
10
5
0
26/6622,0 M. 6.50.
20/1628 M. 18.—.
12/5622 M. 14.—.
12/1628 M. 17.50.
Preise plus 25 % für Lohn-Zuschläge
20
15
10
5
0
87/612/5 E M. 4.—.
36/1614 ex M. 6.—.
36/2610 M. 2.75.
44/2612 M. 4.50.
44/1614 ex M. 4.50.
18/1620 ex M. 8.—.
Weichgestopfte Steiff-Spielwaren aus Ersatzstoffgewebe
Die eingesetzten Preise sind Ladenpreise für Deutschland.
KNOPF IM OHR
Schutz-Marke
No. 328. 6. 19.

***Illus. 520**: Catalog page circa 1919 with toys in substitute materials.*

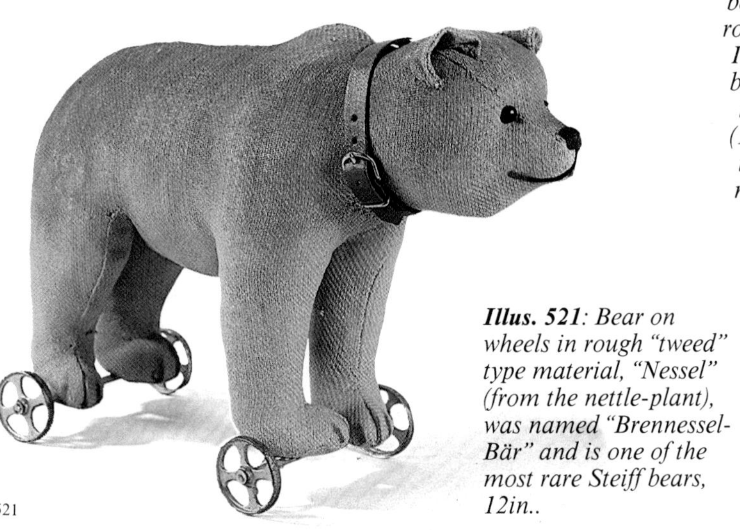

521

***Illus. 521**: Bear on wheels in rough "tweed" type material, "Nessel" (from the nettle-plant), was named "Brennessel-Bär" and is one of the most rare Steiff bears, 12in..*

***Illus. 522**: This bear is made of a rough wood-fiber. In five sizes. The bear in the photo is marked 5622, (13in.). 19,556 of these bears were made from 1919 until 1921.*

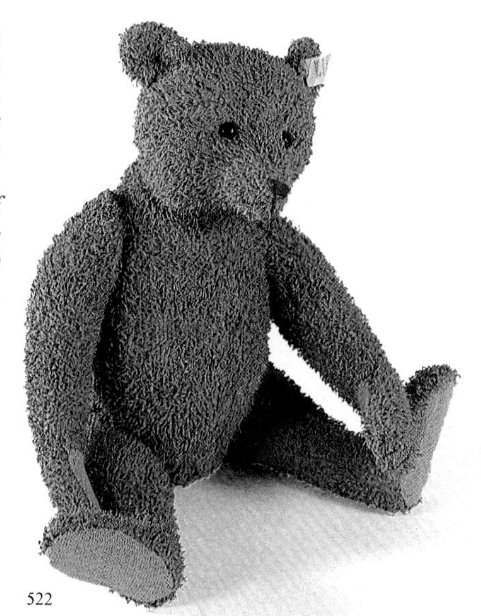

522

employed by the Bing Toy Company in Nuremburg in an advisory capacity for their doll department.

World War I began on Aug. 2, 1914. Steiff's prolonged rise to the top was halted slightly at first, and then finally stopped. The three company directors, Richard, Paul and Hugo Steiff were called-up to serve their country. The company was not without leadership, but its most important directors were sorely missed. 800 workers were employed at the factory at this time and 400 home-workers were also listed.

The chief clerks, Meck and Rabus, guided the toy factory through these difficult times. Important problems were solved by means of a circular sent out to the three Steiff brothers. Difficulties arose when the brothers expressed different opinions. Richard, Hugo and Paul Steiff tried to reach unanimous decisions by exchanging letters from their various posts. A complicated method which only helped to patch-up the problems temporarily. At first all were full of hope! The war would surely not last long. In 1915, Richard Steiff sent a postcard to Giengen. He urged the management: "Naturally we have to deliver the best to make a profit. Everyone wants a French soldier doll for their sons (and a Russian, too!). Cheap, of course, but good as well."

However, two months later, after a visit to Giengen, his personal experience prompted a more sober approach: "I saw that much had to be improvised in order to fulfill the Army Orders and still overcome the material and coal shortage so that they would not take our machinery as well." There was absolutely no thought of export – all borders were closed. Although at the beginning of 1916 it was still possible to send goods to America via Holland, production at the factory was reduced to an absolute minimum.

***Illus. 523**: Stamping the cloth.*

***Illus. 524**: Filling with excelsior.*

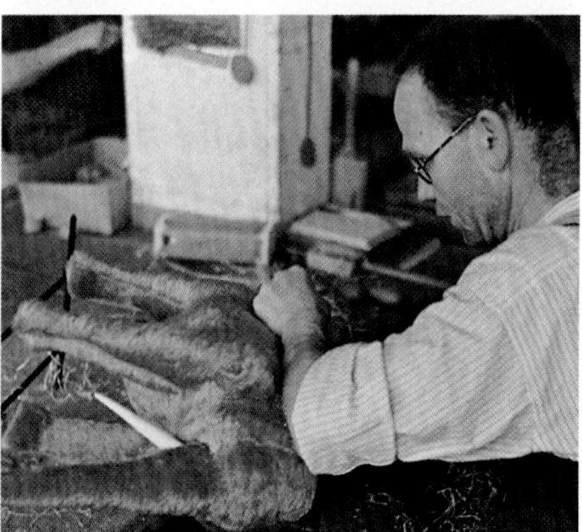

***Illus. 525**: Completion of an elephant.*

***Illus. 526**: Attaching a saddle.*

Steiff were ordered to produce supplies for the War effort. Now, the toy factory produced: "gas-masks for horses, feed-bags, wooden ammunition boxes, hand-grenade handles, percussion fuses, anvil-screws, split loop-rings and metal fittings for the building of airplanes in Friedrichshafen."

There was no shortage of man-power, since most of the work could be done by the women at the factory, or by the cottage workers. But the raw materials were missing. Felt was imposssible to obtain, since the "United Felt Factories" were only allowed to supply the Kaiser's Army. What could they do in order to ensure that the production of toys did not stop completely? They had to find other materials. Thus a small collection of toys in paper-plush was now produced. "We are only using alternative materials of the best available quality. The design and manufacture remain the same as for our 'real' cloth toys."

New products helped them through this difficult period. There was still plenty of wood available, so Steiff produced building-sets and childrens' furniture. Military items for children were also made: lunch boxes, flasks, rucksacks, tobacco-boxes, ammunition-boxes and uniform-caps. Very little was altered in their animal program during these war years. The shortage of raw materials greatly limited the program. When the war ended in 1918, the Margarete Steiff GmbH. was left to clear up the debris at their factory. Their overseas contacts had been interrupted, and the shortage of material naturally made a new beginning extremely difficult. A shortage of funds hampered the essential import of mohair. Business friends in the U.S.A. came to their rescue in this moment of need with generous dollar loans. A difficult period of improvisation began in Giengen, but as in the past, this was soon mastered. Somehow, ▶

Illus. 527: *The conveyor-belt was introduced in 1921. A conveyor-belt (between the pillars) for the suspended caskets can be seen clearly on this photo. The sewing tables are also divided by a conveyor-belt, which carries the finished pieces on to the next stage.*

Steiff managed once again, to achieve the high standards which had made them world famous. In 1920, wooden animals, wooden building sets, and childrens' furniture were newly designed. The company brochure for the 50th jubilee states: "In 1921, our childrens' increasing interest in active play was recognised, and the production of scooters began. First came the Steiff-Skiro and the Steiff-Skirit; these were soon followed by the immensely popular Bubi-Rad (Tricycle)."

In 1922, the Schlopsnies-Steiff doll entered the world of toys as a "Künstlerpuppe" (Artist doll). These dolls had unbreakable bodies of felt, but what made them especially interesting was the so-called "Aprico" painting (a technique developed by Schlopsnies which involved painting the dolls heads on the inside, thus giving them a "peach" tint resembling a child's complexion). This method also ensured that the paint could not be scratched off.

Steiff's directors began looking to the future. They built a new factory complex, several buildings of which were in reinforced concrete. A connection between the Steiff factory and a bridge over the River Brenz provided a direct link with the local railway.

In 1923, Richard Steiff decided to emigrate to America with his family. He was of the opinion that he would be better able to serve the Company's Export and Marketing departments from the U.S.. A number of letters written by him during this period are still in Steiff's possession. In these letters one can find many encouraging suggestions with which he hoped to motivate and help his brothers in Giengen. However, more of these, later.

Steiff was once again on the road to success. Their program was adapted to suit the demands of the customer. Teddy-bears were now replaced by dogs. The much loved Steiff "Molly" was the first representative of this new line. With tremendous success! Felt articles were now less popular than their mohair counterparts; and the early ride-on animals and rocking-horses were replaced by scooters, tricycles and pedal cars.

1920/21 were the years in which production methods at the Steiff factory were modernized – the result was a definite reduction in costs. Hugo Steiff introduced the conveyor-belt to the factory. "Discovered" in 1870, in the slaughterhouses of Chicago, and developed to perfection by the Ford Motor Company in the U.S.A., this new machinery fascinated the Steiff brothers. The new installation accelerated production to such an extent that it was no longer necessary to store half-finished ▸

***Illus. 528**: Steiff advertising stamps with several motives (1914).*

***Illus. 529**: Steiff advertising stamps with several motives (1920s).*

articles in the warehouse; and this in turn meant huge areas were left free for storage, which saved having to order large quantities of materials in advance. In 1921, the conveyor-belt was first used on the Steiff scooter.

Although this modernization required large investments at first, these soon proved worthwhile. One by one the other articles on Steiff's inventory were adapted for these new procedures; including their extensive line of plush animals. The Steiff Company had withstood the crises of war and inflation, and was once more highly visible on the world market.

An account written at this time illustrates clearly the work procedures of the individual departments responsible for producing toys:

“The factory complex with its translucent glass buildings has a superstructure of 162,755 sq.feet. The first hall is used for material storage. Huge bales of felt and plush in every available quality and color can be found here. The patterns are painstakingly drawn to ensure that there is no wastage of cloth. These patterns are designed and tested in the Sample Department, where each article is altered several times before it is finally released for production. The so called ‘Finished Line’ is housed in another large hall. The employees sit at long, low tables in this building. The cut-out pattern pieces are placed on the conveyor-belt at definite intervals (the speed of which can be adjusted according to the article), and arrive at each employee's workbench. The first seamstress removes her piece from the conveyor-belt, and with a swift push on the foot pedal of her machine, she sews the material together so quickly the eye can hardly follow. The second, third and fourth seamstresses continue in the same manner. Once the complete article has been sewn and turned inside out (often a difficult process) the toys are passed on to those responsible for the filling. Each of these employees has specialised in a particular part of the ‘body’: heads, legs, torso. Next, the pre-finished ears and tails are sewn on, the eyes are attached and the noses stitched. Gradually the ▶

Illus. 530*: Glimpse inside the design department (1922).*

product begins to take shape, and one can see if the toy is a cat, a dog, or some other animal. The conveyor-belt then carries the animal to the 'artists', where they are given their final 'make-up'. Animals on wheels however, involve a longer production procedure. Their metal skeleton frames are cut by an automatic machine, then formed and welded electrically. These metal frames, which provide the animals with their remarkably sturdy weightload capacity, are then carefully inserted into the cloth bodies. Finally the iron base is fitted with finely painted wheels covered by a rubber tire.
Each completed article is then marked with the appropriate tag ▶

Illus. 531*: The patterns for Steiff dolls and animals were sketched at these tables.*

532

***Illus. 532**: An annual meeting of Vedes, the Retail Toy Dealers association (1922).*

***Illus. 533**: A family reunion at Steiff, 1927.*

1. Reihe: 1) Fr. Eva Köpff Aalen 2) Fr. Lucie Schall Ellwangen 3) Frl. Martha und 4) Frl. Maria Schall Zuffenhausen 5) Frl. Margarete Köpff Aalen 6) Hugo und 7) Erich Wolff Giengen 8) Eugen Brehm Ulm 9) Karl Schmidt Geislingen 10) Emilie Maier Giengen 11) Georg Köpff Aalen 12) Robert Steiff Neu-Ulm 13) Robert Schneider Ulm

2. Reihe: 14) Hugo Steiff Giengen 15) Richard und 16) Frl. Gertrud Steiff Stuttgart 17) Fr. Johanna Steiff Giengen 18) Otto Schall Ellwangen 19) Frl. Margarete Werner Geislingen 20) Fr. Mina Brehm Ulm 21) Eugen Schneider 22) Frl. Ruth Köpff Aalen 23) Frl. Else Maier 24) Frl. Margarete Steiff Giengen 25) Frl. Elfriede Steiff Giengen 26) Frl. Ruth Schneider Ulm 27) Fr. Lidya Steiff Neu-Ulm 28) Otto Steiff 29) Leonhard Maier Giengen

3. Reihe: 30) Wilhelm Köpff Aalen 31) Erwin Rentschler Laupheim 32) Fr. Mini Steiff Giengen 33) Fr. Emma Rentschler Laupheim 34) Theodor Steiff Stuttgart 35) Frl. Pauline Steiff Vaihingen 36) Friedrich Güthner Biberach 37) Karl und 38) Emma Schmidt Geislingen 89) Paul Steiff Giengen 40) Frl. Halene Steiff Stuttgart 41) Fr. Pauline Maier Giengen 42) Frl. Johanna Steiff Stuttgart 43) Fr. Fanny Huber Tuttlingen 44) Paul Wolff 45) Fr. Berta Steiff Giengen 46) Frl. Gertrud Steiff 47) Fr. Emma und 48) Otto Steiff Geislingen 49) Fritz Steiff Giengen

4. Reihe: (sitzend) 50) August Schmidt Tuttlingen 51) Frl. Emilie Steiff Geislingen 52) Frl. Emilie Schneider Ulm 53) Fr. Berta Güthner Biberach 54) Fr. Berta Steiff 55) Frl. Tusnelde Steiff Stuttgart 56) Fr. Mathilde Steiff 57) Frl. Babette Steiff Stuttgart 58) Fr. Eugenie Stein Hinzistobel 59) Fr. Emilie Wolff Giengen 60) Fr. Berta Sandholz Hinzistobel 61) Fr. Klara Steiff Giengen

Kinder: 62) Irmgard Schall Ellwangen 63) Hans Köpff Aalen 64) Robert Steiff 65) Hans Steiff Giengen 66) Erika Steiff Neu-Ulm 67) Klara Steiff Geislingen 68) Doris Steiff Giengen

533

and Button-in-Ear before it is passed on to quality control. Another hall in the factory complex houses the 'Metal-work' department. Next to this is the department responsible for making the different voice-boxes used in each animal. Here one hears 'bow-wow', 'moo-moo', 'miaow', 'he-haw' and the powerful growl of the bear. In the next room the horses are saddled, and their manes are fixed in place; the oxen are given soft horns of leather, and the Roloplans are tied together and packed. Some of the Roloplans are placed on one side for 'Test-flights', so that the quality of production can be checked.

The department for childrens' cars, scooters etc. is housed separately in another building. The strong wheels are punched out, then pressed and welded by large machines. The mudguards and coachwork for the cars as well as the metal-parts for the scooters, are also made by these machines. All metal parts are then painted and enamelled at considerable technical expense before they are finally assembled."

This account does not disclose the number of employees working for Steiff between 1925 and 1930. In fact, 1,800 people were employed at the factory, and countless others worked from their homes.

Steiff's felt character dolls suffered particularly as a result of the poor quality material which was all that was available after the war. In 1925 they were withdrawn from the program. Another reason for the decision to discontinue the dolls, was the disturbing "center-seam" in the face. However, customers were not happy with this decision; they wanted the Steiff dolls back in the program. Giengen remained firm. Later, their decision was not only regretted, it was acknowledged as a mistake. (New dolls, with pressed felt faces were produced in 1936; but not until Spring 1987 was a satisfying doll-series included in the Steiff program once again.)

Steiff's program became really "colorful" in 1927. The predominantly natural tones used for the animals (rabbits, ducks, bears, dogs, etc.) were now replaced by plush in dazzling colors. Hugo Steiff designed the first childrens' cars; the pedal-car, the sportscar, and the "Triplmobil". Quality was of the utmost importance and legal patents for designs and patterns were obtained "to protect the company from their copy-cat competitors!"

The youngest of the Steiff brothers, Ernst Steiff, joined the company in 1927. He had spent fourteen years in the U.S.A. working as an electrical engineer. Now he wanted to devote his knowledge and energy to the family business.

In 1929 the ride-on animals were fitted with an improved steering-mechanism, but their most important improvement was the new metal disc-wheels with rubber tires. Thus playing indoors on vulnerable floor surfaces was no longer a problem. "Teddy-baby", the little bear cub was also created at this time, and was enthusiastically received by Steiff's customers.

At the beginning of 1929, plush animals marked with a tag in the left ear, suddenly appeared on the market. These were not from the Giengen manufacturer, and Steiff were naturally incensed. A legal battle seemed inevitable and Steiff prepared themselves by taking unusual measures. In January they sent out questionnaires to numerous toy stores in order to find out how many of these copies were already on the store-shelves. Four weeks later numerous replies had arrived in Giengen. The stores were behind Steiff. Encouraging and approving letters document the close-knit relationship between the Giengen manufacturer and the suppliers. Ernst G. Meyer of Hannover, wrote: "Yes. The public insists on the Steiff 'Button-in-Ear' with the tags. I have checked all the merchandise in my warehouse and find that all other manufacturers attach their trademarks to the animals' collars, or sew them onto their chests." Carl Schäffer, Osnabrück, wrote: "Customers expect that when they buy an article with the 'Button-in-Ear' trademark, they are buying a Steiff article." And Heinrich Roskothen, purveyor to the court, Duisburg, wrote: "The 'Button-in-Ear' is the rightful trademark of a Steiff product." The chain-store owner, Leonard Tietz of Cologne, wrote: "A more appropriate place for your trademark would be difficult to imagine. Also, each salesperson only has to point to your trademark when selling one of your products for the customer to be satisfied."

In 1930, Steiff celebrated their 50th anniversary with an expensive celebration. The speeches were full of hope; the daily papers referring to the difficult economic times remarked optimistically that: "a strong will and unshakeable motivation" were visible, so that "a further upward trend is almost guaranteed". Steiff agents from home and abroad arrived in Giengen and joined visitors invited from far and near. A huge luncheon was arranged in the restaurant "Zum Lamm" (which still exists today), and the ensuing tour of the factory was extremely well attended.

In the Steiff archives there are only a few insignificant references relating to new designs, production or business policy during the 1920s and 1930s. A few handwritten letters of Richard Steiff's remain in the company's possesssion. These letters were written in America between 1925 and 1935 and are addressed to his brother Paul, his sister Lina, and the company secretary, Rathgeber. They are unique documents, in which Richard Steiff tried to guide the production of plush animals in faraway Giengen, toward improvements which were ▸ 210

A man's best friend is his dog; so goes the old saying. Indeed, no animal is as close to mankind as the dog. In ancient times, in the Middle Ages, and in modern times, dogs have been the constant companions of the human race. A dog is alert, obedient and in the truest sense, "faithful until death". He is also a playmate. No wonder dogs have an established place in the history of mankind. No-one can explain why, but the 1920s were the most successful "Dog Years" in the history of the Toy Industry. The dog replaced the Teddy-bear. His popularity began in England and in the U.S.A., and in 1924/25 there were toy dogs of every breed. Steiff followed the trend. In long-haired plush; in pink, lilac, light-blue, green, lavender and orange; soft-filled with Kapok, wearing huge silk ribbons – sometimes with greatly exaggerated features. These cuddly four-legged creations did not simply appeal to children – ladies were captivated too. Squeeze voice-boxes imitated real barking. The 1920s were truly "crazy, dog years".

534

***Illus. 534**: The plush dog "Molly" was Steiff's greatest success after the Teddy-bear. Offered for the first time in 1925, it remained in the program until the 1950s: Available sitting, standing, as a bag, pin-cushion, music-toy, hand-puppet, Molliette or pendant.*

***Illus. 535**: Belgian Toy Store with special department for Steiff products (1925).*

"Beauty" was the name of the young collie who was the heroine in a series of English adventure stories. J.K. Farnell & Co. manufactured her in plush for the English market, and she was a sales hit! A notice dated January 15, 1925 from the Steiff archives, reads: "Mr. McDonald has just told me that the English dog Beauty is an absolute hit now, whereas two years ago, no one wanted her . . . ." Steiff requested manufacturing rights, but these were not granted. Their original design was so cleverly adapted that the copyright laws were not broken. The dog developed from this design was named "Molly" and became a huge success. At the Spring fair in Leipzig in 1925 "Molly" made her first appearance. Soon the dog was available, sitting, in 7, 9, 11 and 14in.. and standing, in 4, 6, 7, 9, 10 and 12in.. Musical Molly, as a pendant, a handpuppet, a bag and a pincushion – Between 1925 and 1932, over half a million "Molly" products were made. Even in the '50s, "Molly" was one of the best-loved Steiff animals.

535

Whenever an interesting and lucrative toy appeared anywhere in the world, the Steiff agent in the area immediately sent an example of it to Giengen. Here the toy was studied in detail; quality was assessed, and its manufacturing possibilities were calculated. This was normal procedure in the trade. On October 29, 1926, a package from England arrived in Giengen. Inside was a "Tango Puppy" – a dancing dog manufactured by the English Chad Valley Toy Company. The dog had extra long legs and when held by the arms he executed dancing movements. Chad Valley made five models under the name "Tango Toys". In 1927, the dog was re-named "Molliette" by Steiff. The body, a replica of the Chad Valley model, was of bright velvet, in vivid colors: orange, pink, purple, yellow, green or light blue. This series was named "Charleston Tiere" by Steiff. The heads were taken from the dogs "Molly", "Cheerio", "Fluffy" and "Bully". There was also a rabbit head. The new animals were named "Molliette", "Cheeriette", "Fluffiette", "Bulliette" and "Rabbiette". These fashionable products were not simply sold as childrens toys they were also sold as Boudoir-Room and Auto-Dolls.

***Illus. 536**: "Molly" in the "Molliette" version – a Boudoir- or Auto-doll rather than a toy (1927).*

538

***Illus. 538**: "Molliette" in 12 and 17in. (1928).*

537

***Illus. 537**: Charleston-animals, Play and Auto Dolls in bright colors. A popular fashion accessory in the 1920s.*

***Illus. 539**: A design by Paul Steiff – "Treff" created from the English version, " Dismal Desmond", 6in. (1928).*

539

***Illus. 540**: "Dismal Desmond" Illustration by George Hildebrandt.*

***Illus. 541**: American Patent for Paul Steiff's design – "Treff".*

***Illus. 542**: "Treff" in all variations (from the left) back: as a dressed-doll and Charleston-animal (1929) front: velvet, 4 and 6in. Also available in plush, in 4, 6, 7, 9, 11, 14, 17 and 21in. (until 1938).*

542

The design for Steiff's mournful looking dog "Treff" was adapted from the English Dalmation, "Dismal Desmond", made in velvet by Deans Rag Book Co. of London. The "Lady of the World" according to the English advertisers, carried Desmond with her wherever she went – to parties or simply shopping. Steiff refined the dog's appearance, altered his pose, developed a new method of making the eyes, and changed the Dalmation into a bloodhound; cute, not at all dangerous-looking, rather with an expression which aroused a protective instinct. The pattern was sent from Giengen to Geo. Borgfeldt in New York. They were confident that "Treff" would be a success, and had the design patented. Borgfeldt informed Steiff on August 31, 1928: "We are holding the first delivery of 'Treff' until the patent has been applied for. In the meantime, however, we shall stamp the paper tag on 'Treff', with the words 'Patent pending'." Borgfeldt also wrote: "We should also patent the dog's head, with its typical and appropriate eyes; the slanting, half-covered eye-ball, which gives this dog's face a particularly thoughtful, intelligent expression." At the same time, Steiff's American partner warned the company to pay special attention to quality: "We advise you to make absolutely sure that this slanting, characteristic pose and exact modelling is obvious on all 'Treff' dogs, so that our patent application remains correct." In Germany, too, a DRGM was applied for, since the attaching of "Treff's" eyes was a previously unknown procedure developed by Steiff. The application stated that the eyes were not simply sewn onto the cloth, rather that: "the cloth covering has special slits for the eyes." The eyes were then attached beneath these slits. By adapting the eyelids the dog would have many different and comical expressions. For instance, "if both the bottom lids were hidden behind the eye, the eyes would give the impression of drooping downwards, creating a sleepy or melancholy expression. If both lids were in front of the eyes, the dog would appear to be squinting or blinking." Steiff's "Treff" was available sitting or standing; in velvet or mohair; on wheels and also with head-movement. Velvet dogs were available in 4, 5 and 7in.; plush dogs in 4, 5, 6, 9, 11, 14, 17 and 20in. Manufactured until 1937/38.

543

544

***Illus. 544a**: Chow-chow "Blanco" on a pink pin-cushion with pink bow, very feminine, 7in. (1930).*

The dog as a fashion accessory – only an insatiable market could allow such frivolity. Instead of a design for realistic looking dogs, a more feminine but unnatural appeal was now required. How inconvenient that a living lap-dog could wet the carpet. How much more convenient and clean a little plush dog would be – and no trouble at all! One could always sit him in the corner and there he would stay. The soft-toy industry was over-run by new ideas for this latest craze. Plush animals must be made to cuddle and pamper, they must invite stroking. The elegant vamp must carry a soft-filled lap-dog of silky mohair in her arms. Steiff advertised: "Unmistakably Steiff, with all the characteristics of the breed, with appealing expression and intelligent air, the soft-mohair just right for stroking . . .."

***Illus. 545**: The West-highland white terrier "Zotty" with squeeze voice-box was only popular for a short time. 4, 6, 7 and 9in. (1926-1929).*

***Illus. 543**: Red-Cross dog "St. Bernard", standing and sitting, 7in. (1934).*

***Illus. 544**: "Chin-Chin", the royal Chinese dog; in cheaper version, felt, 9in. (early '30s).*

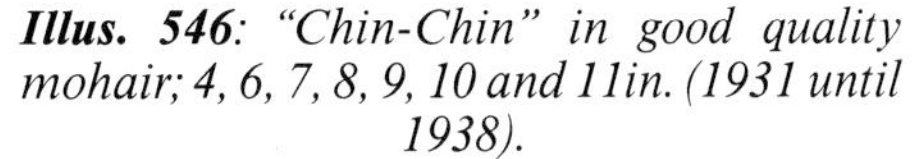

***Illus. 546**: "Chin-Chin" in good quality mohair; 4, 6, 7, 8, 9, 10 and 11in. (1931 until 1938).*

546

547

548

***Illus. 547 + 548**: Almost unbeatable in the popularity stakes: every third dog registered in America was a German Shepherd made famous by the movies "Strongheart" and "Rin-Tin-Tin". In 1925, Steiff produced their first German Shepherd "Sergeant Police Dog" for the U.S. market and "Polizeihund" for Germany. Sitting German Shepherd (**Illus. 547**), 7in. in felt (1932). **Illus. 548**: Later, a new model, 9in.; larger sizes with open mouths.*

***Illus. 549**: Fashionable breeds from mid 1920 until the end of the '30s (from the l.): "Scotty" in black, white and on wheels, 7in. (1930); "Prince", 9in. (1920); "Sealyham", 7in. (1938); "Snip", 7in. (1929); "Skye Terrier", 6in. with snap-fastening to attach to tricycle (1939).*

***Illus. 550-552**: "His Masters' Voice" Trademark of the Electrola Record Co., was the prototype for this fashionable dog of the 1920s. This fox-terrier was made in several versions. In 1928, a new design for a "box-shaped" head was developed – to give the dog*

549

550

*a more natural appearance. The Electrola-Fox (**Illus. 551**) of the 60s, in: 5, 7 and 10in.. **Illus. 552** shows three typical Fox-Terriers (from the l.): "Strupp", 9in. (1928), "Strupp" with head movement, 6in. (1931) and "Fox", 7in. (1930).*

551

552

553

The French Bulldog, darling of Parisian Salons in the mid 1920s, served as a model for Steiff's "Bully". He did not have short ears though, quite the opposite, his ears seemed particularly big. Their secret: The outside seam was strengthened by wire so that the ears could be bent into the desired position. "Bully" was registered as a design, and a trademark, in 1927. Naturally he was soon copied by other manufacturers (as was the custom in the toy trade) and Steiff sought legal action yet again. In 1925, the factory owner Willy Weiermüller was legally ordered to present all his books for court inspection since he had supplied the trade with exact copies of "Bully". Weiermüller was ordered to hand over all his profits to Steiff. The dog with the huge ears proved to be a long-standing success for Steiff. Their catalog text read: "Bully Bulldog, with his realistic facial expression, detailed painting, glass eyes, jointed neck with collar, and voice box." "Bully" was available sitting, standing, on wheels; as a ride-on toy, a pull-toy and on eccentric wheels; as a hand-puppet, a handbag, a pin-cushion; with a music-box or, as a cleaner for gramophone records in 1932. "Bully" was available in velvet, (black, gold or blue/white) and in plush (gold/white or black/white, brown) in sizes from 4 to 20in.

554

555

***Illus. 553**: "Bully" in 7 and 9in. sizes (1927 until 1930).*

***Illus. 554**: Further variations of "Bully" were (from the l.), in plush and velvet, standing and sitting (1928-1930) on eccentric wheels (1929); and in front: reclining "Bully" as gramophone-record cleaner.*

***Illus. 555**: "Villa Bully" an advertising photograph.*

***Illus. 556**: "Bully" with Trademark label from Jan. 28, 1927. In velvet, 6in.*

Illus. 557*:* *Advertising sheet for "Bully" and "Pip" (see page 205). Over 250,000 "Bullys" were sold in the first five years of production.*

557

STEIFF BULLY

ORIGINAL KNOPF IM OHR

STEIFF BULLY

originell und von treffendster Charakteristik, der schnell zum Lieblingshund geworden ist.

Sitzende Serie aus feinem Plüsch in den Farben: schwarz/weiß, braun/weiß, gold/weiß. Mit drehbarem Kopf u. Haarhalskrause.

No. 11/3310 . . . . p. Stück Rm. 1.60
„ 3314 . . . . „ 3.25
„ 3317 . . . . „ 4.30
„ 3322,2 mit Bellstimme „ 7.20
„ 3325,2 . . . . „ 9.30
„ 3330,2 . . . . „ 11.—
„ 3335,2 . . . . „ 15.50
„ 3343,2 . . . . „ 24.—
„ 3350,2 . . . . „ 32.—

Sitzend, aus Samt, in den Farben: gold/weiß, blau/weiß, schwarz/weiß.

No. 11/3410 . . . . p. Stück Rm. 1.60
„ 3414 . . . . „ 3.25
„ 3417 . . . . „ 4.30

Lieferbar auch auf Rädern bis 50 cm hoch.

STEIFF PIP

komisch und grotesk, erfreut sich diese drollige Bulldogge großer Beliebtheit und Nachfrage.

Wir liefern ihn in Mohairplüsch in mais, lila und blau.

No. 16/6308,0 . . . . p. Stück Rm. 1.70
„ 6310,0 . . . . „ 3.25
„ 6312,0 . . . . „ 3.90
„ 6317,02 . . . . . „ 7.80

In feinem pastellfarbenem Samt in blau, grün, rot und gold.

No. 16/6408,0 . . p. Stück Rm. 1.70
„ 6410,0 . . „ 3.25
„ 6412,0 . . „ 3.90
„ 6417,0 . . „ 7.80

PIP

Bully

MARGARETE STEIFF G.M.B.H., GIENGEN A. BRENZ (WÜRTT.)

ERSTE FABRIK WEICHGESTOPFTER SPIELWAREN

399 d. 3600. 927.

Illus. 558*:* *"Bully" in striped plush with head-movement, 10in. (1931).*

Illus. 559*:* *"Bully" in all available sizes. This dog was made well into the 60's; although the pattern was altered.*

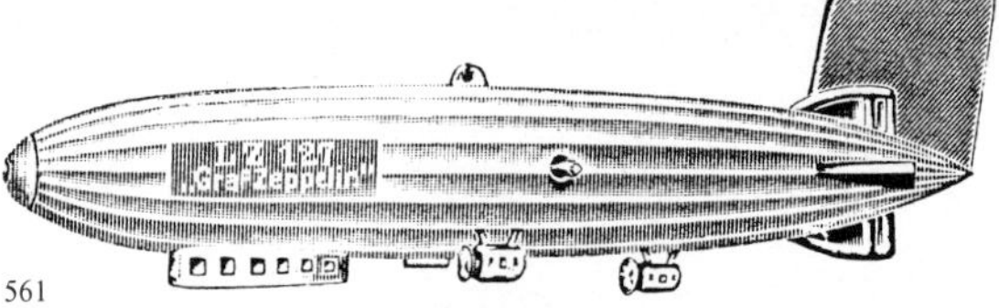

561

562

564

560

***Illus. 560-564**: The little Chow-Chow "Veedol" after his successful landing (**Illus. 560**) in Friedrichshafen on Lake Constance. – **Illus. 561**: Airship LZ 127 as a tin toy. – **Illus. 562**: Photo of "Veedol", mascot on the America-Germany flight. – **Illus. 563**: Chow-Chow "Brownie", the Zeppelin mascot. This is the first model from Dec. 20, 1928, a few weeks after the U.S. visit of LZ 127. – **Illus. 564**: The improved version of "Brownie" was the Chow-Chow "Blanco", from the new pattern. Available sitting or standing, on eccentric wheels; in several sizes, in white or brown.*

October 11, 1928. The German airship "Graf Zeppelin" (LZ127) took off on a flight to America. Among others on board, was a little canary which was presented to a distinguished guest on arrival in New York. The newspapers were full of reports about the little souvenir from Germany and exactly one day later, the airship's captain, Ernst A. Lehmann, was officially presented with the gift of a substitute mascot – a little chow dog named "Veedol". On the return flight (October 29, 1928) the little guest on board the airship was spoiled by crew and passengers alike. He was even fed cake! Captain Lehmann wrote wittily in his journal: "The young puppy devours the newspapers, either through vanity because he is mentioned, or because he actually enjoys the taste." The chow remained in the best of health, survived the flight and on arrival was given over to the care of the helmsman, Sammt. This story became so popular in America, that it was not long before Steiff were advised by their New York agent, Geo. Borgfeldt, to include a chow in their program. The name proved to be a problem at first, and the original "Veedol", was changed to "Brownie". The design was registered on December 20, 1928. The round Steiff tag was marked "Chow-chow Brownie" on the front, and "Zeppelin-mascot" on the back. Several models were available: light-brown, standing, in mohair, 9, 11 and 14in.; standing on eccentric wheels, 7 and 9in., standing on wheels, with squeeze voice box, 11 and 14in.; and sitting, with silk ribbon, 4, 6 and 7in., with voice box, 9, 11 and 14in. Another variation was "Blanco", a white chow, available in the same sizes as "Brownie". The advertising text read: "He has been showered with affection from all sides, ever since he was adopted as the Zeppelin mascot on the West-East flight of the LZ 127. His virtue was certainly the reason he was chosen, and is envied by all the world. As a toy or decorative item, we have portrayed his characteristics as carefully as possible: large, wise eyes; white, pale or chocolate-brown plush coat, and a good 'barking' voice-box."

563

The exploration of the South Pole made headlines at the end of the 1920s. The mighty icebergs, the reports of expedition failure in these white deserts, impressed the public worldwide. Richard Evelyn Byrd, an American marine officer and pilot was one of the explorers of the South Pole. In 1929, together with the Australian, Wilkins, Byrd undertook his first expedition to the land of eternal ice. The pair had spent two years preparing their journey. From their base camp at Ross-sea, they made several "informative" flights over the South Pole. In the thin, icy atmosphere, they were able to achieve the necessary height in their airplanes only by throwing out everything they could possibly do without; including their food. Without the help of their faithful Huskies, the expedition would not have been possible, revealed Byrd later in one of his accounts. The most important weapon in any Polar expedition is the Husky, or Eskimo dog, as he is sometimes called. No other breed of dog could cope with such extreme conditions. Byrd's favorite dog in the camp at the Ross-sea was the Husky, "Chinook". Steiff paid their own tribute to the breed by making a mohair version of Chinook in 1930. The penguins, too, whose comical antics Byrd described in his travel reports, were soon featured on the pages of the Steiff catalog. A display piece was created featuring a Polar scene. This was not only on display in the windows of several stores, but "The Polar Expedition" was sold nine times to the trade.

565

566

Illus. 565 + 566*: The King Penguin "King Peng" (= South Pole Bird) in four sizes: 6, 7, 9 and 14in. Fitted with head movement and with a hook in his open mouth to attach messages. Only 1,675 were made.*

567

Illus. 567*: South Pole explorer Byrd, with "Chinook" his faithful companion on his expedition.*

Illus. 568*: "Chinook – Byrd's Antarctic Expedition Dog" was available in standing, sitting and lying versions; also with head movement. In four sizes 1930 until 1931 only 2,493 examples made. With head movement: only 257 examples made! A rare collectors item!*

568

569

Soft, cuddly, fluffy animals were in great demand in the 1920s. Customers demanded them – adults as well as children. Naturally mohair cats were especially suitable, but instead of looking realistic they had to have expressions to suit the public's taste. Steiff had already produced similar animals, even before the First World War, based on the illustrations of children's writer Grace Drayton. Steiff "exaggerated cats" with huge "googly" eyes were a great hit in Russia in 1912. The googly eyes were the special design of Steiff's supplier, Amandus Eichhorn-Nelson, from Lauscha in Thuringia. At the time "Molly" the dog joined the Steiff program, they also created a cat in white mohair "Fluffy". "Fluffy" is a name often used for pet cats in English speaking countries. Steiff's other cats were also given names suggesting softness, gentleness and snuggling: "Kitty", "Tabby", "Siamy" and "Susi". Much to the delight of children, the cats were adorned with large silk bows, miaow voice-boxes and even with a special head movement. In 1933 an original design for a "Drinking-Cat" was patented. By pressing the body (which encased a rubber ball) the cat could lap up water or milk through a thin pipe. An extremely rare collectors piece, since the cat was only made from 1933 until 1935. Total Production: 345 examples.

570

571

572

573

Illus. 569-573*: Comical animal sketches by Grace Drayton (****Illus. 569****) provided the incentive for Steiff's products –* ***Illus. 570****: "Überkatzen" was the title of the sketch for this design of cats with googly eyes – made for the Russian market in 1912. –* ***Illus. 571****: "Tabby" (left), 7in., and "Fluffy", 10in. (both circa 1929). –* ***Illus. 572****: A little later "Susi", 6in. (1936), and "Kitty" (right) with head movement, 6in. (1931). –* ***Illus. 573****: The two Siamese cats "Siamy" also had the new head movement; 7 and 9in. (1931).*

***Illus. 574**: Rare examples of "Kitty". Left: with head-movement 7in., marked with tag "Made in U.S.-Zone Germany" on left front paw (1952). Right: standing version of "Kitty" with a grey felt mouse in her mouth, 9in. (1930).*

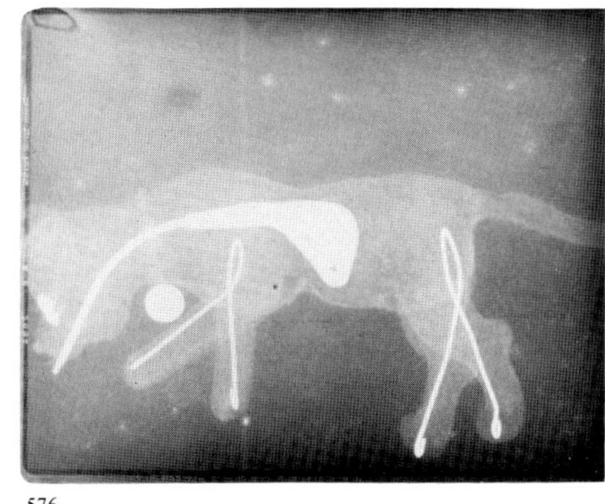

576

***Illus. 575 + 576**: "Drinking-Cats" can lap-up liquid from a bowl, by pressure on their bodies; 6in. (1933-1935), only 345 examples made. – **Illus. 576**: X-ray picture of the "Drinking-Cat".*

575

***Illus. 577**: Advertising photo; "The white monkey", novelty of 1926, with "Jocko".*

In 1925 Steiff began searching for new ideas spurred on by Richard Steiff in America. Traditional designs were adapted to suit the times – "The Roaring Twenties" full of ideas and originality had affected everyone on both sides of the ocean; even those in faraway Giengen. Changes were visible in almost all Steiff products, even the monkeys. An initial oversight was rectified and the design for "Jocko" was now patented. "Jocko" sold especially well in America, where he was featured in the comic series, "Smitty". When John Galsworthy's book "The White Monkey Climbs Higher" became a bestseller in 1925, Steiff developed their own "White Monkey" within a couple of months. However, although the book achieved record sales, the Steiff monkey could not match the success of his literary counterpart. Even a completely new type of monkey, produced in 1930, only achieved modest success. The Orang-Utan "Orangu" with his "Mimocculo" eyes, was made in long, rust colored mohair, with jointed arms and legs. His unique eye-mechanism was worked by a lever behind his right ear. The lever activated the mechanism which allowed the monkey to roll his eyes right or left and up or down. The advertising text which was affixed to each "Orangu" read: "By moving his right ear backwards and forwards the monkey assumes comical expressions, looking left or right. By moving the ear up and down the monkey can be made to look friendly or angry, moving his eyes up and down. By moving the right ear in circular motion, (not turning) the monkeys eyes can be rolled. Do not turn the ear around – just push it." "Orangu" was available in six sizes: 3, 4, 5, 6, 7, 9 and 10in. Approximately, 1,970 pieces were made between 1930 and 1931.

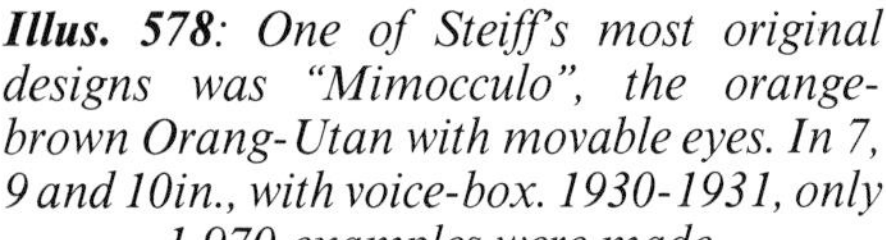

***Illus. 578**: One of Steiff's most original designs was "Mimocculo", the orange-brown Orang-Utan with movable eyes. In 7, 9 and 10in., with voice-box. 1930-1931, only 1,970 examples were made.*

***Illus. 579**: Novelty in 1927: Animal purses with zipper-closing; lined with colored velvet movable head, squeaker in tail. Chimp, Bully, Bear, Charly, Fox-Terrier, Molly, Scotty, Strupp, Chow-Chow, Brownie, Camel, Treff and Pinscher were all used. Between 1927-1931, only 806 examples of the Chimpanzee were sold.*

The "Salto-Monkey" worked through delayed mechanism. He was placed on a simple tumbling device "with a release tripping mechanism." This toy was christened "Salto Salti", and could be matched up with other animals. In 1924, over 27,820 sold.

***Illus. 580**: Two very different monkeys. The larger, 10in., has sewn eye-lids (1928 until 1929).*

STEIFF Salto-Salti

D. R. P. a.

Bolzen des Sprungbrettes vollständig in das Loch drücken und durch den Riegel feststellen. Kleines „Knopf im Ohr"-Tier auf das Sprungbrett setzen und Riegel auslösen. Mit einer gewissen Verzögerung wird das Tier im Salto hochgeschleudert.

Die Verzögerung ist mit Schlitzschraube regulierbar u. zwar erfolgt die Auslösung **schneller durch Linksdrehen, langsamer durch Rechtsdrehen.**

581

582

***Illus. 581 + 582**: Salto Monkey with regulated delay-movement. The monkey was placed on the catapult, the mechanism released, thus propelling the monkey through the air. Other small animals from Steiff's program were also recommended for the "Salto-Salti" program. In 1924, 27,820 examples left the factory.*

583

After the difficult war years Steiff had not forgotten that the Teddy-bear had been "born" at their factory. They decided to recapture their earlier success with these plush companions. However, it still took over a decade for them to develop a completely different looking bear. 1920: Because of the shortage of mohair as a result of the war, Teddy-bears were made in short plush or paper plush. Color: gold. – 1921: The rule now was to give all Teddys and animals glass eyes with black pupils. All sizes available before 1914 were once again available. – 1922: In order to pep up Teddy-bear sales Steiff developed a "Bear-Ladder" for window displays. The ladder was painted red, 43in. high and in great demand. Between 1922 and 1925, 897 ladders were sold to the trade. – 1924: Steiff placed all their hopes on the Teddy-bear. Their new-colored catalog (10 x 12in.) available for the Spring Fair in Leipzig, featured a huge Teddy-bear on the titel page. – 1925: Richard Steiff wrote to his brother Paul, from New York: "Our teddies, in the show-room here in New York, appear colorless, sober and insipid. I feel inclined to decorate all the teddies we have left with huge, colorful silk ribbons; only then can we ask a slightly higher price." American taste had outgrown traditional Steiff products and Steiff had omitted to develop new designs. It was important that they adapt quickly to keep in touch with the market. The feminine touch was required – Bears, soft filled with kapok, with squeeze voice-boxes, manufactured in extra-long, silky mohair. The hard, excelsior bears were now impossible to sell. Steiff fulfilled the demands of their American customers. Modern colors, gold and pink, were also used, although most of the bears in the program were white, blond and dark brown. A "better quality" long-haired mohair was available in white, or brown with white tips. "Teddybu", the Teddy-bear boy was offered in white, blond or dark brown, with a colorful felt vest. He too was especially made for the American market, in four sizes. In the U.S. the customers loved to furnish their teddies with complete trousseaux. Everything an elegant Teddy might require was included: comb, brush, glasses, umbrella, clothing – right down to pajamas. The program was enlarged – "Tali-Bear", a talisman for cyclists; complete with flag and clip to attach to the handle-bars. – 1926: "Teddy Clown" arrived. In brown/white tipped mohair with a clown's hat and neck ruff; also available in pink or gold. – 1927: "Petsy", the bear cub was first seen on the market. – 1929: Teddy-baby, a smiling, happy bear-cub was developed through Richard Steiff's encouragement. – 1930: Colored pads and a lively expression were the distinguishing characteristics of the "Dicky" bears presented at the Leipzig Fair. – 1934/35: Steiff introduced a new numbering system. Until this time bears had been measured in sitting position, now the sizes given were for the whole animal. Included here were the original Teddy, the Teddy-baby and the "Dicky" bear. If the tag in the ear is present, one can establish from the size given whether the bear was made before or after this date. – 1938: The first Panda bear left the Steiff factory.

584

585

***Illus. 583-586**: "Teddy-Bu" (Bu = Bube = Boy), wore a colored felt vest (**Illus. 583**) and was made in white, gold or dark brown mohair. Sizes: 9, 10, 12 and 13in.. 2,438 examples made between 1925 and 1927. – **Illus. 584**: "The Mayfair Playthings Store" in New York offered a Teddy-bear trousseau with Steiff bears, in 1929. The trunk contained a complete trousseau for the "elegant travelling bear": pajamas, shirts, jackets, umbrella, toilet articles, glasses, shoes etc. – **Illus. 585**: A mascot for cyclists was "Tali-Bär" (left) who could be attached to the handlebars (1925-1926 = 6,541 examples). Also available as "Tali-Affe" (monkey). Right: "Tali-Bär" as a toy bear, both 4in. – **Illus. 586**: Window decoration – the "Bear-Ladder", 44in. high. Between 1922 and 1925 = 897 bear-ladders (without bears) were sold.*

586

587

588

589

Illus. 588 + 589*: Pink or yellow bears in extra-soft lang mohair were made in sizes not used for regular Teddy-bears: 33, 36, 44 and 48 cm (1925 until 1930 = 5,271 yellow and 4,794 pink bears).*

590

591

Illus. 587 + 590 + 591*: The famous "Teddy-Clown" was patented in the U.S.A. in 1926. In brown-tipped mohair with clown's hat and two-colored ruff; Kapok stuffing (light and soft). Squeeze voice box, in eleven sizes, from 9 to 45in.. Also in pink or gold mohair, 13, 14 and 17in.. 30,000 examples were made until 1928. –* ***Illus. 587****: Advertisement for "Teddy-Clown". –* ***Illus. 590****: "Teddy-Clown" in gold mohair, 13in. –* ***Illus. 591****: Parade of "Teddy-Clowns" in brown-tipped mohair all sizes.*

***Illus. 592**: Two versions of "Petsy" – left: with brown eyes and black nose; right: with blue eyes and stitched red nose. Both 14in. (1928).*

***Illus. 593**: "Petsy" in the "Record" version; available in two sizes: 8 and 10in. (1928 until 1929 = 1,462 examples).*

***Illus. 594**: Pattern for a Baby Teddy-bear with new head-design, 1927. Tipped mohair. It is not known whether this bear was put into production.*

A design registration dated 1927, does not reveal for which bear it was intended. Four bear-head patterns were presented at the Petty Court: "Bär, rosa, 5325 pattern for the head, each with one head seam. Bär, brown/white tipped 5325, 3- and 4 pieces, or 3 piece seam." A bear made from this pattern is in the Steiff archives, but it seems doubtful that it was ever put into production. Similarly worked is another design from 1928: "Buschy" with wired ears, blue eyes, stubby nose and red ribbon. "Buschy" became "Petsy", the bear-baby. "Petsy" was jointed, soft-filled, and made in long haired brown mohair, with white tips. His large posable ears were fitted with wire. Petsy had a red nose, blue eyes and a sqeeze or automatic voice-box. Available in sizes: 6, 7, 8, 9, 10, 11, 13, 14, 17 and 20in. (sitting). Petsy was also available as a handpuppet and as "Record-Petsy". Today he is one of the most sought after Teddy-types. 10,668 pieces were made, until 1930.

***Illus. 595**: Advertising photo – Clown with "Petsy" (1928).*

Illus. 596: *"Teddy-Babys" from the Patent registered in 1929, in dress or pants, pink slippers, white bib, 10in..*

In 1927 Richard Steiff urged his brothers to design animals with "smiling faces which come alive." The new designs took Steiff one year to develop. They were registered immediately, and in great detail, in order to ensure protection against plagiarism. Several versions of the "Teddy-Baby", probably Steiff's most humorous bear, were registered: "1. Standing, gold mohair; 2. Standing, gold wool-plush, voice-box; 3. Dark brown with gold face and paws and 4. Dark brown wearing baby-cap, light brown face and feet." Further changes followed quickly, which resulted in a better facial expression and a very definite shape of head. This pattern too was sent straight to the Patent Office. Whilst the first "Teddy-Baby" series went into production, Steiff's patent application was rejected. However, the labels on the first "Teddy-Babies" were marked "Teddy-Baby D.R.P.a." (a= angemeldet = pending). Through this label one is able to determine whether a bear is from the first series, or of a later date. Immediately after the patent was rejected on October 18, 1930, the next labels were marked "Teddy Baby ges. gesch." The Patent Office justified its refusal thus: ". . .nevertheless the use of gussets and tucks in the sewing of a cloth-covering, does not mean that the experienced seamstress has discovered a new method, but rather that she knows how to make the best of age-old measures." The new pattern continued to be used, however, since it was especially suitable for producing the "fat cheeks" which were so appealing. "Teddy-Baby" was a success in the toy-stores. Several versions were developed. For instance, an open-mouth version with felt teeth (2 at the top and 2 at the bottom) with a laughing expression. "Teddy Baby's" large feet and slightly bent front paws created a droll appearance. Another version wearing dress or pants, pink slippers and a white bib was made. Several colors were used for the collars, and "Teddy-Baby" was available in twelve sizes, from 3, 4, 5, 6, 7, 8, 10, 11, 13, 14, 17 and 45 in. (standing). "Teddy-Baby" was also avaible as a hand-puppet. He remained a "hit" in Steiff's program until well into the 50s. The advertising text read: "Model of a lifelike comical young bear-cub, whose friendly face speaks volumes; may be made to stand upright, or sit, as desired."

597

600

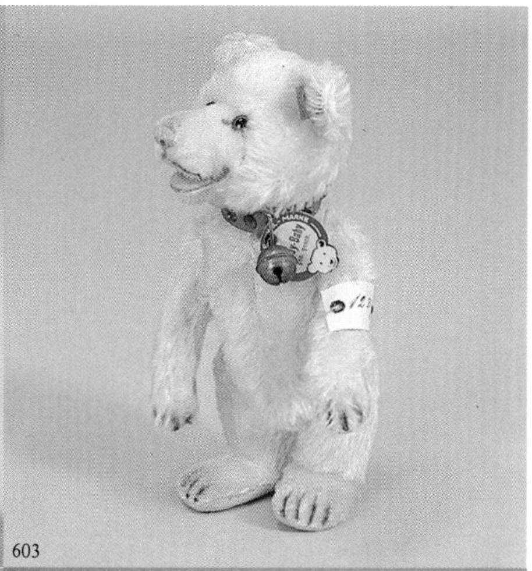

603

598

601

604

599

602

605

606

***Illus. 597-606**: "Teddy-Baby" (**Illus. 597**), left: laughing, open mouth, 5in. (1930). – **Illus. 598**: "Teddy-Baby" in blue mohair, 12in. (1929). – **Illus. 599**: "Teddy-Baby" in artificial silk mohair, 12in. (1940). – **Illus. 600**: "Teddy-Baby", in wool-mohair, 17in. (1930). – **Illus. 601**: "Teddy-Baby", left: white with blue collar, 11in. (1930), right: dark brown with red collar, 11in. (1935). – **Illus. 602**: "Teddy-Baby" – in a dress, 10in. (1929). – **Illus. 603**: White, with open mouth, 12in., with 1929 patented design. – **Illus. 604**: "Teddy-Baby" with laughing open mouth and felt teeth, 15in., (1929). – **Illus. 605**: "Teddy-Baby" in wool plush with open mouth, 12in. (1930). – **Illus. 606**: "Teddy-Baby at home", a display piece from 1930. Sold 21 times.*

***Illus. 607**: "Dicky Bear", gold mohair, (14in.), in front of a sample-board of colors for the pads (1930).*

607

***Illus. 608**: "Dicky"-Bear in white mohair; 9, 10 and 12in. (1933 until 1934).*

"Dicky" was designed at the same time as "Teddy-Baby" in 1930. "A new, improved and less expensive Steiff Teddy-bear", claimed the advertisements in 1930. "Attractive design, newly formed head, strong squeeze growler, soft-filling, blond or white mohair with painted pads, movable head and joints, famous workmanship." "Dicky's" characteristics were his happy face and colored pads. A fascinating model. The gold version had a corn-gold set-in snout, nose and ears painted red and the nose stitching was in black. "Dicky" was available in blond, in 6, 8 and 9in.; in blond or white in 10, 12, 13, 14 and 16in. In 1936 a cheaper version was available for a short time in 10, 12 and 13in. sizes, as well as 14 and 17in. with double growler. This version had a set-in snout in short plush. Between 1930 and 1936, 14,646 bears were made in gold, and 11,029 were made in white.

608

Illus. 610: *Novelty in 1937 was this "Roly-Bär" from a new pattern and design. 777 examples sold between 1937 and 1941.*

Illus. 609: *An interesting comparison: left the usual Steiff Teddy-bear as a tea-cosey; and right an example influenced by "Teddy-Baby" and "Dicky" bear designs (circa 1930).*

610

609

Illus. 611: *Display piece "The Bears Wedding", from 1925. Unfortunately the photograph is not very clear, but for documentary purposes, we have published it. "The Bears' Wedding" was on display in San Francisco, for the American Children's Day on June 18, 1927. (Perhaps this exhibition was reponsible for promoting the rumors of the White House Wedding of President Roosevelt's daughter, for which Steiff bears were said to have been used as table decoration).*

611

Illus. 612*: Baby-Bear on wheels, lying on his back, 8in. (1939).*

Illus. 613*: This sample of the Koala bear, patented by Steiff in 1932, is from the Steiff archives. It was probably not put into production.*

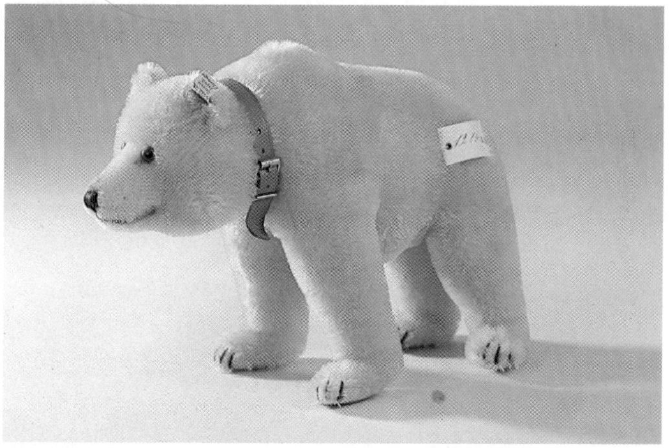

Illus. 614*: House sample "Jungbär" (Bear-cub), made in three sizes, 7, 9 and 11in. (1929).*

Illus. 615*: Wool Teddy from the miniature wool series, made in good quality mothproof wool. Fully bendable, because of wire skeleton frame. Only one size, 9in. (Photo right). 955 examples made from 1936 until 1938.*

616

Illus. 616-618: *"Pindar the Panda" (**Illus. 616**), prototype for the Panda toys, drawn by English cartoonist, Low. – **Illus. 617**: A Panda-Parade from the '50s; in 6, 9, 11, 14, 17 and 20in.. – **Illus. 618**: A 1950s Panda from the Steiff archives, 14in..*

617

Panda Bears are among the most rare animals on earth and more in danger of extinction than ever before. Their history can be traced back to the year 621, when they were mentioned in a Chinese chronicle. Even then they were not found in large numbers and were obviously a rare species. The panda appears to have lived a charmed life until the beginning of the 1930s – when bad luck finally caught up with them in the persons of Theodore and Kermit Roosevelt (sons of the ex-U.S. President, Theodore Roosevelt). Like their father, they were enthusiastic big-game hunters. They captured a giant panda in China, in the Hsifan mountain region, and with this coveted trophy (the bear's skin) they gave programs and talks which aroused "ownership feelings" in zoo directors all over the world. The "Panda-Hunt" began. Seven bears lost their lives between 1930 and 1938 for so-called scientific study – too many for a species in danger of becoming extinct! Captured animals often die during transportation, and the first giant Pandas to survive a long journey, were "Su-Lin" and "Mei-Mei" who arrived at Chicago Zoo in March 1938. "Su-Lin" died shortly afterwards when she fell from a tree-stump. "Mei-Mei" settled in well and became extremely popular with visitors. In December 1938, London Zoo also received its Panda, a seven month old female cub named "Ming". The "Evening Standard" soon featured the story of "Pindar – the Panda" written by Peter Howard and illustrated by B.Low. The toy industry in England followed the lead; cuddly pandas were soon found in toy stores all over England. On January 12, 1938, Steiff also registered a design for a 12in. Panda Bear. A total of 1,293 Pandas (12in.) were produced by Steiff until 1941. In 1939 Steiff made a second size, 6in. larger, but this version was only sold 145 times. In the same year they designed a small 7in., Panda, standing on all fours. After 1948, Pandas were included in Steiff's program once again. At first in one size, (12in.) but from 1951 they were available in six sizes: 6, 9, 11, 14, 17 and 20in. The Panda was now produced in large quantities and remained in production until the '60s.

618

In 1919 "Barney Google", a comic character, created by Billy De Beck, an American cartoonist, was featured in the Hearst Newspapers. "Barney Google" was popular-readers loved him. He embodied the "little man" who simply could not cope with his everyday problems; mostly because of his own stupidity. In 1922, Barney received company: "Spark Plug", a racehorse with an extra-large horse blanket. The two were later joined by the ostrich, "Rudy". Barney's comical adventures now featured his two companions; and the three also captured the hearts of their fans in a hit song composed by Billy Rose. In 1924, after several attempts, Steiff finally brought out their own Barney Google Series. "Barney" was 5in. tall, "Spark Plug", 7in. and "Rudy", 8in. Another version were the "Gallop"-animals (on eccentric wheels with a galloping movement) Series: "Barney Google" with "Spark Plug"; "Rudy" with "Spark Plug" and "Barney Google" with a dancing bear. "Spark Plug" was stamped on the sole of the back foot: "Copyright 1924 – 1925 by King Features Synd. Inc." Only 700 examples were sold between 1925 and 1927 (in the Gallop Series; 613 examples were sold between 1926 and 1928).

Illus. 619: *"Rudy" the ostrich (8in.), and "Galop-Rudy" (5in.). Probably only made as samples (1927).*

Illus. 622: *"Barney Google" and "Spark Plug", 6 and 7 inches, (1925-1927 = 613 examples).*

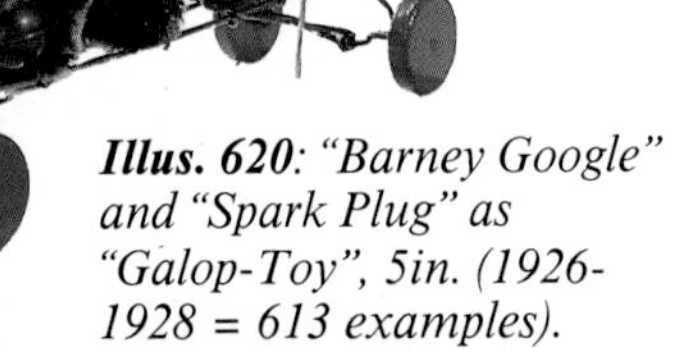

Illus. 620: *"Barney Google" and "Spark Plug" as "Galop-Toy", 5in. (1926-1928 = 613 examples).*

Illus. 621: *Original copies of the artist De Beck's drawing, from the Steiff archives.*

622

Between 1927 and 1931, Steiff sold a total of 2,780 examples of "Jack Rabbit". "Jack Rabbit" was a character whose adventures were told in an American childrens' book. The book was publised by Grosset & Dunlop Books, New York. For this reason, each "Jack Rabbit" paper tag was marked on the back "copyright by Grossert and Dunlop". The lollipop, which Steiff's "Jack Rabbit" held in his right hand was marked "Jack Rabbit of Uncle Dave Cory, copyright by Grossert and Dunlop." (Editors note: The name Grosset was mis-spelt). Steiff manufactured the rabbit in two sizes: 9 and 11in.

623

624

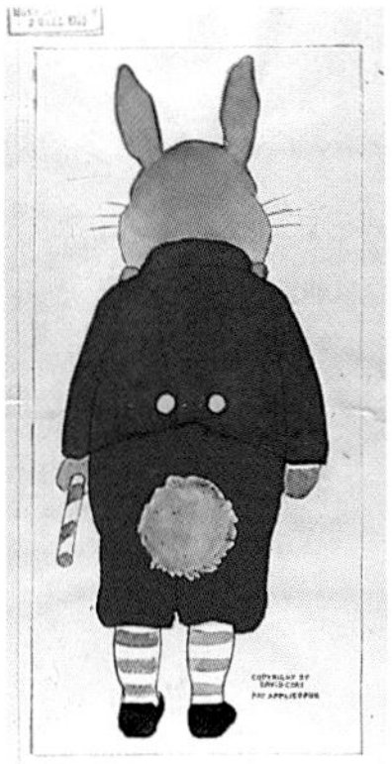

625

Illus. 623-625: Drawings and designs for "Jack Rabbit", by David Cory.

626

Illus. 626: "Jack Rabbit", with giant lollipop, as suggested in the original designs. In two sizes: 9 and 11in. (1927-1931 = 2,780 examples).

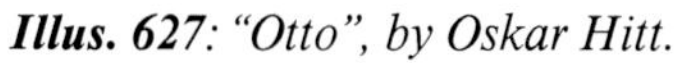

Illus. 627: "Otto", by Oskar Hitt.

628

Only one example, (a so-called "house-sample") exists of "Otto", a sullen, grouchy dog, (11in.), dressed in pants. The sample is well taken care of in the Steiff archives, and serves to show that not everything which was designed was automatically accepted into the program. "Otto" was the creation of the American illustrator Hitt. Geo. Borgfeldt, New York, placed the original order for "Otto" in 1929, but they were not satisfied with the Steiff design. "We feel that in spite of all the trouble you have taken, you should not go ahead with production of this 'Otto' design" wrote Borgfeldt on April 10, 1929.

***Illus. 628**: Only this one sample of "Otto" has been retained, 11in..*

***Illus. 629**: Steiff samples of "Bonzo" in all variations. 115 examples were made, but these remained unsold, as Steiff could not get licensing permission.*

***Illus. 630**: "Bonzo" from a comic strip by the Englishman, G.E. Studdy.*

629

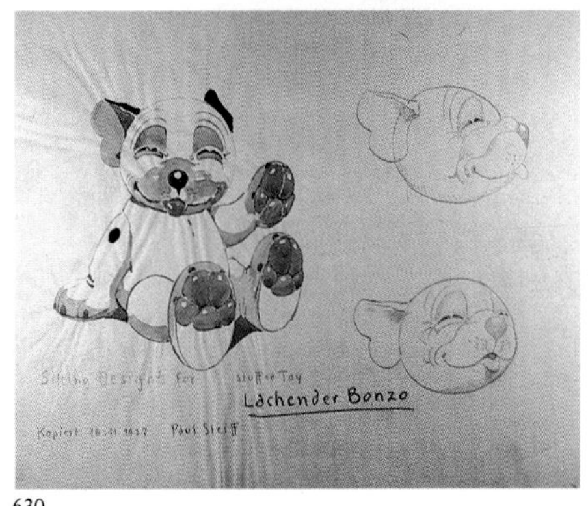

630

Steiff missed a golden opportunity in 1927, when they failed to secure the manufacturing rights for "Bonzo", a comical young fox-terrier puppy, created by the English illustrator G.E. Studdy. Studdy was completely responsible for marketing his creation, and handing out licensing rights. Bonzo books became best-sellers, and "Bonzo" himself extremely popular. Steiff sent a sample to England for approval, but they were rejected in favor of the Chad Valley Co.. Studdy did not like Steiff's version of "Bonzo" at all. He felt their "characterization" was too "vulgar". Also the similarity between Studdy's drawings and the Steiff sample had not been achieved. Paul Steiff wrote defiantly on the letter of rejection: "We can't and don't wish to make an exact replica of "Bonzo". The Steiff archives possess seven Bonzo samples: 5, 6, 7, 8, 9, 10, 12 and 17in.. A total of 115 examples were made.

Since Steiff were unable to obtain licensing rights for "Bonzo" their designers developed a pattern which looked remarkably like the original. The company directors were now determined to go ahead with their production and the design was registered in Paul Steiff's name in 1929. Steiff's new model was named "Cheerio". The design was an exaggerated portrayal of a smiling puppy; he had movable blue eyes (a few examples were also made with brown eyes) and an open mouth with his tongue hanging out. "Cheerio" was made in white/light brown mohair, standing, with movable head and voice box in five sizes: 4, 5, 7, 9 and 11in. In begging position he measured 7, 9 and 11in..

***Illus. 631** + **632**: The laughing Puppy "Cheerio" (**Illus. 631**). From the left: begging, 9in.; standing, 9in. Especially comical, the huge movable eyes. (1928-1932 = 4,771 examples; and 170 with music box). – **Illus. 632**: U.S. Design Patent for "Cheerio", by Paul Steiff.*

632

631

633

***Illus. 633**: A.B. Payne's comic from the "Daily Mirror". "Pip, Squeak and Wilfred" provided the incentive for Steiff's dog "Pip" (1920s).*

***Illus. 634**: The exeggerated Bulldog caricature "Pip" in bright colors, with movable googly eyes, in 4 sizes; 3, 4, 5 and 7in. (1925-1931).*

Also belonging to the dog family was Steiff's caricature of the bulldog, "Pip". "Pip" was developed from the drawings of A.B. Payne, whose cartoons had been featured in the "Daily Mirror" in London since 1919. Steiff offered "Pip" in 1925 for the first time. The standing version in pink or gold mohair (or velvet) in sizes from 3 to 7in.; and the seated version in light blue, green or orange velvet. All the dogs had large movable "googly" eyes in glass. "Pip" could not be sold in England, and was removed from the catalog in 1931.

634

635

"Bertha" the "Siberian Cheesehound" a creation of Rube Goldberg, was featured in the American Sunday-comic series: "Boob Mc Nutt" from 1915 until 1934. "Bertha" joined Steiff's dog family in 1927, in two sizes, 7 and 9in. 24 examples were made in brown/ tipped mohair with sewn, painted or glass eyes. Another version, with a metal box on the tail was planned, but since there was little demand for "Bertha", production was soon stopped.

636

***Illus. 635**: "Bertha". Original sketch by R.C. Goldberg, (1925).*

***Illus. 636**: "Bertha" was only produced as a sample (24 examples) in 7 and 9in. (1917).*

637

***Illus. 637-640**: Mops, exaggerated (**Illus. 637**), 6in. Sold in the U.S.A. as "Pug-Dog", (1925-1927 = 819 examples). – **Illus. 638**: Comic with "Putzi", (1932). – **Illus. 639**: Design sketch from Steiff. – **Illus. 640**: "Putzi" in white wool-plush; sizes, 7, 9 and 11in. (1932-1935 = 2,542 examples).*

638

"Putzi" was a comic little dog whose adventures were also featured in German Newspapers (Thuringia General Newspaper = TAZ). The U.S. company, King Features Co., neglected to legally protect their character in Europe, thus allowing Steiff to manufacture "Putzi". The toy merchant Otto Ritter, of Erfurt, placed a huge order for Steiff's "Putzi", but insisted on being given sole rights to sell the dog in Erfurt, Weimar, Gotha and Arnstadt. "Putzi's" label read "I am Putzi, of the TAZ." The dog was produced in three sizes; 7, 9 and 11ins.. He was soft-filled, his muzzle and claws were black, he had a tongue and eyebrows of red felt, and black glass buttons for eyes and nose.

639

640

641 642

***Illus. 641 + 642**: Original "Flip the Frog" (**Illus. 641**), by Ub Iwerks. – **Illus. 642**: Only one sample of "Flip the Frog", 11in., remains today. Velvet, with felt clothing.*

In 1933, "Flip the Frog" was registered. His design was taken from an clay figure sent to Steiff from the Geo. Borgfeldt Co., New York. Paul Steiff noted that he had seen the frog in a cartoon, at the end of a Mickey Mouse show, and he found the frog to be "just as funny and famous" as "Felix the Cat". "Flip the Frog", was a creation of Ub Iwerk, who had also designed Mickey Mouse. Steiff's "Flip" was in black and white velvet, and wore green felt pants and a hat. However, because of the political situation in Germany in 1933, "Flip" was not put into production. There is only one sample in Steiff's archives.

FLIP THE FROG

A big star of silent movies in the 20s was "Felix", the Cat. Together with his girlfriend "Muschi" he was a milestone in the history of cartoons. Created for a comic series by the illustrator Pat Sullivan (and Otto Messmer, his studio chief), "Felix" soon developed his own lifestyle. Felix was featured regularly in the American Sunday-comics from 1923, and he achieved such popularity that in 1927, Geo. Borgfeldt asked Steiff to supply a prototype. The first designs were a catastrophe so Steiff had to develop new patterns. This time the ears and face were in felt instead of plush, and Borgfeldt was happy at last. However, Steiff's management remained sceptical, for "Felix" was "drab", he could only be made in black and white, like his screen counterpart. Paul Steiff's was a decisive voice against the order. He was convinced that black and white toys were unsaleable. And he was right! Between 1925 and 1927, only 605 examples were made. The handpuppet version (15,300 examples) and the "Rekord-Felix" (2,100 examples) were more successful.

643

***Illus. 643 + 644**: Darling of the silent movies (**Illus. 643**), "Felix the Cat". – **Illus. 644**: "Felix the Cat", left as an earthenware model, and right: Steiff version, 9in. (1925-1927 = 605 examples).*

644

645

Illus. 645 + 646: *Photograph of Walt Disney (**Illus. 645**) from the "Berliner Illustrirte" (1930). – **Illus. 646**: "Mickey Mouse" and "Minnie Mouse" by Steiff (1931). "Mickey Mouse" in 4, 6, 9, 12, 14 and 19in.; "Minnie Mouse" in 5, 7, 9, 12, 14 and 19in.. (1931-1936, over 67,000 examples).*

647

646

648

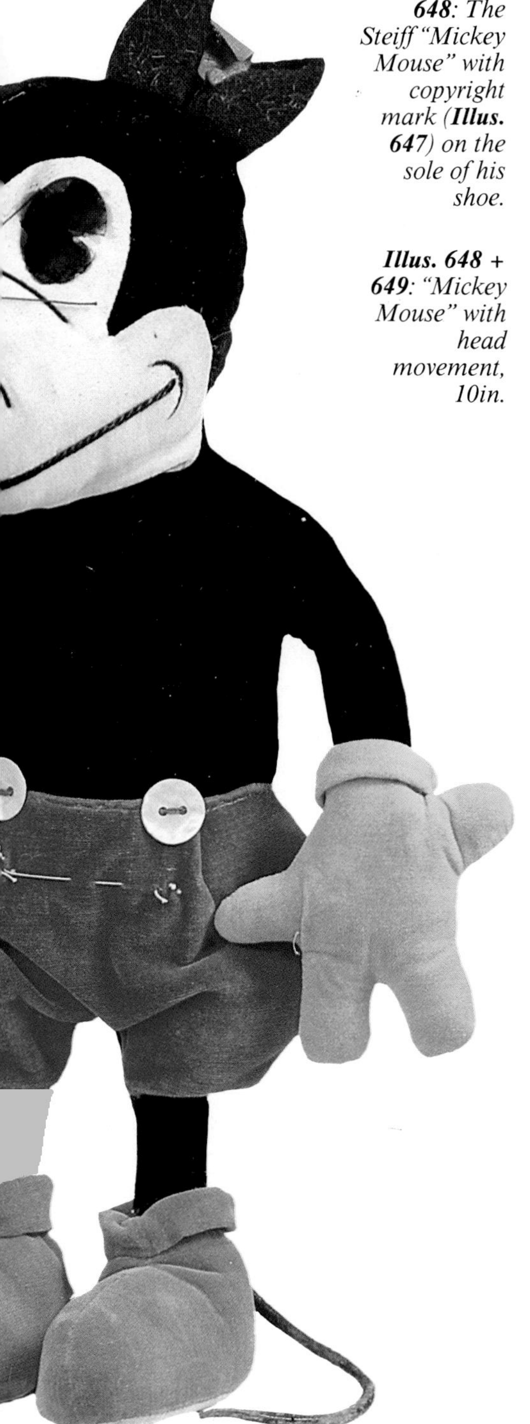

***Illus. 647 + 648**: The Steiff "Mickey Mouse" with copyright mark (**Illus. 647**) on the sole of his shoe.*

***Illus. 648 + 649**: "Mickey Mouse" with head movement, 10in.*

Mickey Mouse

"Mickey Mouse, star of the talking-movie era." With this advertising slogan, a tiny cartoon mouse began his global conquest in 1929, and his breathtaking success has remained constant until the present day. "Felix" the cat, Mickey's forerunner, had disappeared from the movie theaters because his creators were unable to think up new adventures. "A mouse has defeated the cat" wrote the "Berliner Illustrirte". Ub Iwerks, creator of the Mickey Mouse character, worked as a cartoonist long before he was discovered by Hollywood. His first movie cartoon was "Oswald", the crazy rabbit. When Ub Iwerks signed a contract with Walt Disney and produced the first talking movie cartoon with his Mickey Mouse character; he also created the most fascinating comic figure of all time. Walt Disney Studios produced two Mickey Mouse movies a month, and these were shown in movie theaters in Germany and the rest of the world too. The popularity of the lively little mouse soon swept through the Toy and Souvenir Industries. Naturally, Steiff joined the race! Paul Steiff once travelled with his chauffeur, Herr Ratter, to a movie theater in Stuttgart in order to see a Mickey Mouse film. On June 26, 1930, he noted: "We sat in the very last row and appeared to be the only ones who laughed over the film. Either no-one in Germany is yet able to understand a cartoon film, or life at present is so sad that no-one has the heart to laugh; or are these films unsuitable for the majority of people?" He called the agile character "lively, three-dimensional, comical, understanding, funny, droll and happy." Walt Disney sold all the commercial rights for Mickey Mouse to Geo. Borgfeldt & Co. in New York. One could only obtain a license to market the "wondermouse" through the Borgfeldt Company. Obviously Steiff had a head-start on their competitors in the race for marketing rights, for Borgfeldt had been Steiff's sole agent in the States for decades. It was not long before the first examples of Mickey Mouse left the Toy Factory in Giengen. In sizes ranging from 4, 6, 9, 12, 14 and 19in. almost 30,000 pieces were manufactured in 1931. Dissatisfaction arose, as the Steiff prototype of Minnie Mouse arrived in New York for approval, in 1932. Fred Wander, Chief buyer at Borgfeldt was appalled by the quality of the Steiff sample. Minnie's bottom lip was not at all similar to the original. On July 19, 1932, Wander wrote a letter to Steiff: "Mr. Disney is very disappointed, I shall quote you his exact words: 'No matter how Steiff feel my Minnie Mouse should be made, I insist she be made the way I want, or not at all. Minnie Mouse's head is identical to Mickey's and Steiff has made it completely different. Her face is thin, and the open mouth is ugly, so that I do not wish to have any more delivered. . .' Mr. Disney does not want the bottom lip to droop downwards, it has to be made exactly as sketched on the accompanying designs. By attempting to make an open mouth, you have robbed Mickey Mouse of his most distinguishing feature. You cannot do this. They can remove any article from the market which does not meet the specifications of their model. The Disneys can cause us a lot of trouble if you insist on continuing your production." And at the end of the letter, an important detail: "A further sore point with Disney is that you have sewn on a four-sided tail!" Steiff altered Minnie Mouse as desired, and all further designs of Mickey and Minnie Mouse were given rounded tails. Steiff were able to keep these articles in their program until 1936; their export was arranged through Holland during the last three years. Steiff produced their Mickey Mouse over 53,000 times, whilst with Minnie, they only managed a production figure of 13,000. Incidentally, the business relationship between Walt Disney and Steiff was re-established in the 50s with the fawn "Bambi" and other toys.

649

RICHARD STEIFF
ORIGINATOR OF STEIFF TOYS
610 HARWOOD STREET
JACKSON, MICHIGAN

Nov. 26. 1931.

Lieber Bruder Paul!

Illus. 650: *Richard Steiff's letter-head.*

imperative to the export market. The fact that he remarked critically on some products, was part of his job as the New York representative of the toy company. (The Margarete Steiff & Co. Inc. was founded in partnership with the Geo. Borgfeldt & Co. U.S.-Export Company, to stimulate export. The company headquarters were in the Borgfeldt-building, 111-119 East 16th Street, New York.)

In his clear, distinct penmanship, Richard Steiff composed situation reports on the American toy industry, as well as detailed analyses of faulty merchandise, and suggestions for the design of new products.

On February 6, 1925, he informed his brother Paul, in Giengen: "I am asked almost daily for new products; and I always have to answer that we do not really want to develop new products, since we can hardly cope with the delivery orders we receive for our old toys. However, the stiff competition here means we must be on our toes. Our customers here are not simply satisfied with 'good German quality' and they are not interested in our problems with fulfilling our orders. They insist on: (1) new designs, (2) cheaper products and (3) a more attractive inventory – by which I mean neat workmanship, artistic design and good material!"

Richard Steiff tried to co-erce his brother into making some improvements: "The faces of the police shepherd dogs are too carelessly modelled." He also placed great emphasis on a much more careful control of the finished products: "In Giengen, there is still one important step in the work process which is being neglected. The quality control when our products are finished! Mass production involves an exact work process and the division of this process into as many parts as possible." He explains further: "I know, of course, that when visitors to the factory see that a toy which has been completed (in their opinion!) is subjected to even further checks, they think to themselves 'no wonder their toys are so expensive, if their work is so old-fashioned.' Nevertheless, I believe that only with such careful attention to detail can we continue to have success. And these bunglers will continue to wonder at our success, for they will never be able to fathom it."

On February 18, 1927, Richard Steiff wrote to Paul about the encouraging economic stability which the toy company in Giengen had once again achieved after the crises of war and inflation. "Perhaps we were too cautious and we expected the future to be blacker than it was; but at least we can relax now, and it is our turn to laugh at those others who are just beginning to worry. Yes, I know for a fact that the Steiff family are much better off than even some similar families here in America, because these families are not making much money today and have not learnt to save and live prudently." But he also warned, "You can easily do something really important for the company if you do nothing else but spend a couple of hours daily checking the finished products, right there in the Packing Room. Check them without consideration for anyone (for considerate people are hardest on themselves!) and either through written or spoken instructions send everything back which you don't like . . . the most important thing is that our toys have the nicest, drollest expressions."

Richard Steiff's personal intervention from America was soon visible in the company's steadily increasing profits. On February 22, 1925, he wrote proudly to his sister Lina: "Sales figures over here seem to be improving all the time, but as far as I'm concerned, the most important thing is that once again we have achieved our old position of respect; with the customers and competition alike. Both believe that Steiff are somehow able to achieve success through some secret method, something which no-one else seems able to do!" He continues: "People are no longer content simply because the animals have nice symmetrical faces. I want to produce a series with comical facial expressions which come alive. This new animals series also has to serve as a type of doll – we must be able to dress and undress them like the Teddy-bear." Richard Steiff goes on to explain: "The money spent in our design department – the best in New York – has ▶

proved to be our most lucrative investment. Our designs visibly hypnotize the buyers, who would otherwise throw our splendid catalogs straight into the waste basket. My business colleagues here constantly assure me that my advertising and my other (display) methods have certainly been responsible for our present success..." And in order to convince the sceptics in Giengen, he adds: "They are prepared to confirm this in writing if the management in Giengen so wish..."

In 1928 advertising spots for Steiff Teddy-bears and animals were heard on over one hundred radio stations throughout America, and the daily papers were flooded with photo-advertisements for the toys from Giengen.

The economic depression at the end of the twenties caused Richard Steiff to warn his brothers that costing must be more strictly managed in the future. They were no longer to compete with high quality, but rather with lower prices. "The actual costs now have to be cut through rational management" wrote Richard Steiff to the company secretary, Rathgeber in 1931. "The need to cut the costs in production often makes people inventive, and usually brings more, not less profit, for all involved... Therefore, you must help to dictate the production costs... you will often have no choice but to remove products which are not selling, from the program, and then concentrate on items you may not consider as good (but which sell)..."

Finally, a letter written by Richard Steiff on March 26, 1931, not to one person in particular, but to the "Steiff Company, GmbH." urges the management to "americanize" their thinking in order to remain competitive in the U.S. "The fact that most German manufacturers are simply not on the same wavelength as their American

Illus. 651: Special postmark, 1942.

customers has certainly damaged their sales-capacity over here more than anything else. It is no longer true that one can design a luxury article in an impoverished small town like Giengen, which will then automatically capture the hearts of the worldly Americans, and be able to compete with similar local products. Today the new designs evolve here (!) and the Germans must not simply follow suit, they must stay on their toes in order to learn of these new designs at all. Many of today's toys are totally American, since a German designer naturally cannot conceive an Americn toy..."

The political atmosphere in Europe at this time was cloudy and uncertain, and soon halted any plans which Steiff had for conquering the overseas markets. In 1933 Hitler came to power. Production within the whole German toy industry was slowed considerably at first and finally came to a complete halt.

World leaders in their industry for decades, even for centuries, the German toy industry, recovering slowly from the effects of World War I and the ensuing economic crisis, now died swiftly with the birth of the racial madness in the country. For not only were many of the doll and toy companies in Jewish hands, almost all the export houses had been successfully run by Jews for decades. George Kolb, of the Geo. Borgfeldt Company, New York, indicated possible difficulties in a letter dated June 16, 1933. "... the drop in quality, and finally the Hitler boycott, leave us with little hope that we shall get any future orders for German products."

Richard Steiff had an especially difficult time in America – he was advised to return to Germany. However, he stayed. "Our business here is now at rock-bottom, thanks to the Hitler propaganda," wrote Richard Steiff to his sister Lina on September 24, 1934. Somehow they had to make it, even if: "I sell the animals myself" (in the toy stores), he added.

The toy factory in Giengen, also felt the new political force ▸ 234

Illus. 652: Festive floats in honor of the Steiff Company's 50th Anniversary.

Illus. 653: Catalog supplement 1931; animals with new head movement.

Supplementary catalogue E 31 contains all new lines created since we have edited Catalogue E/9. There are indeed very many and the significant progress as to lifelike reproduction of the models in colour, character and beauty is obvious to everybody.

The year 1931 has presented us with the animals with the new head movement. Immediately these animals were shown in the market every buyer saw the enormous improvement on their value and since then decided preference is given to them also by the public.

The simplicity of the mechanism, through which the splendid movement is produced, cannot be beaten, yet it is unbreakable and allows lifelike play, full of variety and mimics. The monkey moves merrily, the Elephant plays with his trunk, Molly- Bully- and Rattler Dog look beggingly, watchfully or ill humoured just at wish, while Fluffy Cat flatters.

When buying new supply in plush toys

please be sure to include the STEIFF animals with the new head movement; all numbers equipped with it are marked **"H"**.

"The ingenious head-movement makes Steiff animals appear alive." With this slogan, Steiff advertised the simple mechanism which allowed their plush animals to move their heads around in any direction. The designer of this mechanism was Hugo Steiff. Both the German patent (No. 552 223, January 17, 1931) and the American counterpart (January 19, 1932) certify: "connecting joints between two pieces, which remain connected in different positions, especially suitable for toys and dolls." "Rattler" the dog was the first animal to be fitted with this new head-movement. "Rattler", a Schnauzer, with a coat of good quality mohair, whose distinguishing marks were a bristly beard and bushy eyebrows. "When Rattler's tail is turned around, the dog appears remarkably life-like. If his head is positioned upwards, he seems ready to pounce; positioned towards the right he looks 'cunning'; whilst posing the head towards the left makes him appear 'faithful'. 'Rattler' has a truly sorrowful, reproachful appearance if his head is posed downwards." Steiff also gave explicit directions on how to carry "Rattler" in the arms, so that he most resembled a living dog: "One carries the Steiff dog on the lower part of the left arm, with tail pointing towards the right. With the right hand hidden from any audience, one holds tightly to the base of the tail." The Toy Factory Schreyer & Co. (Schuco) of Nuremberg, whose Yes/No mechanism had already been on the market for a long time saw little possibility of legally objecting to Steiff's new design, and their protests were accordingly weak. 25 animals were given this new head-movement: "Rattler", "Dachshund", "Molly", "Fluffy" (cat), "Treff", "Strupp", "St. Bernard", "Kitty", "Scotty", Chimpanzee, standing bear, "Baboon", rabbit (sitting and begging), elephant, "Bully", Poodle, Siamese, lamb, duck, penguin, goat, German shepherd, "Chinook", and "Mickey Mouse". Important: The Teddy-bear is missing completely from this list. Steiff Teddy-bears with head-movement were first made in 1955 (see page 242).

654

***Illus. 654**: Left duck with head movement brown/green mohair, 10in. (1933-1936 = 1,046). Right: yellow duck with head movement, 9in. (1931-1933 = 468).*

***Abb.655 + 656**: Patent designs for DRP 592 223 and a U.S. Patent.*

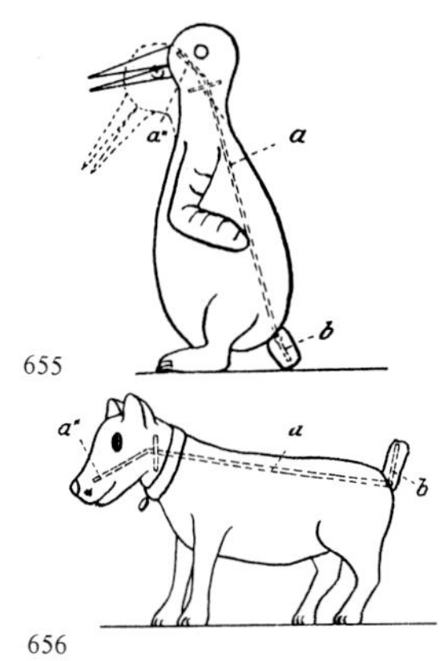

655

656

***Illus. 657**: "St. Bernard", sitting, in brown and white mohair, with head movement in 4, 6, 7, 9, 11 and 14in. (1931 until 1934).*

659

***Illus. 658**: Mr. and Mrs. "Rattler"; window decoration, 1931 (46 examples sold).*

***Illus. 659**: "Rattler" the rat-catcher, the famous Schnauzer with head movement. In sizes 3, 4, 5, 7, 9, 10, 11 and 14 in.; manufactured in large numbers from 1930 until 1935.*

***Illus. 660**: Animals with head movement had this label attached to their tails.*

***Illus. 661**: "Circus Bear", 13in.. These photos show the various stages of the bear's movement (1935 until 1939 = 897 examples made).*

662

The new neck-mechanism lent the animals their head movement, and soon additional snap-joints increased the scope of "play possibilities". Thus the Circus-bear and the Circus-elephant were developed. Both these animals could not only move their heads, thanks to the new flexible snap-joints, they could be positioned to sit, crawl or stand upright. The Circus-elephant was available from 1931, and the Circus-bear from 1935. There was also a doll with this new snap-jointing, the "Dream Baby No. 103". The head was made by the Rheinische Gummi Co. (turtle-mark), and filled with excelsior. The body was in good quality felt, and the doll had a "Mama" voice box. The doll had the new jointing in the legs, so that it could assume both sitting and standing positions. Four versions of this doll were made – all 11 inches tall, with white skirts, colored sweaters and caps: "Greta" in light green; "Blonda" in light blue; "Rose" in pink and "Angeli" in orange. (1934-1937 – total production = 4,553).

***Illus. 662**: "Rose", 11 in. with turtle-mark head "103". She wears pink knitted clothing and bonnet (1934 until 1937).*

***Illus. 663**: Sample from Steiff's archives: "Dicky-Bear", 10 in. with head movement and snap-joints in his hands and feet (1936).*

663

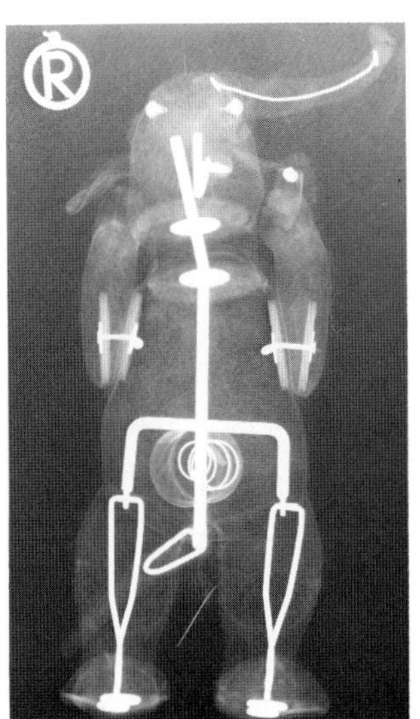

664

***Illus. 664 + 665**: X-ray photograph of the "Circus-Elephant", which shows the design of the head movement and snap joints more clearly.*

***Illus. 666**: The "Circus-Elephant", 1931. Right: in gray and white mohair, 10 and 12in. (until 1940 = 1,040 examples). Left: a house-sample, "Jumbo" in light brown mohair, 12in. Both animals have snap-joints in the legs, their mouths can be opened or closed, their pads are painted, and they have blue glass eyes.*

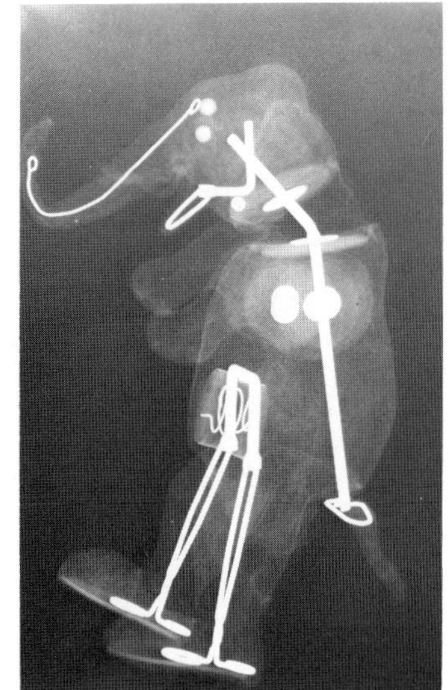

665

666

667

668

669

670

The jointed "Record-animals" gave pleasure to both young and old Steiff fans from 1912 onwards. In the 1920s many new models were added: "Record Felix", "Record-Petsy", "Record-Puck", "Record-August", "Record-Teddy-Baby" and "Record Bunny", (some of these with voice boxes). In the 1930s these "Record" toys were offered once again. – In 1924, the first "cycling" toys were seen in the catalogs. Plush animals on metal tricycles with pull-string and large wooden wheels; the "Rad-Affe" (monkey) and dolls; "Rad Heinz" or "Rad-Hilmar". "Dry-boy" had a very original tricycle; his feet were attached to the wheels so that he imitated a "pedalling movement" when pulled along. Toys with a "see-saw" movement rounded off the Steiff program: toys on wheels "Wiwag" with monkeys or Teddy-bears. The animals rocked to and fro when the toy was pulled along. Or: wooden, pull-along motor-cycle with sidecar. "Puck" the dwarf was the rider, and "Teddy" was his passenger. – At Steiff all things were possible! A three-wheeler with clock-work mechanism was made in 1925 for the American market, a "Monkey Car" ("Monk King"), a white monkey with a felt crown on his head, sitting on a metal tricycle. The robust clock-work mechanism allowed the monkey to cycle around several times before it stopped. The front wheels of the tricycle could be positioned in three different directions. Other clockwork Tricycle-riders followed: "Urfips" and "Urboy" (chimpanzees). A monkey, "Urpeter" and teddy, "Urteddy" on four-wheeled carriages joined the clockwork group. The monkey was in white plush and both toys had a "pedalling" movement. The "Roly-Droly" toys were attached to a metal frame with wooden wheels. Each toy had two mohair animals – teddys, monkeys, chickens and rabbits. Animal pairs were also used in 1926 for the "Galop-Toys". These carriages had eccentric wheels, and each animal had a bell, a silk bow or a ruff around the neck: "Galop-Teddy" (white/brown bear); "Galop-Molly" (dog/cat); "Galop-Jumbo" (elephant/lion); "Galop-Fuchs" (Fox/rabbit); "Galop-Tanzbär" (Dancing bear/Barney Google); "Galop-Barney Google" (with Spark Plug) and "Galop-Boxer" (two goats).

***Illus. 667-670**: "Wiwag" with Teddy and monkey (**Illus. 667**) in five inch size (1926 until 1928 = 330 examples), in 3 inch size (687 examples). – **Illus. 668**: "Galop-Teddy" white and brown bear (1926 until 1929 = 9,000 examples). – **Illus. 669**: Motor-cycle and side-car with "Puck" the dwarf (8in.) and Teddy (4in.), as a pull-toy (1926-1927 = 151 examples). – **Illus. 670**: "Record Teddy-Baby" with cap, 8 and 10in. (1929-1933 = 1,741 examples).*

***Illus. 671**: "Dryboy", 7in. on wooden tricycle to pull-along (1926 – 1928 = 480 examples).*

671

672

***Illus. 673**: Clockwork-toy "Urpeter". A special design for America, "Monk-King" with felt crown, 7in. (1920).*

673

***Illus. 674**: Clockwork-toy "Urteddy", 8in. (1926-1929 = 1,583 examples).*

674

***Illus. 672 + 675**: "Urboy" clockwork-toy with wooden wheels, (1926-1928 = 724 examples).*

675

676

677

***Illus. 676 + 677**: Polar bear on eccentric wheels (**Illus. 676**) with nodding movement of the head, 9in. (1928-1932). – **Illus. 677**: metal skeleton for nodding movement, from the patent DRGM 1051513 (1928).*

By combining the eccentric wheels with a metal rod going from the axle to the animals' head, Steiff gave their toys an additional "nodding" movement. In 1928 this new mechanism was granted a patent (DRGM). The droll nodding movement was activated by the rolling of the wheels as the toys were pulled along. The catalog text read: "A natural bouncing movement with nodding head. Sturdy mechanism; simply has to be pulled-along." Four of these waddling animals were available: "Polar-bear" (9in.); "Elephant" (9in.); "Lamb" (10in.); and "Goat" (11in.). From 1931 until 1932.

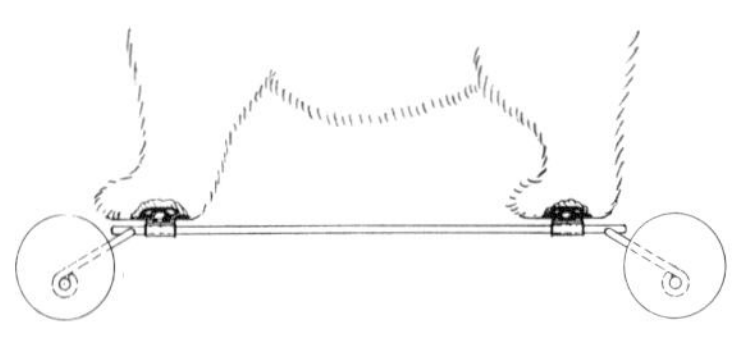

***Illus. 678**: Drawing from Patent, DRGM 1051523 for "Faspi"-animals.*

"Driving" animals were generally firmly attached to their carriages. Steiff's "Faspi-Tiere" were an exception. These were "drive" and "play" animals at the same time. The secret: The animals feet were attached to the carriages with snap-fasteners. These snap-fasteners were inter-changeable, so that only one "carriage" was necessary for all the "Faspi-Animals". There were five animals in this series with snap-fastenings on their feet: "Faspi-Bär" (bear); "Faspi-Ele" (elephant); a "Faspi-Sealyham", "Faspi-Skye Terrier", and "Faspi Dax" (dogs). Available until 1939 in limited numbers.

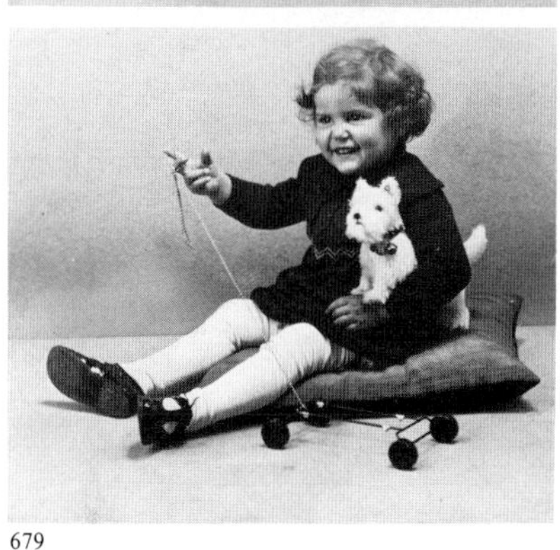

679

***Illus. 679**: Advertising photographs for ride-on animals which could be removed from wheeled-base.*

680

***Illus. 680**: "Faspi" elephant in cheaper substitute material, 7in. (1936-1939 = 646 examples).*

681

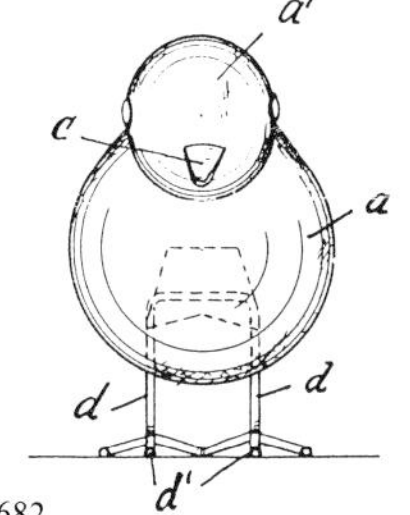

682

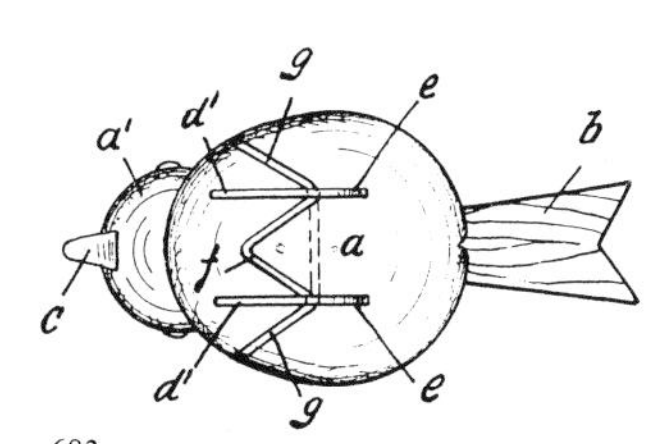

683

__Illus. 681-684__: Special design: a group of wool miniature animals (__Illus. 681__) with a little Teddy-bear, 8in. long (1936). – __Illus. 682 + 683__: Drawing from DRGM 1173143 "Bird". – __Illus. 684__: Advertising photograph for wool miniatures from 1935/1936.

"If it's good, it's expensive." This motto of the Steiff company's was firmly contradicted with the production of their "Wool-Animal" series. The new "wool-birds" cost 50 Pfennig (30 cents) each. They were modelled on six different European songbirds. Heads and bodies were made of moth-proof wool, and the heads were jointed. The bodies were attached to metal legs which provided the birds with stability so that they could be moved back and forth. Beaks and tails were in good quality felt. "A toy for our youngest customers; therefore we have not used stick-pin eyes – the eyes are firmly sewn in." The trademark was a linen ring around the left foot, to which the metal Steiff button was attached. Additions to the program were "chirping birds" (with chirping voice-box). In 1934/35 other animals joined the "wool" birds: rabbits, cats, lambs, mice, lady-birds and dogs. Small birds attached to trees or branches were available; a "wool" starling on a bird box; and a parrot on a stand could also be ordered. Large numbers of these woollen animals were made, and in the 1950s they appeared in the program once again.

684

685

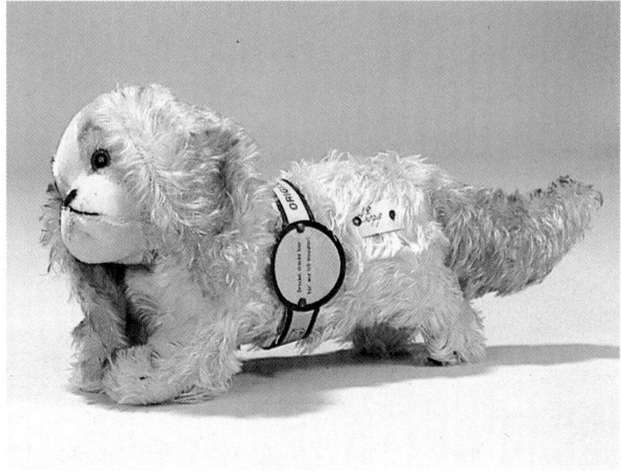

686

687

688

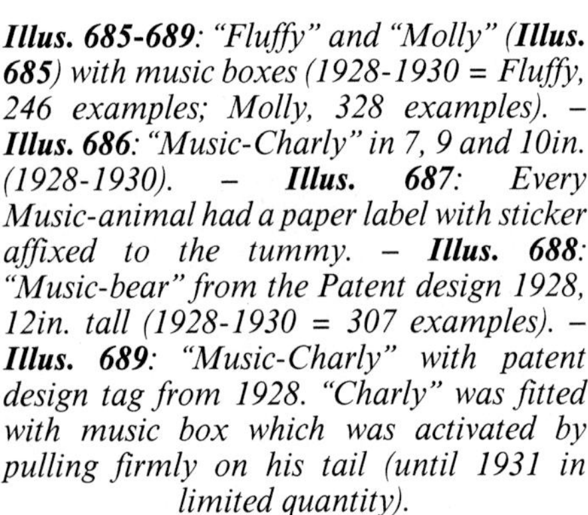

***Illus. 685-689**: "Fluffy" and "Molly" (**Illus. 685**) with music boxes (1928-1930 = Fluffy, 246 examples; Molly, 328 examples). – **Illus. 686**: "Music-Charly" in 7, 9 and 10in. (1928-1930). – **Illus. 687**: Every Music-animal had a paper label with sticker affixed to the tummy. – **Illus. 688**: "Music-bear" from the Patent design 1928, 12in. tall (1928-1930 = 307 examples). – **Illus. 689**: "Music-Charly" with patent design tag from 1928. "Charly" was fitted with music box which was activated by pulling firmly on his tail (until 1931 in limited quantity).*

The "Music-Animals" of 1928 were introduced for "cuddling and snuggling-up-to before falling asleep". A Swiss musical box fitted inside the body so that it was invisible, was activated by pressing the animal's body to play the melody. A clown (14 and 17in.) and approximately 20 animals (7 to 12in.) were put into production: "Teddy", "Petsy", "Bully" and "Charly" (standing and sitting), "Treff", "Molly", "Fluffy" (cat), "Cheerio", "Fellow" and a lamb. Another model was fitted with a voice box which was activated by turning the animal's tail. However, sales of these animals were minimal and they were last sold in 1930/31. In the 1950s Steiff returned "Music-Animals" to their program: a Teddy and a Monkey were now available with music boxes.

689

690

691

"Everything for your child's nursery." Under this motto Steiff first developed their hand-puppets in 1912. These puppets had already been registered at the Patent Office in Heidenheim in 1909;(Handpuppet-bear in jacket, cat in jacket, King Charles Spaniel as a farmer) but they first appeared in the catalog three years later. These mohair puppets named "Punchy" were available as: monkeys, bears and King Charles spaniels in one size, 7in., and cost between 2.25 and 2.70 Marks. A true "Mr. Punch" figure in his original form was first produced in the '60s as a puppet by Steiff; although a fox-terrier, a fox and a cat were added to the Steiff animals already in production. John Hess, the owner of a showroom in Hamburg was not at all happy with the new Steiff puppets. In a letter dated August 15, 1912, he wrote to inform Steiff that his son had been promoting the "Punchy Monkey" in Bad Kissingen, and: ". . . .would recommend that you re-issue the 'Punchy Monkey' in a new design – so that it has two legs with feet dangling down in front, and that on the back (of the hand), a long tail should be sewn on." A suitable pattern was made up, but because of the extravagant costs the design was never put into production.

692

Illus. 690-692*: Steiff hand-puppets (****Illus. 690****) for a puppet-theater from the 1920s. Advertising photo. –* ***Illus. 691****: Catalog drawing. –* ***Illus. 692****: American advertisement for Steiff hand-puppets.*

***Illus. 693**: Advertising photograph for building sets, 1920.*

***Illus. 694**: Wooden building set.*

***Illus. 695**: Dolls furniture from the building set.*

***Illus. 696**: Rabbit-team with "Puck".*

***Illus. 698**: Racing-car (late 1930s).*

Wooden toys were offered in Steiff's program as early as 1910 – primarily as accessories for their dolls and animals. School-benches, wheel-barrows, post-coaches, and furniture were offered in the catalogs. Later an army barracks complete with lockers, guard-house, tables and benches was also available. Owing to the shortage of materials for their cloth toys during 1918/19 (First World War) Steiff offered a wooden building set with blocks which could be assembled as desired, or according to the enclosed pattern-sheets. In 1921 a wooden-train was featured in the catalog and a gradual increase in the variety of wooden-toys offered by Steiff was soon visible. Pull-along wooden animals and animals on eccentric wheels (geese, hens, rabbits) and an elephant on a tricycle were available: "Top quality wood, rounded edges and smooth surface, detailed painting." A wooden rocking horse was introduced, and wooden cars, trolleys and airplanes were fitted with a steering mechanism so that children could stand and push, or steer their toys. Everything for the child: Wheel-barrows, wooden-carts. Steiff produced every wooden toy conceivable during this period. Designs for outside play were also offered: bows and arrows, and "Stratosplan", an airplane which could be catapulted up to the tree-tops by a strong rubber-band.

***Illus. 697**: Steerable airplane (1925).*

***Illus. 699**: Birds on eccentric wheels (1921).*

Illus. 700: *Steerable-Tram (1925).*

Illus. 701*: Village building set (1920s).*

Illus. 702*: Wooden horse (1930s).*

Illus. 703*: Wipp-toy (1920s).*

Illus. 704*: Sand-barrow with horse (1922).*

Illus. 705*: Bow and Arrow (1922).*

Illus. 706*: Racing-car (late 1930s).*

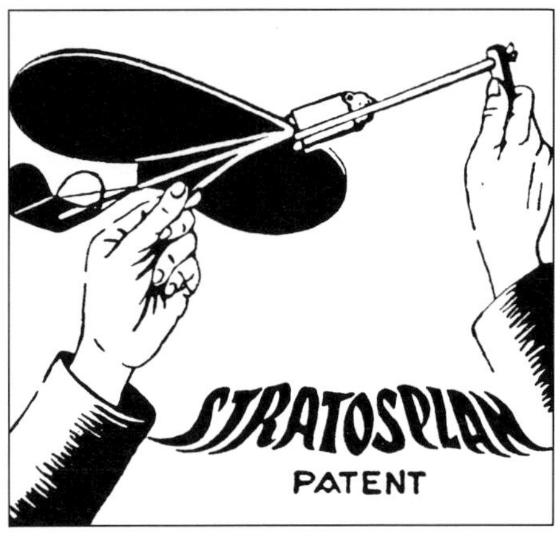

Illus. 707*: Advertisement (1931).*

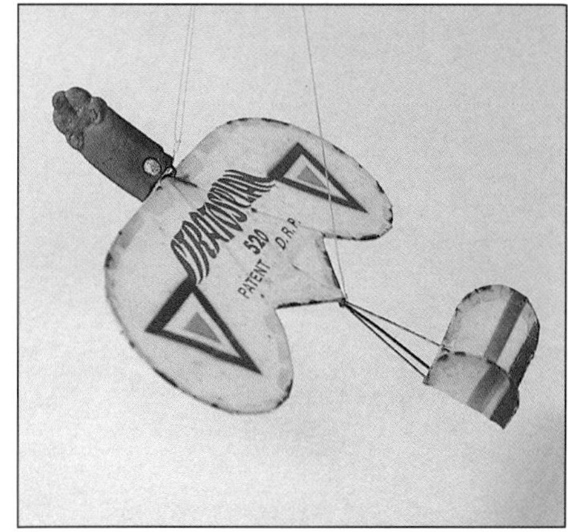

Illus. 708*: "Stratosplan" (1931).*

Illus. 709*: Wooden toys from 1922 onwards.*

Illus. 710*: Steiff-toys in sand-cars (1926).*

711

712

713

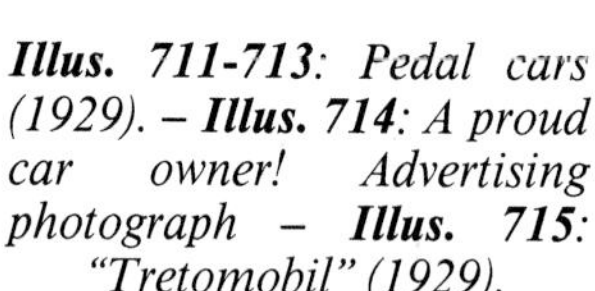

Illus. 711-713: *Pedal cars (1929).* – ***Illus. 714***: *A proud car owner! Advertising photograph* – ***Illus. 715***: *"Tretomobil" (1929).*

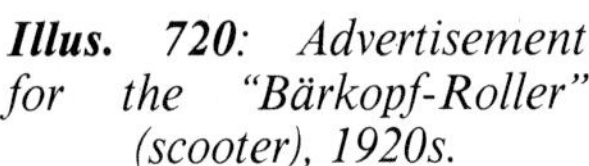

Illus. 720: *Advertisement for the "Bärkopf-Roller" (scooter), 1920s.*

Childrens' transport at Steiff also kept pace with the world's motorization. Advertised first in 1927, four vehicles were offered in the 1928 catalog. They were produced on the conveyor-belt and demand was surprisingly high. Their construction was indestructable; road-performance, safety and life-span were praised. The 1930 advertising text reads just like a real auto brochure: "Light and sturdy frame, well designed metal coachwork, chrome-plated radiator, metal-disc wheels fitted with snugly-fitting rubber tires, front axle of high-grade steel, rolling brakes, chain-wheel drive steering, comfortable, wide seats; extras: loud horn, indicators." Four streamlined models were available in 1930: "Littlmobil", "Sportmobil", "Tretomobil" and "Triplmobil". The same high demand was enjoyed by Steiff's "Bärkopf-Roller" (scooter), the first item to be produced on the conveyor-belt in 1921. "The sturdy construction, smoothly rounded wooden frame, and rear wheel brakes (also serve as rear-guard) and the unseamed special rubber-tired disc wheels guarantee our workmanship is safe for children." The scooters "Uniroller", "Skiro", "Skirogi", "Rennrogi", "Skirogo" and "Rennrole" were solidly built, and remained well-loved toys in Steiff's program until well into the 1960s.

714

Illus. 719: *"Bear-head Scooter" and "go-cart" (1937/38).*

715

Illus. 718: *"Bubirad" (1938).*

Illus. 717: *Pedal-scooter (1938).*

Illus. 716: *With Steiff-scooters on a tour of Europe.*

Illus. 721: An admiring crowd in front of the Steiff display-pieces at the Leipzig Fair in 1930.

Illus. 722: Steiff's advertising train on its journey through Leipzig, (1900).

Spring and Fall Trade Fairs in Leipzig had been the biggest events in the Toy Industry's calendar since approximately 1890. Steiff was represented at the Fair from 1897 onwards – their exhibits growing more impressive each year. Their large display items were first presented for public-viewing at the Leipzig Fair: 1910 – an army barracks; 1911 – Circus Sarassani; 1912 – Fire Brigade; 1913 – Noah's Ark; etc. etc. From a balcony in one of the large exhibition halls, (where Steiff had their stand from 1908 onwards) a mechanical display was set up for the thousands of toy buyers from around the world: 1926 – two advertising figures; 1927 – Six animals seated at a table; 1928 – a scene from a six-day marathon; 1929 – "Around the world with the Steiff animals"; 1930 – a "globe" house with groups of figures on either side. Steiff not only caused a sensation with their display figures, they organized large "floats" with life-sized animals which they pulled through the huge crowds visiting the exhibition grounds. Their fabulous costumes easily captured the visitors attention. Leipzig remained Steiff's advertising window until 1945. After the war, from 1949, Nuremberg became the center of the newly established "Toy Fair" and Steiff has had representatives at this fair each year.

Illus. 724: Giengen – Leipzig, the whole world.

Illus. 723: The first exhibition sign (pre 1897).

***Illus. 725**: Body of the Schlopsnies doll; on the right, the celluloid head filled with excelsior.*

726

***Illus. 726 + 728**: Advertising photo **(Illus. 726)**, circa 1922. – **Illus. 728**: Catalog 1921.*

***Illus. 727**: Schlopsnies-dolls: (from the left), "Axel" in winter outfit; "Hosenmatz"; "Rolf" in muslin shirt and pink pants; "Adele" in jumper.*

Madeleine Richard Marius Sepp Marga Anna

728

727

1921 until 1925 – Schlopsnies dolls at Steiff. The basic model was the celluloid head "Bebi N" made by the Rheinischen Gummi and Celluloidwaren Fabrik, Mannheim Neckarau (Turtle-mark), which was delivered to Steiff in its natural state. It was then painted from the inside, glued together, and filled with excelsior. The head was marked "32" with a turtle (with and without the diamond shape). "An epoch-making discovery", advertised Steiff. The main characteristic was the completely new "Apricot" painting technique which gave the dolls' faces a soft, peach complexion: "resembling the faces of real children." The heads were washable, durable and: "dirt or spots may be washed with soap or rubbed with sandpaper, without damaging the paint or the soft-coloring in any way." Each doll had a band on its arm, and in addition, a "bear's head" charm around its neck. DRGM (Patent) Text: "Armband for

Illus. 729: *Schlopsnies dolls' labels; also available in blue and red.*

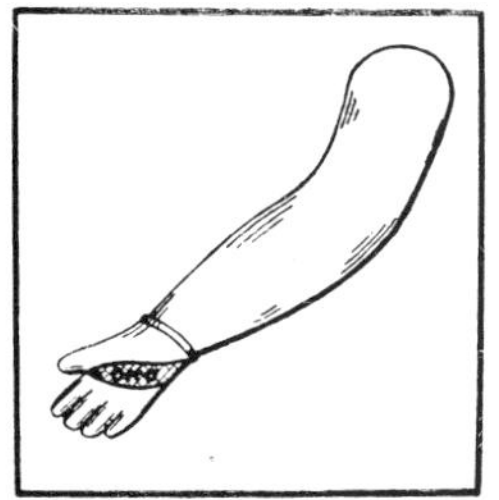

Illus. 730: *"Bracelet" patented in 1921, also in blue and red.*

731

cloth dolls to which the Steiff tag is fixed to the hand through a string." The doll's body was adapted from the pattern for the original Steiff dolls – in good quality felt, soft-filled, with the characteristics of a "toddler" (3 year old). The doll, 16in. tall is offered in a dirndl, or wears clothes suitable for spring, summer, fall or winter; in pajamas, in an underskirt (Hemdenmatz); and also with a white-face, as a "Pierrot" or as a colorful clown. A black doll was also made. All clothing was tastefully created "by expert, artistic designers" and made-up in top quality materials. "The child's wish to dress and undress her doll is fulfilled, and in her doll's outfits she can recognise her own clothing, right down to the smallest detail." However, the Schlopsnies doll was not a great success. It was available for four years – from 1921 until 1925; only 9,158 were manufactured.

732

733

Illus. 731-733: *Steiff advertisement (**Illus. 731**) from 1922. – **Illus. 732**: "Agnes" in winter outfit. Partner to "Axel"; snow-shoes and sleigh could be ordered. – **Illus. 733**: This portrait of "Agnes" illustrates the "Apricot" complexion with its rosy shimmer. Some dolls also had dark-brown painted hair.*

734

736

In the 1920s Steiff were no longer able to remain as competitive in the doll market as they had been in earlier years. They searched continuously for new designs and ideas, but by 1920 their comic dolls had almost completely disappeared from the program (especially the American models) as a result of the First World War. The models offered at this time were those which appealed to the German market: "Max and Moritz", "Struwwelpeter", "Dwarves" and "Clowns" were dominant – and character dolls were given new costumes. In 1922, "Alphonse", "Gaston" and "Hooligan" were made once again for the American market; a "Tramp-doll" ("Strolch" – in Germany) also enjoyed short lived success. Steiff's management were not happy with their "Doll-Policy". Schlopsnies dolls could not achieve a breakthrough, and their own design, unpopular because of the "center-seam" running through the face, was removed from the program. Only the gnomes and dwarves remained popular and were successfully sold items in the Steiff program until the 1930s. By 1925/26, production of all the Steiff character dolls had come to a halt. They had been available in 9, 11, 14, 17, 20, 24 and 30in. and special orders could be placed. The following presentation shows just how hard Steiff tried to cultivate the doll market. Unsuccessfully!

735

Illus. 734-737*: From the Character-Doll Program (****Illus. 734****) at the beginning of the 1920s. –* ***Illus. 735****: Prototype of the cloth "Doctor Dolittle", doll, 11in. (1931). –* ***Illus. 736****: The last of Steiff's felt-dolls was "Tramp" for the U.S. market. He was available as "Strolch" in Germany, 14in. (1922-1925 = 616 examples). –* ***Illus. 737****: Advertising photograph with "Tramp", 1923.*

737

738

***Illus. 738 + 739**: Comic character "Adamson" with his book.*

"Adamson" was a comic figure from Sweden. He was created in Stockholm by the artist O. Jacobsson, for a Swedish comic magazine. The first sketches led to a whole series of cartoons which greatly increased the magazines popularity and circulation. "Adamson" became a household name in Scandinavia; and very soon daily newspapers, not only in Europe, but also in America, published his popular antics. The secret of his success lay in his attitude to all human weaknesses. "Like all of us, 'Adamson' wages a tough and brave battle with his better self, and just like us, he wins most of the time and is deservedly punished." In 1925 Steiff adopted "Adamson" into their program, after several trial attempts. For "Adamson" was not easy to portray; he had a cigar in his mouth which he rarely removed. 997 examples of "Adamson" were sold between 1925 and 1929.

739

***Illus. 740**: A selection of Steiff products from the early 1920s.*

740

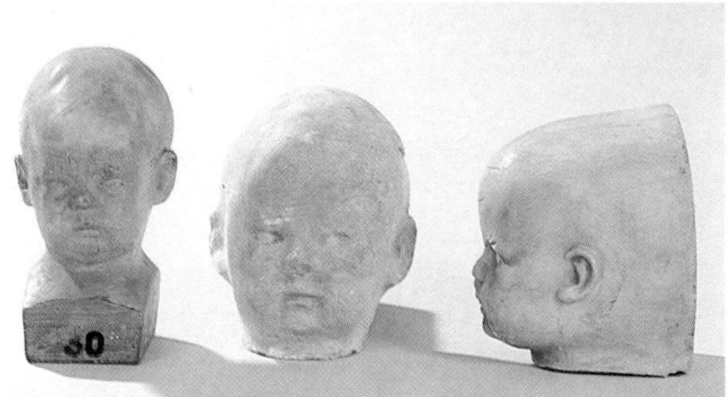

Illus. 741: Francois Duquesnois's model from the Steiff archives. Beside it are plaster samples of forms for the pressed-felt heads (face-masks without seams). Models for dolls from 14 to 17in.

743

*Illus. 743 + 744: "Tilde", 17in. (**Illus. 744**) not put into production. – **Illus. 743**: A large blue metal-button, the trade-mark for "Tilde".*

742

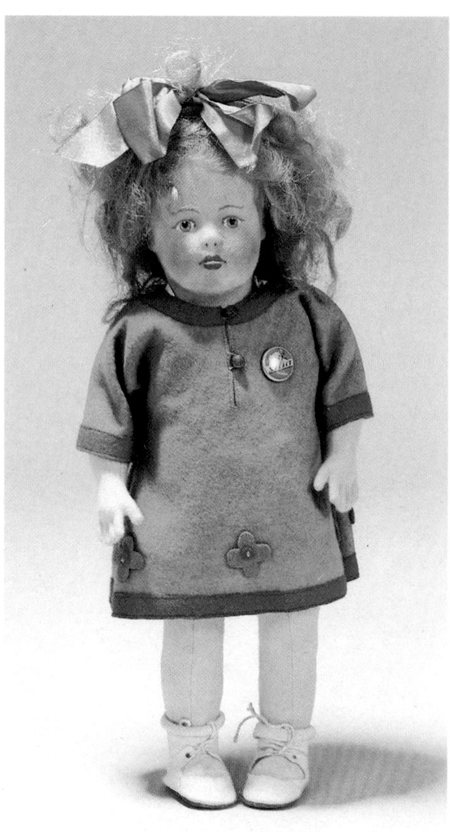

744

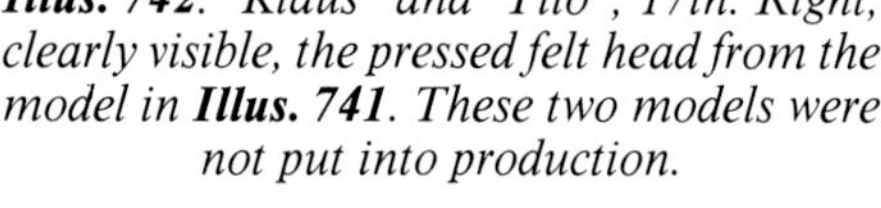

*Illus. 742: "Klaus" and "Tilo", 17in. Right, clearly visible, the pressed felt head from the model in **Illus. 741**. These two models were not put into production.*

745 746 747

*Illus. 745-747: "Rosemarie" (**Illus. 745**), 17in. doll with seamless pressed-felt face and glass eyes. Inserted Mohair wig (1938-1941). – **Illus. 746**: "Rosemarie", 14in., seamless face, glass eyes and plush wig (1938-1941). – **Illus. 747**: "Hedy", 14in. with painted eyes (1950).*

Steiff made several attempts to create a suitable doll for the 1920s. They were even prepared to "borrow" the designs of other doll manufacturers. In order to eliminate the troublesome center-seam they experimented with a one-piece doll head in pressed-felt, a procedure which the Käthe Kruse Workshop had always used. They turned to the successful child sculpture of the Italian artist, Francois Duquesnois. This sculpture is not unknown in the doll world: Käthe Kruse used it, and many of the doll manufacturers in Thuringia made porcelain versions of the Duquesnois child's face. However, attempts to make a mask of pressed-felt and still retain the original facial contours of a child, met with little success. In 1925 Steiff nevertheless patented their head, and the pattern; three of these dolls are in the Steiff archives today: "Klaus", "Tilde" and "Tilo". "Tilde" has a blue metal button on the front of her dress. It is highly probable, that these dolls are the only samples, and that the series was never actually put into production. A further eleven years were to go by before Steiff finally produced their dolls with pressed-felt faces. These were shown in 1936 at the Spring Fair in Leipzig: a clown, a sailor and a soldier. On August 31, 1936, "Ria", the new childlike doll modelled on the Duquesnois sculpture was put into production. The pressed-felt face was backed by a celluloid mask to ensure stability. The ears of these dolls were especially complicated to produce: by dipping double-

748

***Illus. 748 + 751**: Dolls with glass eyes: (from the left) "Ruth", 14in. (1945/46); "Frieder", 14in. (1938); "Zensi", 14in. (1946/47); "Lissy", 14in. (1949) see **Illus. 751** – all these dolls were only made in small quantities.*

sided felt pieces in a celluloid solution and then pressing them into a form, the ears were stiffened, modelled and joined together, before they were attached to the dolls' heads. The eyes could be sewn on or inserted from behind into holes cut into the felt face. Otto Steiff wrote: "Then the completed felt face would be soft-filled, and a mohair wig (in light or middle blonde) was attached before the head was fixed to the body by disc-jointing." Some also had inserted mohair wigs with braids. The dolls were given their rosy cheeks by Steiff's artists, and their curls from the company's hair stylists. The manufacturing procedure for these dolls was constantly being improved, and refined. The advertising text read: "Continuing the tradition of our early, popular, Steiff dolls, we now present our new dolls, with their sleek, long-lasting workmanship and appealing, engaging expressions." The clothing and underwear was made of top quality material in realistic childlike designs. All clothing could be removed. The new dolls were 14in. tall. "Mella" (jumper, pink coat and hat); "Rosemarie" (blue-print jumper); "Heidi" (striped dress with belt); and "Gudrun" (spotted blouse and light blue skirt). Soon afterwards the dolls were made in a second size – 17in.; and in 1939 a further 15 models were added to the original series – including dolls in regional costume. Produced until 1941 and then re-introduced for a short time in 1949.

749

***Illus. 749**: "Orla", 14in. glass eyes with closed painted mouth.*

750

751

***Illus. 750**: Boy with cap, 14in. with closed painted mouth and label, "Made in U.S. Zone Germany", 1950.*

***Illus. 752 + 753**: "Roly-Poly Clown" (**Illus. 752**) with glass eyes, 10in. (1937). – **Illus. 753**: First doll with pressed-felt face, clown, 14in. (1936-1940).*

752

753

After a break of almost 15 years, Steiff's dressed animals reappeared in the catalogs in 1920. "Teddy-Baby", but also "Bully", "Treff", "Charly" and the extensive series of Steiff cats now wore dresses and pants, or jackets and slippers. In 1932, a series of animals with soft bodies was developed; dangling arms, sturdy, standing legs and mohair heads: dogs, cats, ducks, bears and elephants. They wore Dirndls, or Bavarian dress, sport-shirts with blue pants; pajamas in light-blue/white; rompers in red print; swimming costumes in red/yellow; rompers in bright red; rompers in blue; pants and wool-jackets with scarves. Many of these animals were produced again in the '50s. The Dachshund, "Waldi" in hunting outfit, was especially popular, as was "Teddyli" with his light brown or dark brown head.

754

***Illus. 754**: "Paddy" the sailor. Designed by Brendl, design patented 1939 (118 examples made).*

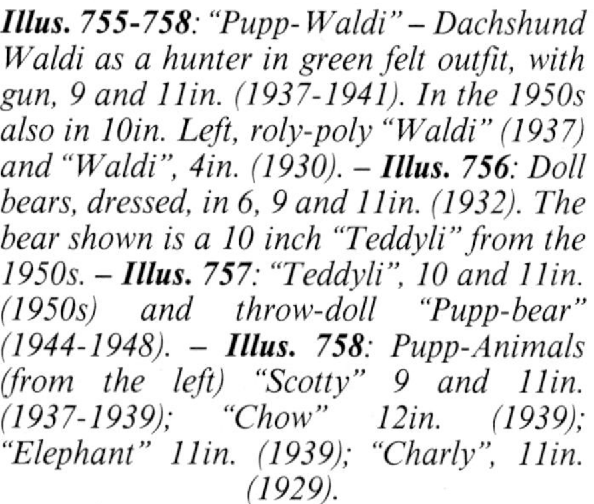

***Illus. 755-758**: "Pupp-Waldi" – Dachshund Waldi as a hunter in green felt outfit, with gun, 9 and 11in. (1937-1941). In the 1950s also in 10in. Left, roly-poly "Waldi" (1937) and "Waldi", 4in. (1930). – **Illus. 756**: Doll bears, dressed, in 6, 9 and 11in. (1932). The bear shown is a 10 inch "Teddyli" from the 1950s. – **Illus. 757**: "Teddyli", 10 and 11in. (1950s) and throw-doll "Pupp-bear" (1944-1948). – **Illus. 758**: Pupp-Animals (from the left) "Scotty" 9 and 11in. (1937-1939); "Chow" 12in. (1939); "Elephant" 11in. (1939); "Charly", 11in. (1929).*

756

755

757

758

759

***Illus. 759**: "Schwefelmännchen", 10in. (1933-1935 = 1,315 examples).*

***Illus. 760:** Advertising Photograph (1933).*

***Illus. 761**: "Schwefelmänchen's" successor, "Glückspilz", 10in.*

***Illus. 762:** Design by H. Oehl, (1937).*

In 1933, Steiff patented the 10 inch "Schwefelmännchen". A little fairy-tale character, "very expressive" of yellow felt with a green hat. In May 1936 Steiff received a letter from a Berlin attorney representing the interests of the artist Charlotte M. Kirchhoff. Contents: "Sales of the 'Schwefelmännchen' are to be stopped immediately, since the little man was a creation of my client." How did this happen? Hotel-Owner, Anton Gross from Hindelang in Bavaria had the little man designed by Charlotte Kirchhoff as an exclusive mascot for his hotel-chain. In 1933, Gross approached Steiff with a sample of the "Schwefelmännchen" and wanted to have it made up in their usual high-quality material. However, he never placed an actual order. Otto Steiff discovered the sample of the little man, and thinking that it was an idea from Steiff's design department, he gave the go-ahead for production to begin. Thus, between 1933 and 1936, a total of 1,315 examples of the "Schwefelmännchen" were made, but production was immediately stopped on receipt of the attorney's letter. A legal hearing followed and Steiff were ordered to pay Kirchhoff compensation for the profits they had made on her design. Steiff paid up, and gave the little felt character a new "look". The "Schwefelmännchen" became the "Glückspilz" ("Lucky-fellow"). He now wore a mushroom-shaped hat, and was made in yellowish-green felt. Between 1937 and 1941, Steiff sold 1,824 of their "Glückspilz".

of the National Socialists. A company this size could not hope to avoid the laws of the new political power. They fit the plans of the power-hungry Nazis exactly, since the agile fingers of women were needed to produce many items necessary for the war effort. "Unnecessary" imports were forbidden because of currency deficiency. Mohair could no longer be bought from England, and the production of mohair plush stopped accordingly. The previously purchased supplies only lasted for a very short time.

Some toy manufacturers attempted to compromise by producing toys which would please the dictators in Berlin. They wanted to prove their "good will" towards the new state-apparatus, in order to circumvent political pressure. Most of these toys were so strange or so badly produced that production was immediately forbidden. Steiff experienced this, too. A letter from the Württemberg Chamber of Commerce dated April 3, 1934, confirms that the Steiff family tried to distance themselves from the political ideals in the first years of upheaval. Herr Engel, (who wrote the letter) ordered "The 9in. doll which the Margarete Steiff GmbH in Giengen has developed, portraying an SS man, is simply an insult to the honor of our national symbol. The manufacture and distribution of this doll would be against the law to safeguard this symbol, and therefore the application is rejected."

Steiff had to conform more rapidly. Personnel changes were made. Hugo Steiff was removed from the management, and a little later Ernst Steiff was dismissed because of his sympathy for a Jewish sales-representative. The Hitler regime placed their own chairmen and confidants in the managerial positions. Preparation for producing war articles began. How would the Steiff Company exist? Their business was now primarily concerned with the production of

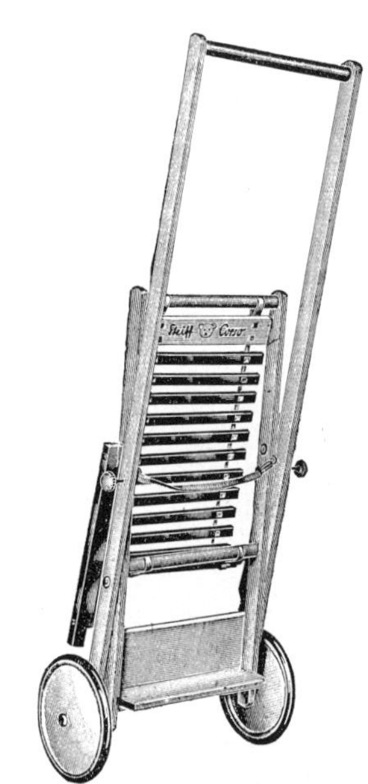

Illus. 763: *"Corso" child's buggy, the first important product after 1948.*

Illus. 764: *Advertisement drawing (1950).*

war articles; toys were of secondary importance.
On March 31, 1939, at the age of 63 years, Richard Steiff died of a heart-attack in Jackson, Michigan. The creator of the Teddy-bear was dead. The Steiff Company ran a huge obituary: "The memory of the deceased will live on in our hearts and his name will always be honored in the history of our company." The trade newspaper, "Wegweiser" wrote: "A man who created the most important, and now indispensable, toys; who not only developed revolutionary production methods but also organized novel advertising, which even today sets us all an example."
The start of the war on September 1, 1939 reduced the production of toys to an absolute minimum. Steiff's valuable, skilled employees were called-up to go to war. Almost three months earlier Steiff had warned customers in a newsletter: "The new items of 1939 will be temporarily removed from our program . . . Difficulty in obtaining materials, and the grave shortage of workers particularly affects the wooden toys and the motor cars."

On February 5, 1940 a complete list of "unavailable" items was sent to toy stores; almost all the plush animals were on this list. A postscript added: "It is also highly probable that as time goes on, other items will be added to this list. We are now compelled to use the best-quality substitute material which is available whenever it is necessary, or at all possible (i.e., paper plush)."

As of September 1940, each customer was allocated a definite number of products. "Any attempts to order extra items will not only result in unnecessary and time consuming correspondence, but are also totally pointless." On May 16, 1943, the production of toys stopped completely. A small gray postcard informed trade customers: "To our honored customers! We wish to inform you that the responsible Reichstelle (governing

body) has forbidden the manufacture of toys in any form, to take effect as of 15.4.1943 . . . Our warehouse is completely empty since the production of toys has been kept to an absolute minimum in the last few years."

Steiff became a munitions factory. On February 21, 1944, Otto Steiff, who had remained at the factory until the end, died. As the war came to an end in Spring 1945, nothing remained of the worldwide toy company, except the completely intact factory complex, and the extensive inventory of machinery.
1945. The war was over. American troops occupied Giengen. They stormed through the factory, but only found left-overs from the munition production. Thanks to an absolute stroke of luck the extensive archives with almost every doll and animal ever made by Steiff, remain in the company's possession today. For the American troops searched all the toy factories (even in Sonneberg-Thuringia) and "confiscated" anything which appealed to them, to send as souvenirs to folks back home. Today, no-one is certain who gave the order for the extensive archives to be packed into wooden crates and stored outside the factory complex (in private garages, and in the unused bowling alley of a local inn).

These wooden crates were taken back into the factory many years later, once times had become more settled. The crates were stacked one upon another and remained closed and forgotten in one of the many store-rooms. Only shortly before the authors of this book began their work by sorting through the Steiff archives, were the crates opened: everything was saved, intact and unfaded, including numerous written documents concerning production.

Fame, quality and their polished image helped the Steiff company to overcome what appeared to be a hopeless post-war situation.

Illus. 765*: Title page from the Price-List, 1950.*

Illus. 766*: A return to the old quality was available once again: Dachshund "Bazi" and "Fox" (1949).*

Contact with American officials was quickly established. In October 1945 Steiff answered requests thus ". . . we are able to produce small quantities of our toys with the permission of the American military government, as far as the shortage of materials allows. The products may only be sold to the American troops and at present we are not allowed to distribute any toys at all to the civilian sector."

A slight relaxation of this law was visible in July 1946 as Steiff informed inquirers: "As far as cloth toys are concerned we are still confined strictly to export, which is understandable in these times. However, we continue to make an effort to distribute wooden toys . . ." Four months later: "We are striving to arrange the distribution of our popular products within the internal market, but this can only be expected once the laws concerning the rationing of materials is relaxed. Until then, we ask that you remain favorably disposed toward the Button-in-Ear trademark."

Those who still placed an order for a doll received a rebuff from the local authority, the Dept. of Trade and Industry in Stuttgart: "Unfortunately, it is my duty to inform you that your request for cloth dolls and animals cannot be granted, since the production of the Steiff company is still reserved for export only. This export is necessary in order to obtain additional provisions for the American sector." It was later disclosed that the currency which Steiff brought into the country with its U.S. exports was used to purchase wheat from overseas, for the hungry population in Baden-Württemberg.

In January 1947, the company was allowed to make its first offer to the trade. "A buggy, Corso 2870, hammock seat, with wooden bars, as comfortable as a deck chair. The foot board offers sturdy support for the legs; can be folded together." ▶

Illus. 767: Walt Disney with "Perri" the squirrel (1958).

However, there were conditions attached to delivery. If a customer wanted 100 push-chairs, not only was it necessary to pay 2,400 Reichsmark but also the customer had to supply Steiff with 2,5 sqm. of cut plywood or 600 kg of iron to help cover the material needed for the order.
Finally, in February 1947, the long awaited circular went out to customers. Steiff were happy to announce that inland orders could now be fulfilled. A modest catalog showed which items could be ordered: "on condition that you have permission to buy from your local authority." An almost insurmountable hurdle was the further condition: the order had to be paid in dollars. 1 Reichsmark = 40 cents.
Steiff was on the way up again, and tricks were often necessary. Orders were placed through an agent; Broederna Ivarson A.B. in Osby. In Germany the separate military zones (American, English, French and Russian) were impossible to bypass. The only loophole was through overseas agents. Through these agents it was possible to deliver goods almost anywhere. Steiff wrote to their "honored customers": "We are pleased to inform you that orders for Fall this year can, for the main part, be delivered in our famous, mohair-plush quality." Ride-on animals and pull-along animals on eccentric wheels were included in the program once again. "We hope to be able to show these designs at the Export Fair in Hannover from May 22 until June 6, 1948. If you can find your way to Hannover, we would be honored to greet you at our stand, No. 45, in Hall VII."
However, Steiff were unable to obtain the required mohair themselves. Delivery was made possible by the Swiss company Boneta A.G. of Basel. Boneta was Steiff's general agent in Switzerland at this time. "The new designs are once again true 'Button-in-Ear' products, and will surely meet with your approval." 1949: The monetary-reform stabilized the German economy, and political development relaxed the trade laws. Steiff was once again visible on the market.
After the difficult years, confidence returned to Giengen: "Steiff plush animals, and our special discovery, the Teddy-bear are the beloved playmates of all children. Their lifelike expression, attractive design, durability, and value are all inimitable. They are unbreakable and thus save tears. The soft hygienic filling, securely sewn glass eyes and fast, non-poisonous colors are completely safe for children. The trademark 'Button-in-Ear' guarantees Steiff quality in each article."
The upward trend in the economy, the demand for toys after years of deprivation, numerous overseas customers who had been waiting since 1933, and determination to succeed wherever possible, encouraged optimism in management and employees alike. In 1949, 550 ▸

Illus. 768: Film-star Liz Taylor with a Steiff tiger.

employees were already on the Steiff payroll (seven years later the staff numbered 2,000).
Also in 1949, Steiff returned to New York. After an absence of 16 years the new products of an old friend, the Margarete Steiff Company, were displayed at the German Trade Fair. And the display succeeded in winning back American customers; and also in establishing new and long-lasting business contacts. Steiff was represented at the Leipzig Fair on two occasions after the Second World War. Ten paper plush animals were offered; enough to obtain orders for many months of production!

Buyers from inland and overseas were also attracted to the Steiff stand at the first German Toy Fair (held annually in Nuremberg since 1949). The Steiff team returned to Giengen with their order books full. Therefore, it was hardly surprising that Steiff soon found it difficult to keep their deliveries up to date; production could not keep up with the orders. Steiff sent this apology out to customers because many of their Teddy-bears no longer had growlers: "Several letters from our customers express the fear that our Teddy-bears will now be produced without growlers. These fears stem from the fact that shortly before Christmas we were so inundated with orders for Teddy-bears, that our 'voice-box department' was no longer able to keep up with the demand, and most of our customers at this time agreed to accept the bears without growlers, simply to be able to get bears at all. Since the beginning of the New Year all the bears will have growlers once again, and even our smallest Teddy is now fitted with a greatly improved squeeze voice-box."

The new program also included a large number of pre-war items. The ever-popular chimpanzee, hand-puppets, pull-along toys, as well as dolls and a go-cart were all featured in the catalog once again. Steiff had survived the rationing of materials, and now they were also able to do without the additional deliveries of old iron and newspapers.
In spite of the currency reform Steiff kept to their old prices. "We realize that merchants must be given a larger rebate at the appropriate time", they said. At this time only the Teddy-baby and Teddy-bears could be further discounted by ten percent. This reduction satisfied customers and Steiff were rewarded with larger orders thanks to their closeknit relationship with the trade.
Toys with a "sporting" function were in great demand in the post-war period. The "Bubirad", a wooden tricycle; and the "Flitzro 73", as well as a practical scooter stand, which backed-up the sale of scooters and a small pull-along wagon "with a carrying capacity of one ton" were put into production. A small group of selected customers were offered a limited number of ride-on animals: "Once you have seen these animals you will surely share our opinion that we have not simply re-established our pre-war quality, but have greatly improved it. Our "Button-in-Ear" trademark will continue to set the trend in the future."

Illus. 769: International Exhibition in Helsinki. Ludwig Erhard, the German Minister of Trade and Commerce at this time admires the Steiff quality, 1950s.

On February 23, 1950, Steiff informed their German customers: "The Steiff Export Collection is now available for immediate delivery to our inland customers. However, preference must still be given to overseas buyers, so we recommend that you place your orders for Fall delivery as early as possible."
Many items from the Steiff factory made their debut at the Nuremberg Toy Fair in 1950. "Don't miss a visit to our stand; the huge Steiff display at the entrance will show you the way." Among other items presented, was the "Bärkopf-Roller" (Bearhead-scooter) a toddler's scooter with two or three back wheels which was to become the hit of the 1950s.

Severe criticism of the Steiff Teddy-bears was also received from Switzerland. "The arms and necks are too long, and the head is too small. We feel it is our duty to point out these flaws immediately." Giengen acted at once. The Teddy-bear was given shorter arms, and the head was modelled to meet the demands of this period.
1951 – a year which also found its place in the Company's history. This was the so-called "Mecki" year, the year of the cartoon character which was created before 1939, but which first achieved real popularity after the war, thanks to the Radio guide "HÖRZU" (Listen!). Mecki was thought up, designed and put into story-form by the company Diehl Bros., of Graefelding, near Munich. It was this company which also finally granted Steiff permission to produce a "Mecki doll", after a long and boring exchange of contracts. "The 'Mecki Boom' which followed, can definitely be compared with the 'Bear Boom' at the turn of the century" states one report. Since it was impossible to produce the head in felt, the design department developed a head of molded rubber, which later had to be replaced by a plastic-type head, owing to the cracking of the rubber. The management of the Margarete Steiff Company has always tried to do everything possible to ensure that their employees have pleasant working conditions and a congenial working atmosphere. Part of the company's tradition is to ▸ 253

***Illus.** 770: "Mecki" was Steiff's greatest success after the Second World War. The hedgehog was the mascot of the Radio Magazine "HÖRZU". Pictured here is the first example, which was made by Steiff on March 17, 1951.*

"Mecki" is a German comic character. His creator was Ferdinand Diehl, who sketched the first designs in 1940. The cartoon star became extremely popular thanks to his regular appearance in the T.V. Magazine "HÖRZU", at the beginning of the 1950s. He became famous overnight, and started on his career as an editorial hedgehog. Even today, after celebrating his 40-year hedgehog anniversary, his popularity does not seem to have waned. There are "Mecki" clubs, books, postcards, records, haircuts (and soon a T.V. series, too). And naturally, "Mecki"-dolls, exclusively by Steiff – since 1951, when the Diehl Film Co., Munich, granted the Giengen company licensing rights. At first, there were Mr. and Mrs. "Mecki" (later to become Mrs. "Micki"). They were 11 inches tall, and the heads were poured from a rubber-like latex mixture, which unfortunately cracked very easily. From 1962, the heads of the two figures were made in vinyl. The early "Mecki" dolls have red/white/blue checked shirts, another version has a red/white vertically striped shirt. "Micki" wears a blue/white/black checked blouse, or a dark blue/white patterned blouse. Later the clothes were standardized, and the designs have remained the same until the present day. In 1951, the "Mecki" figures were marked with a cloth tag on the right arm "Made in U.S. Zone", and on the left arm, a bracelet with the Steiff button (the button was attached to the vest or apron of later models). The back of the Steiff tags in the early years (after 1951) are marked "Der Redaktionsigel der Rundfunkzeitschrift HÖRZU" (Editorial hedgehog of the Broadcasting magazine "Listen"). In 1952, "Mecki" and "Micki" were available in 7 and 20in. sizes. Their children "Macki" and "Mucki" (5in.), followed one year later; their bodies were of rubber, and from 1962, in vinyl. In 1964 a four inch version was available as: mountain climber, footballer, or mechanic. Important: "Mecki's" in 11 and 20in. sizes carried a wooden pipe in their pockets, and there was a hole between the lips to insert the pipe. A huge advertising campaign by the "HÖRZU" magazine was launched throughout Germany – and even reached Giengen. A man in a hedgehog costume arrived at Giengen's sports-field in a helicopter, much to the delight of local boys and girls. A life-size "Mecki" went to greet "HÖRZU" guests on behalf of Steiff, so that suddenly there were two "Meckis" in costume, face-to-face. The role of the "Steiff Mecki" was played by Jörg Junginger, a descendant of Margarete Steiff's – then 13 years old. Today Herr Junginger is the Company Secretary and head of the design department at Steiff. In 1992, Mecki and his companions are due to make a new bid for fame; German television plans to run a new cartoon series featuring the well-loved hedgehog.

***Illus.** 771: Two successful creations. "Mecki" and "Zotty".*

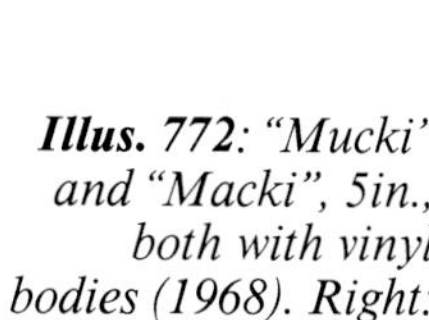

***Illus.** 772: "Mucki" and "Macki", 5in., both with vinyl bodies (1968). Right: "Muck", 4in. (1962).*

***Illus.** 773 + 774: "Micki" and "Mecki" (**Illus.** 773) as "Fuba" (Football fans) and "Alpo", (Alpine-climbers) with pressed vinyl bodies, 4in., – **Illus.** 774: "Mecki", left, fat; and right, thin; pressed vinyl bodies, 4in.*

***Illus.** 775: Club magazine for "Mecki" fans.*

***Illus.** 776: Sample design for "Mecki".*

***Illus.** 777: "Mecki" and "Micki", 11in. (1968).*

***Illus.** 778: "Mecki's" hair is combed for the last time before he leaves the factory! 1954.*

779

780

The 100th anniversary of U.S. President Theodore Roosevelt's birthday in October 1958, was marked by a commemorative celebration in Giengen. Representatives from the American Embassy in Bonn and the American Consulate, joined leading figures from German industry and politics to honor the man whose nickname "Teddy" was given to the toy bears. A life-sized bronze statue of Roosevelt's head, donated by the Steiff company, was unveiled at the celebration, and today has a place of honor in the Steiff museum. The American Foreign Ministry presented the town of Giengen with a glass cabinet containing personal mementoes of the ex-president, including a stuffed jackal which Roosevelt is said to have shot himself. In honor of Roosevelt's birthday in the Fall, the town of Giengen had previously organized a Teddy-Bear Festival in the summer which was attended by 25,000 German and American visitors. The Festival with its huge train of decorated floats, a Teddy-bear ballet and huge party-tent was featured in news shows around the world. Reports reached viewers in Canada, Australia and America. The U.S. television company CBS reported on the festival in great detail, and the program was shown on all the network's channels.

781

***Illus. 779-781**: Advertisement from "The Toy" (**Illus. 779**) for the 50th birthday of the Steiff Teddy-bear. – **Illus. 780**: "Nimrod-Bear", special edition for the company's 50th birthday, 9in. dressed in four different colors, with wooden gun. – **Illus. 781**: "Jackie", the first jubilee Teddy by Steiff. With this bear Steiff said good-bye to their classical Teddy-bear design, and adapted their bears to suit the fashions of the times. In 7, 10, 14in. (1953-1955).*

782

Illus. 782-785: Festive floats in Giengen on the occasion of the Teddy-bear festival in honor of American ex-president Theodore Roosevelt's 100th birthday (1958). – **Illus. 783**: This small Steiff brochure, "Theodore Roosevelt and the Teddy-Bear", was printed in English and German. – **Illus. 784**: Advertising Photograph. – **Illus. 785**: The bronze bust of Theodore Roosevelt, donated to the town of Giengen by the Steiff Company. On view in the Steiff Museum since 1980.

783

784

785

***Illus. 786**: Teddy-bear with head movement, activated by turning the tail, in 7 and 10in. (1955-1956 = 3,539 examples).*

***Illus. 787**: At the beginning of the 1950s, almost all Teddy-bears had a white cloth tag marked "Made in U.S. Zone". (From the left) "Teddy", white, 12in. (1948); "Teddy-Baby", 12in., (1950); "Teddy" in short white plush, 10in. (1950); "Teddy", white, 9in. (1949); "Teddy", caramel, 10in. (1951); "Music-Teddy", 14in. (1952).*

Development of the Teddy-bear after 1945. 1947: Two sizes, 12 and 14in.; Teddy-Baby 12in.. 1949/50: Teddys in white, gold, caramel and dark-brown mohair (4, 6, 9, 10, 12, 14, 17 and 20in.). 1950: Teddy, 9 and 14in.. in caramel, dark brown. New pattern with shorter arms and legs; at first only available in these two sizes. In 1951, white, beige, caramel and dark-brown bears were made in the following sizes: 4, 6, 9, 10, 11, 14, 17, 20, 25 and 30in.. Zotty, long-haired, extra soft, in 7, 9, 11, 14, 17 and 20in.. 1953: 50th Anniversary Teddy-bear, "Jackie" in three sizes, and "Nimrod Teddy", 9in., dressed as a hunter. 1955: "Baby-Bear", with movable head in two sizes. 1961: "Dralon Teddy Petsy", light brown, sitting, dangling arms. 1964: "Zoobär" (Zooby), jointed head, standing. 1966: New face, with short-haired snout. 1967: "Cosy bear", synthetic filling. 1969: "Minki Zotty", fur like material. 1970: Soft-bear "Toldi" with apron. 1971: "Toddel-Bär" in Dralon. 1976: "Teddy", "Zotty" in imitation mink with sponge filling. 1979: "Dormy-Bär", 14in.. 1980: 100 years of Steiff, replica of the first bear in gold colored mohair 17in.; "Orsi-Bär", 12in.; "Molly-Teddy", 22 and 26in..

***Illus. 788**: The differences between the bears from 1950 and 1951 are visible in this picture. Left: The new modernized design; beside him two bears from the old design, 9in. (1949 – this size was not available after 1950); right: small bear from the old pattern, 8in..*

Illus. 789: *The Fifties. "Soft-Bear", seated, only the arms are movable, 9in. (1952); behind him a Teddy in wool-plush, 14in. (1952); "Jackie", Jubilee Teddy, seated, 10in. (1954); and standing 14in. (1953); "Teddy" 14in. (1954); behind him standing "Teddy" with head movement, 10in. (1955); "Teddy-Baby", 10in. (1957) and "Cosy-Teddy" with movable arms only, 9in. (1957).*

Illus. 790: *Panda bears, from the left: "Panda" 6in. (1956); "Panda" 4in. (1972); "Panda" standing, 5in. (1955); and right, "Indian Panda", 5in. (1963).*

Illus. 791: *The Sixties. From the left: standing "Cosy-Teddy" 27in. (1967); "Lully", a baby bear, unjointed limbs, 8in. (1967); seated (from the left): "Petsy" in dralon with sponge filling, 14in. (1961); "Cosy-Teddy", 11in. (1964); "Original Teddy", new design, 14in. (1966); "Cosy Teddy" in white, 25in. (1967); "Cosy Teddy" in brown, 25in. (1968).*

Illus. 792: *The Seventies. From the left: Two "Zotty"-bears, 14in. (left 1969, right 1952); two "Dralon Teddies", 12in. (1971); "Teddy", washable, 10in. (1976); "Hockey-Teddy", 12in. (1972); "Minky" Zotty, 14in. (1975) and a special design for the magazine "Eltern", the "Toddel" bear, (1976).*

791

792

793

794

796

795

797

798

Illus. 799*: Goat, 11in. (1954).*

Illus. 800*: "Reinhold" the rhinoceros, 9in. (1964), specially made for the magazine "Stern".*

Illus. 801*: Ram with top-hat, 9in. (1966).*

Illus. 802*: Rabbits – (from the left): "Rübenhas" (turnip rabbit), 16in. (1951); "Manni", 8in. (1983); and rabbit on wheels, 3in. (1955).*

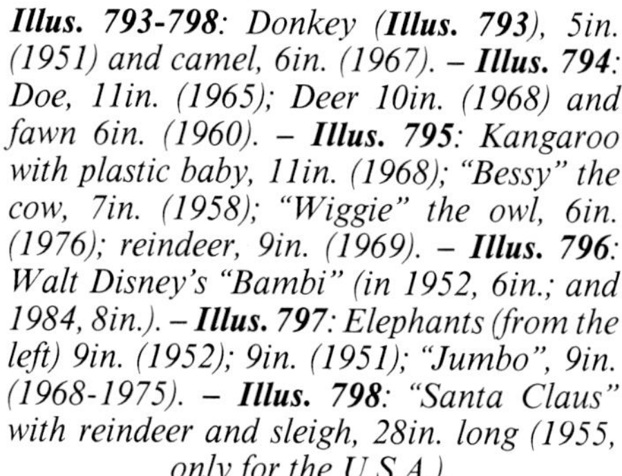

Illus. 793-798*: Donkey (****Illus. 793****), 5in. (1951) and camel, 6in. (1967). –* ***Illus. 794****: Doe, 11in. (1965); Deer 10in. (1968) and fawn 6in. (1960). –* ***Illus. 795****: Kangaroo with plastic baby, 11in. (1968); "Bessy" the cow, 7in. (1958); "Wiggie" the owl, 6in. (1976); reindeer, 9in. (1969). –* ***Illus. 796****: Walt Disney's "Bambi" (in 1952, 6in.; and 1984, 8in.). –* ***Illus. 797****: Elephants (from the left) 9in. (1952); 9in. (1951); "Jumbo", 9in. (1968-1975). –* ***Illus. 798****: "Santa Claus" with reindeer and sleigh, 28in. long (1955, only for the U.S.A.).*

Illus. 803*: Feathered friends (from the left): Goose, 8in. (1954); "Tulla" the duck, 7in. (1952); Hen (with metal feet) 4in. and 7in. (1953).*

Illus. 804: *"Eric" the bat is a desirable collectors' item, 4in. (1960).*

805

806

Illus. 805-807: *Dogs (from the left):* ***Illus. 805***: *"Fox", 7in. (1951); "Revue Susi", 7in. (1959); Basset, 6in. (1961); "Lumpi" the Dachshund (1971); "Waldi" the Dachshund, 7in. (1948).* – ***Illus. 806***: *(from the left): Dachshund, 4in. (1962); "Perri" the squirrel, from Walt Disney (1967); Dachshund, 4in., (1963); "Moosy" elk, 6in. (1963).* – ***Illus. 807***: *Lions (from the left) 4in. (1956); middle, 9in. (1956); 5in. (1951).*

807

***Illus. 808**: Dolls with pressed vinyl heads have been in the Steiff program since the 1950s. Favorites are the dwarves, clowns, Santa Claus, and cowboys, or special editions like "Maggi Fridolin" and the Firemen. This photograph shows (from the left): Shepherd, 7in. (1969) and "Tele Maxl", 8in. (1958). "Maxl" was designed from the "Sandman", a star of childrens' television in Germany.*

***Illus. 809**: From the left: "Larifari" a figure from the Diehl Film Co., Munich, 12in. (1960); "Santa Claus", 11in. (1960), and a Steiff sandman, 10in. (1965).*

810

***Illus. 811**: Plush dinosaurs, (from the left): "Thyrannosaurus" (8in.); "Dinos" (11in. and 28 in.) and "Lizzy" lizard (1959).*

***Illus. 810**: Turtle "Slo", 4in. with plastic shell (1974); "Lizzy" lizard, 2in. and 3in. (1959); "Spidy" spider, 5in. and 9in. (1960); snail, 4in. and 6in. (1962) and "Gaty", alligator 6in. (1967).*

812

***Illus. 812 + 813**: Frog (**Illus. 812**) 4in. (1953). – **Illus. 813**: "Froggy" frog, 9in. (1953).*

813

814

815

***Illus. 814 + 815**: "Crabby" the crab (**Illus. 814**) in three sizes, 4, 7 and 11in. (1963). – **Illus. 815**: Several versions of the snail, 4in. high, shell in plastic material (1962).*

816

817

***Illus. 816 + 817**: From the left, (**Illus. 816**) "Robby" the seal, 9in. (1961); "Paddy" the walrus, 4in. (1958); and a 9in. Penguin (1953). – **Illus. 817**: (left) "Flossy" fish, 9in. (1960); (middle) duckling, 7in. (1967) and "swimming" duck, 5in. (1952).*

818

***Illus. 819**: Left "Dalle" the piglet, 4in. (1977); Middle: "Jolanthe", 7in. (1953) and "Wild Boar", 6in. (1968).*

***Illus. 818**: "Joggi" hedgehog, in three sizes: 3, 4 and 5in. (1961-1975) and mole, 5in. (1964).*

***Illus 820**: Left: Bear-cub, 10in. (1925), and "Cosy Issy", 9in. (1984).*

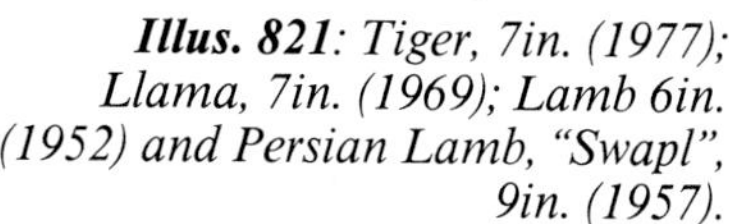

***Illus. 821**: Tiger, 7in. (1977); Llama, 7in. (1969); Lamb 6in. (1952) and Persian Lamb, "Swapl", 9in. (1957).*

821

822

823

***Illus. 822 + 823**: A family of cats (**Illus. 822**). From the left: "Lizzy", 6in. (1968); "Siamy", 4in. (1955) and "Tabby", 6in. (1968). – **Illus. 823**: Dogs, (from the left): German shepherd "Arco", 10in. (1963), Dachshund "Beppo", 4in. (1952) and "Dally" Dalmation, 9in. (1953).*

825

Illus. 824: *"Mungo" the monkey, 14in. (1967).*

Illus. 825: *"Jocko" the puppet, 10in. (1974). These puppets were also made as girls, boys, and naturally, as Teddy-bears.*

Illus. 827: *"Football Monkey, Jocko", 10in. (1971).*

826

Illus. 826: *From the left, Chimpanzee, 14in. (1952); "Jocko" 10in. (1953) and "Coco" the baboon, 6in. (1967).*

maintain the feeling of security and belonging which the first employees enjoyed when Steiff was still a very small family business.
The success of this policy can be clearly measured; since the 1950s an average of 15 per cent of their employees have celebrated 25 years of working for the company, and approximately 32 per cent of the staff have been with Steiff for more than 15 years. Company housing has been available for the employees since the turn of the century.

Until 1930 there was also a staff restaurant with a company kitchen. Today employees go home for lunch or they are able to enjoy subsidized meals at a local restaurant and short breaks for refreshment are enjoyed by all during normal working hours. Naturally the company has a first-aid room with its own nurse and they also engage a social worker. About 30 or 40 company appartments were secured for staff and others were arranged in partnership with the local building union. A company outing, a Christmas Fund bonus and a Pension Fund are also provided. However, in order the qualify for a pension an employee has to have been with the company for at least 20 years. A so-called "Steiff-Aid" is also available to employees who experience financial difficulties through no fault of their own. These employees can receive a one-time payment as assistance, or they may receive continual payments for a longer period with no time restrictions at all.

In 1965, a subsidiary branch, the Steiff Toy Company, was founded in Grieskirchen, upper Austria. The reason for this new company was to establish better export facilities within the complicated European economic market. Over 200 people were employed at the new factory. In the 1970s Steiff suffered a period of stagnation which caused them to revert to their tradition of quality whilst acknowledging the trend for super-soft toys at the same time.

Illus. 828: *Paul Steiff died September 26, 1954.*

The entire Toy Industry suffered a loss of customers as a result of the decrease in the population birth-rate. Profits were difficult to achieve, and the import of cheaper toys from Asian countries decreased sales on the internal market even further. Steiff's answer was to produce cheaper toys; "Allspiel" and "Steinhäuser" (games and blockhouses) – but these attempts were also in vain! In spite of their otherwise close-knit relationship with the Steiff factory, trade buyers were not impressed with the company's new policies. They refused to accept these articles of cheaper quality, and Steiff reached an impasse.

At the beginning of the 1980s the company was finally able to recapture their customers interest when they reinstated their policy of high-quality products. The unexpected Teddy-bear boom in America played an important part in Steiff's comeback. The boom was precipitated by collectors – for Steiff products had suddenly become collectors items. Replicas of the old Teddy-bears were made from the original patterns which had been carefully saved in Steiff's archives. Soon thousands of these replicas left the Giengen factory. The toy factory was on its feet again. Since the beginning of the '80s Steiff's turn-over has almost doubled.
It is true that these replicas were a substitute for the old Teddy-bears and animals, but they soon established their own market, and their original value increased quickly. At the beginning of the 80s the large auction houses in London and New York also began to include early Steiff bears in their Collectors sales.
The company is over 110 years old, and almost five generations of Steiff customers worldwide have learned to love Steiff's products. Their phenomenal success is due to their traditional sales policy and continual high quality; handed down from generation to generation. Steiff – a company name which has developed into a trademark. It is synonymous for Teddy-bears, dolls, and plush animals. What was it that the company's founder Margarete Steiff wrote in the catalog in 1902: "For our children only the best is good enough. This motto remains true today!"

Illus. 829: *Margarete Steiff (Painting by Otto Neubrand, 1947).*

STEIFF-Museum and Archives

Illus. 830: *A glass case in the Steiff museum, showing a display of dolls.*

The layout of the Steiff museum is exemplary. A large collection of Steiff Teddy-bears, dolls, and animals, old and new, are displayed in an area of over 350 square meters. The toys are presented in chronological order, beginning with Margarete Steiff's little felt elephant, and continuing through the years with Richard Steiff's Teddy-bear to the extra-soft toys made at the factory today. Photographs showing the early years at the factory provide an historic portrait of the Steiff story. The complete range of Steiff articles is on view: ride-on animals, plush animals, dolls, Teddy-bears, wooden toys and much more. Visitors are shown a movie, lasting approximately half an hour, which tells the Steiff story and shows the manufacture of a Steiff animal from the first step until the last, when the toy is ready to leave the factory. Opening times: Monday to Friday: 2pm until 6pm. Admission is free. The Steiff archives are housed directly above the museum, but these rooms are not open to the public. However, the Steiff toys on display in the museum are regularly changed around.

Illus. 831: *Historical outline of the Teddy-bear story, with photograph of Richard Steiff and bronze bust of Theodore Roosevelt.*

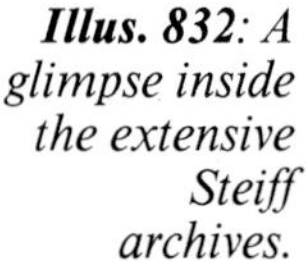

Illus. 832: *A glimpse inside the extensive Steiff archives.*

Illus. 833: *Each pattern ever used for Steiff products is carefully stored in a special room.*

Illus. 834: *Entrance to the Margarete Steiff GmbH factory and to the company museum (left).*

***Illus. 835**: Sample card (1912) with plush samples.*

Steiff's designers have been striving for decades to ensure that the company's toys retain their realistic and attractive appearance. The design is one of the secrets of a products success. The quality of the material used, is another. A great deal of experience is necessary to ensure that each product is made up in the right type of plush. Generally speaking, all materials are carefully sorted out, and only the best quality is used. Woven plush is made up on weaving looms. Whereas mohair was mostly used for earlier animals, the toys today are made of a high-quality woven plush in synthetic fibers. Steiff animals have to be durable and easy to care for. Mohair is also used today, but it is reserved for the collectors editions and better-quality animals. Knitted plush, produced on round knitting machines is created by working a "fuzzy fiber" into each stitch. The result is a fabric of fur-like quality which is extremely durable. The filling of earlier toys was of felt-pieces and excelsior (this is still used for the replicas). However, childrens toys are now filled with synthetic materials, which are often machine washable, and therefore more hygenic. Colors for painting the toys are always free from additives which are considered health hazards. The joints and eyes are securely attached, as they have been for decades. A number of extremely thorough checks are carried out to guarantee that Steiff quality remains constant. An old Steiff motto is: "Only an article which has passed each test has earned a "Button-in-Ear".

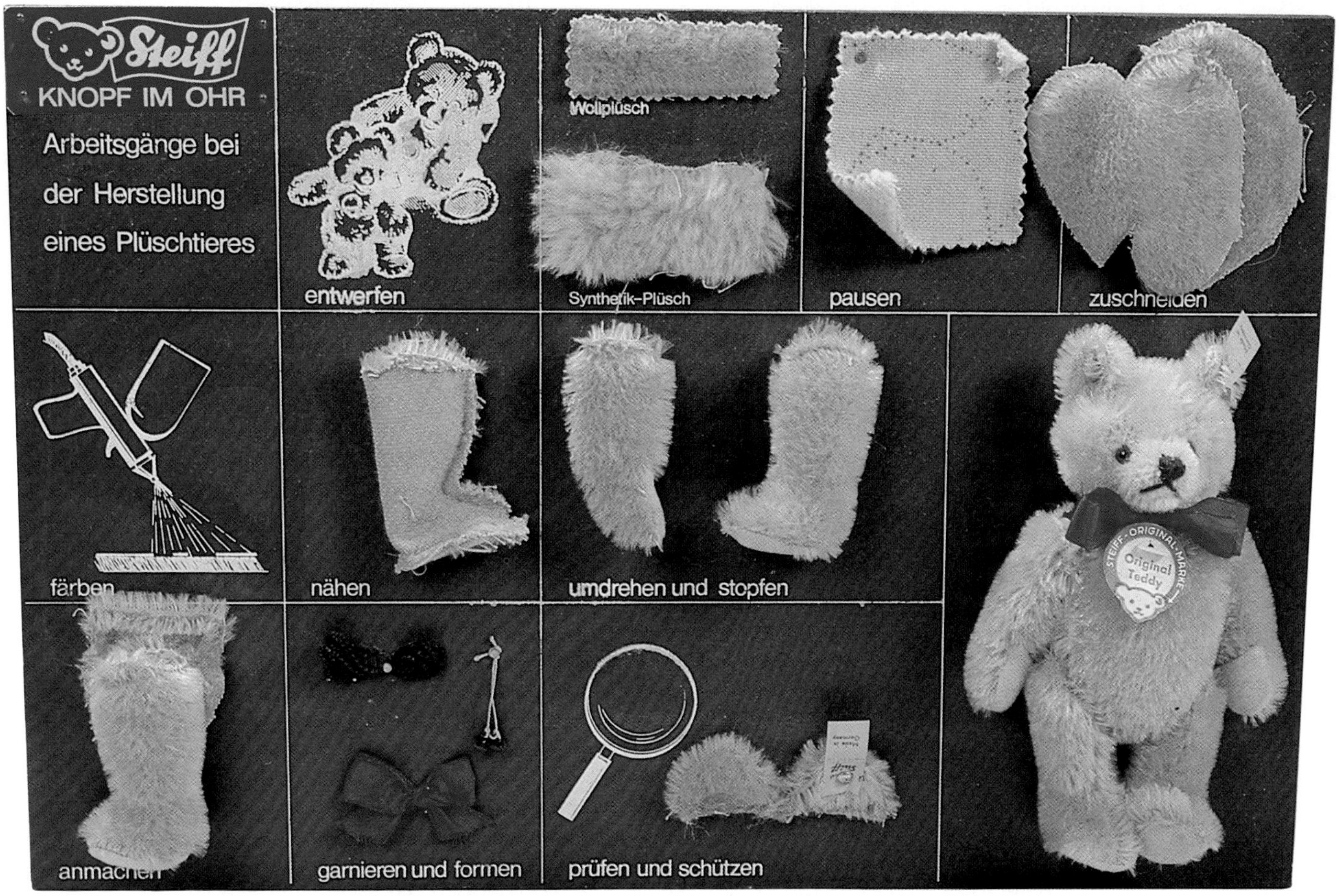

***Illus. 836**: The various steps involved in the production of a Teddy-bear.*

The Steiff-System

In 1905, Steiff introduced an ingenious numerical system for their customers to use when placing orders. These numbers were printed in all catalogs. Each order number consisted of four digits followed by a comma and then one digit. These numbers were also printed on the ear-tags from 1908 onwards. For example: Bear 1350,2 meant: **1**350,2 = standing on wheels; 1**3**50,2 = Mohair; 13**50**,2 = height 50 cm (20ins.); 1350,**2** = automatic voice box. This numerical system has only been slightly altered over the decades, with only new developments supplemented. From 1931 this system was altered to include a two digit serial number in front of the old number (not to be found on ear-tags), and after 1959, this was further increased to a three digit number.

Explanation of numbers (1905)

The thousands indicate the position:

1000 = standing
2000 = lying or crouching
3000 = sitting
4000 = sitting up or dancing
5000 = jointed
6000 = young
7000 = grotesque
8000 = on tricycle
0000 = tumbling

The hundreds indicate the kind of skin:

0**2**00 = Sealskin (Imitation)
0**3**00 = Fine Plush (Mohair)
0**4**00 = Velvet of cotton
0**5**00 = Soft Plush (Lambskin)
0**8**00 = Wood

The tens and units indicate the height of the articles:

00**14** = Size 14 (ca. 5 1/2 inches incl. head)
00**17** = Size 17 (ca. 7 inches incl. head)
00**22** = Size 22 (ca. 9 inches incl. head)
00**28** = Size 28 (ca. 11 inches incl. head)
00**14** = etc.

A number after a comma indicates the special outfit of the animal:

0000,**0** = without wheels (mostly on an elastic string)
0000,**1** = with „cuddle me“ animal voice
0000,**2** = with automatic animal voice, in regard to dolls, „mama“ voice
0000,**4** = simplified
0000,**5** = saddle with support (dismountable)
0000,**9** = with rocker and safety saddle (both dismountable)

Explanation of numbers (1959):

First number = number of serie

000/0000,00 = Serie of species

The thousands = position
000/**0**000,00 = Mimic Animals, Puppets
000/**1**000,00 = standing
000/**2**000,00 = lying
000/**3**000,00 = sitting
000/**4**000,00 = begging
000/**5**000,00 = jointed
000/**6**000,00 = young
000/**7**000,00 = grotesque
000/**8**000,00 = Characters
000/**0**000,00 = mechanic

The hundreds = Kind of material
000/0**0**00 = felt
000/0**1**00 = Height of Big Display
000/0**2**00 = Animals, Large Sizes
000/0**3**00 = mohair plush
000/0**4**00 = velvet
000/0**5**00 = wool plush
000/0**6**00 = Dralon plush
000/0**7**00 = Plastic, Rubber
000/0**8**00 = wood
000/0**5**00 = steel

The tens and singles = height in cm
000/00**12**,00 = height 12 cm

First number after the comma = special outfit
000/0000,**00** = without wheels
000/0000,**10** = on wheels to pull, on excentric wheels, Record
000/0000,**20** = Animals to ride
000/0000,**30** = Animals with steering
000/0000,**40** = wool animals
000/0000,**50** = change part
000/0000,**60** = music animals
000/0000,**70** = boy
000/0000,**80** = girl
000/0000,**90** = Display or on order animals

Second number after the comma = special outfit
000/0000,0**0** = normal
000/0000,0**1** = gold, blond
000/0000,0**2** = caramel
000/0000,0**4** = brown
000/0000,0**5** = grey
000/0000,0**6** = black
000/0000,0**7** = colored
000/0000,0**8** = red, rose
000/0000,0**9** = assorted

STEIFF-Teddy-bears: weight and height

Every collector naturally wants to know: How old is my Teddy-bear? A question which is not easily answered. For basically, the appearance and therefore the design has been altered only slightly between 1905 and 1950. Sometimes only tiny details reveal the manufacturing date of an article. There are however, a few rules, which may be applied as a guide when trying to establish the age of a Steiff product. – The characteristics of the first Teddy-bear, "55 PB" (1903) remain unknown. However, his immediate successor, Bear "35PB" (March 1904), and Bear "28PB" (1904/05), have been studied in depth, and may be clearly defined: 1: Ideally, the "Button-in-Ear" has not been lost. 2: The unusual shape of the head, and the long snout. 3: Shoe-button eyes. 4: sealing-wax nose. 5: Jointing by thread or metal rods. – An additional aid is the length of the bear, and it's weight. Weighing the bear however, is only applicable for the early bears with voice-boxes. After 1908, a heavy mechanical growler was fitted on request, and therefore the weight of the bear did not always correspond with the catalog specifications, especially for the largest sizes. A weight chart follows:

Year	Description	Size (cm)	Weight (grams)
1905	PAB 5317,1	25	90
1905	PAB 5322,1	32	170
1904	PB 28	40	580
1905	PAB 5328,1	40	350
1904	PB 35	50	1050
1905	PAB 5335,1	50	610
1905	PAG 5343,1	60	980
1905	PAB 5350,1	70	1380
1905	PAB 5380,1	115	5400

838

The Teddy Parade below shows Teddy-bears in order of manufacture – dates. Steiff Teddy-bears were available in 14 sizes until 1933/34 (there were no other sizes made!) and 13 of these sizes are pictured. The largest bear, "5380" from 1905, was 115 cm (45 in.) is missing. Important: All Steiff bears were measured in seated position until 1933/34! They were only available in the sizes listed below. – Incidentally: From 1910 onwards, sizes for standing bears were also given in the Steiff catalogs. The item number listed under each bear may be deciphered by this special Steiff-key. For instance: Item No. "5317,2". The first number, the "5", denotes "jointed", the second, "3" = mohair, the "17" = size when seated, and the "2" after the comma = voice-box. These item numbers can be found printed on the colored tags which may sometimes still remain behind the "Button-in-Ear". A change in the numbering system was introduced in 1933/34: all bears were now measured in standing position. A few changes in size were also introduced. A further change in the system followed in 1950. Bears were cut out from a new pattern: larger head, shorter neck, shorter arms and legs, no hump. At first in 22 and 35 cm, but from the mid 1950's twelve sizes were available. In 1966, a completely new bear appeared on the market. In 1980, the first Teddy-bear replicas appeared – the beginning of a series in which the old Steiff models would reappear.

STEIFF-Characteristic of the Teddy-bear 1904/05 – 1950/51

Illus. 841: The first comic doll with velvet face and painted hair (1903).

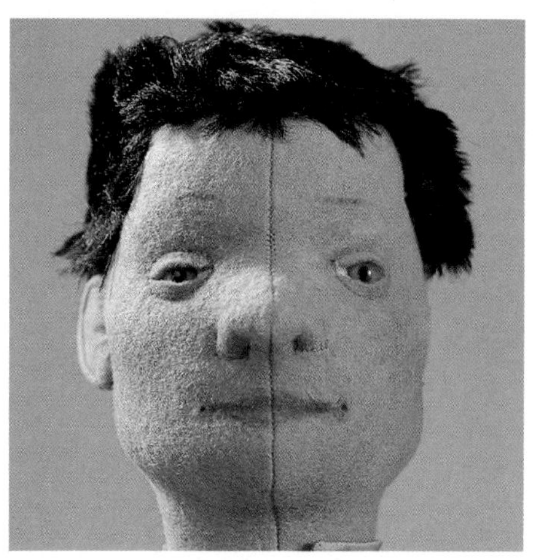

Illus. 842: Doll's head with bulging eyelids and thick lips. (1909).

Illus. 843: The large mouth opening was made like a bag; Sergeant (1909).

Illus. 844: Diagonal seam; a small opening was often left, so that instruments could be inserted (1908).

Illus. 845: Character doll with quilted, set-in mouth (1913).

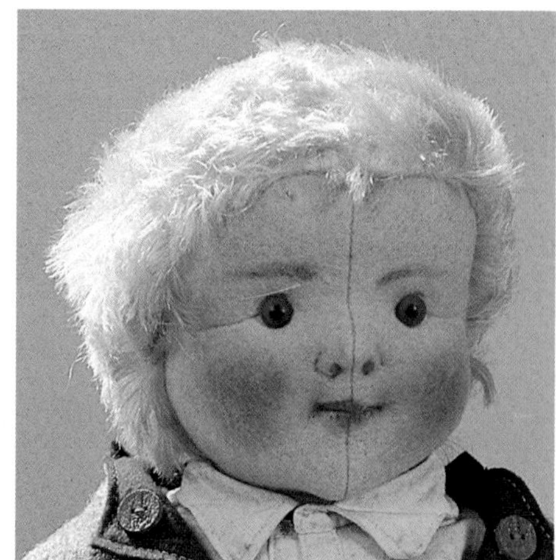

Illus. 846: Character doll with center seam and small seams around the eyes, short mohair wig (1908).

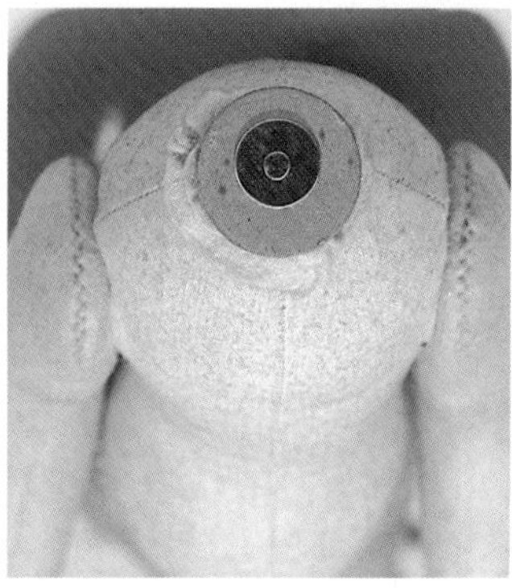

Illus. 847: Disc-jointing of head and limbs.

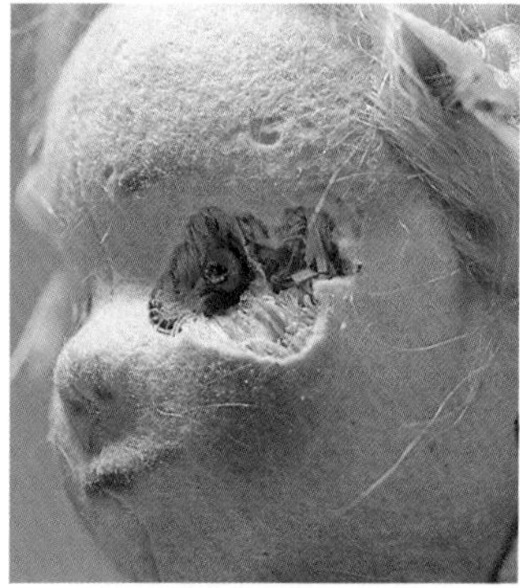

Illus. 848: Powerless against the enemy – the moth!

Characteristic details: center seam or diagonal seam, quilted eyelids or mouth, short mohair wig or long combable hair wig, disc-jointing.

*Illus. 849: Doll's head, DRGM 371 151: "Soft-stuffed toys, whose characteristic pronounced features (i.e. eyelids, lips) were achieved by exaggerated filling of the desired area" (1909), see **Illus. 842 + 845.***

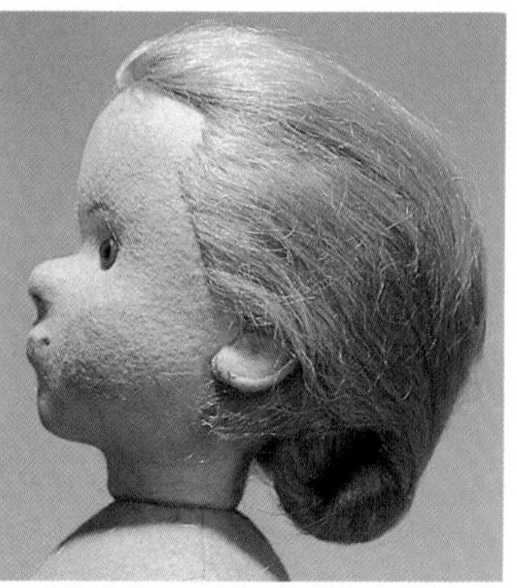

Illus. 850: Doll's head, DRGM 443 868: "Toys with 'rooted' hair, inserted through the material of the scalp, and secured by a putty-like glue at the back of the head" (1910). Were described in the catalogs "H" = hair.

STEIFF-Dolls and their bodies

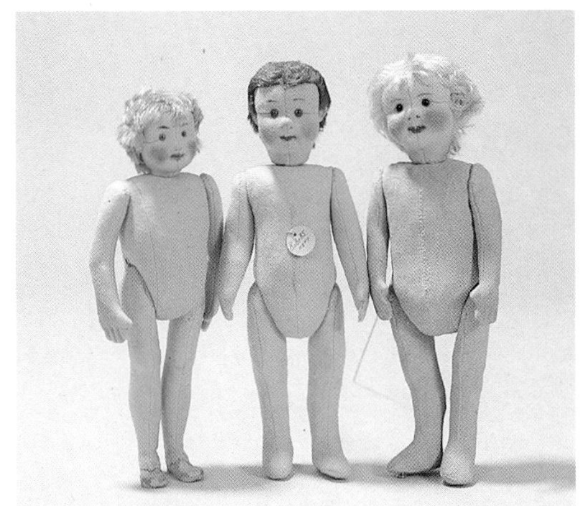

***Illus. 851**: Body of a character doll.*

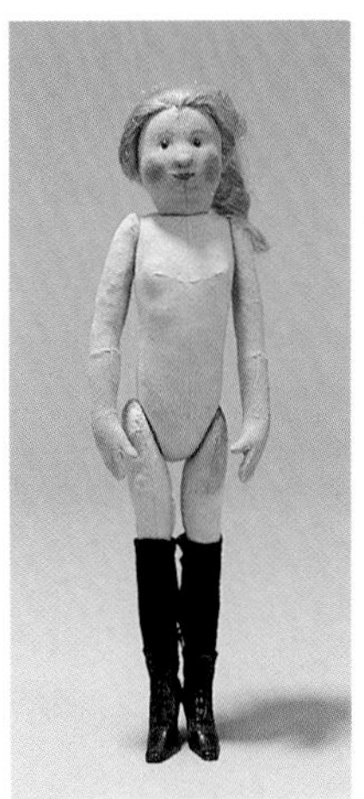

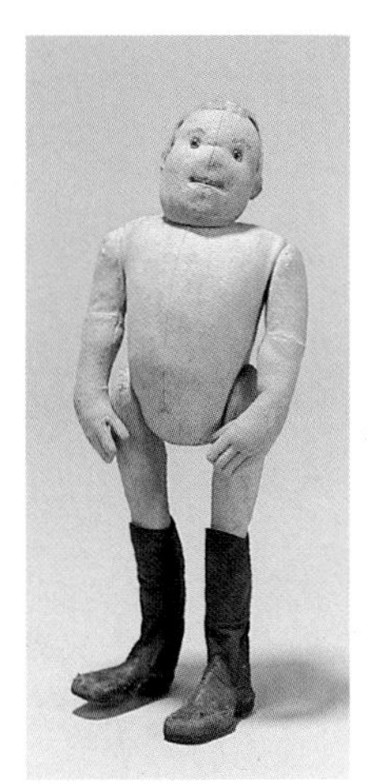

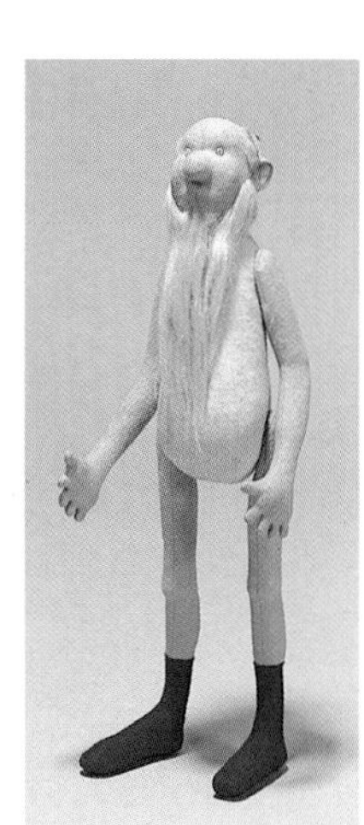

***Illus. 852-855**: Various bodies of the character dolls.*

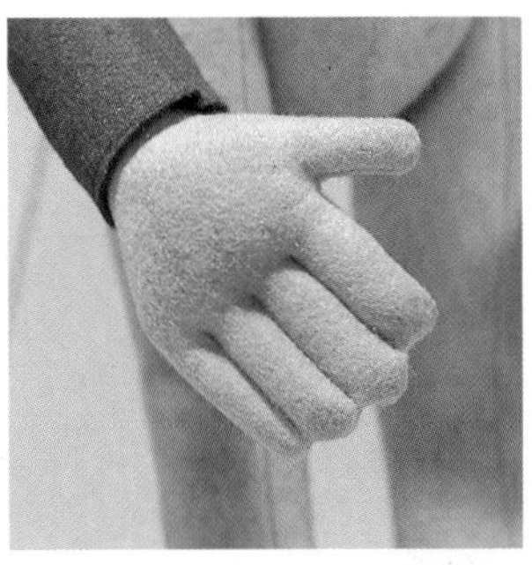

***Illus. 856**: Well modelled hand (the first dolls simply had fists).*

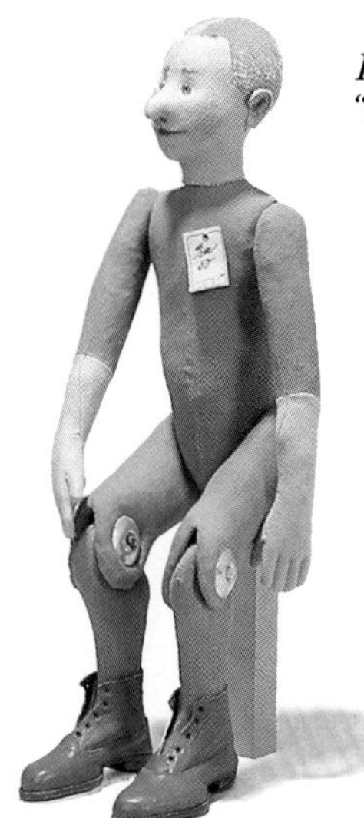

***Illus. 857**: Body DRGM 528 626: "Cloth dolls with special knee-jointing" (1912). Used for dolls 20in. and over.*

***Illus. 858**: Feet DRGM 370 312: "Soft-stuffed toys with separately stitched toes" (1909). Used for dolls and monkeys.*

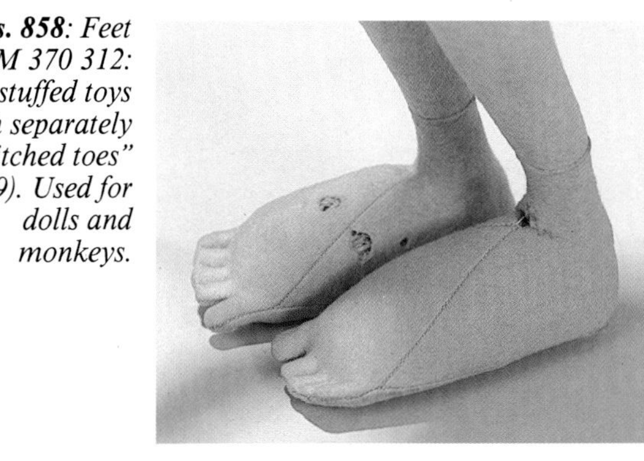

***Illus. 859**: Sewn on shoes.*

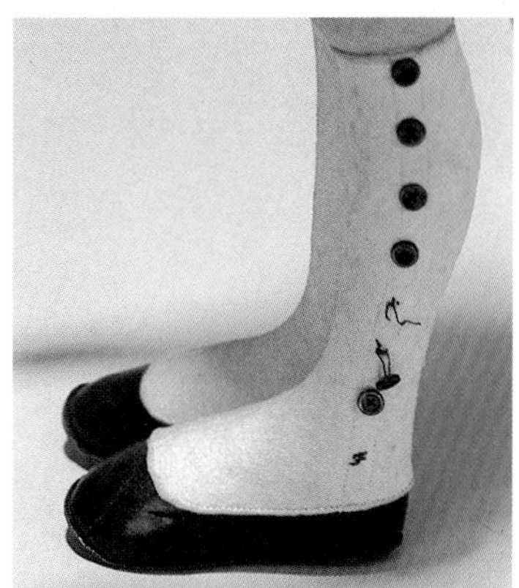

***Illus. 860**: Sewn on gaiters.*

***Illus. 861-864**: Shoes and boots for Steiff dolls were often decorated with Steiff buttons.*

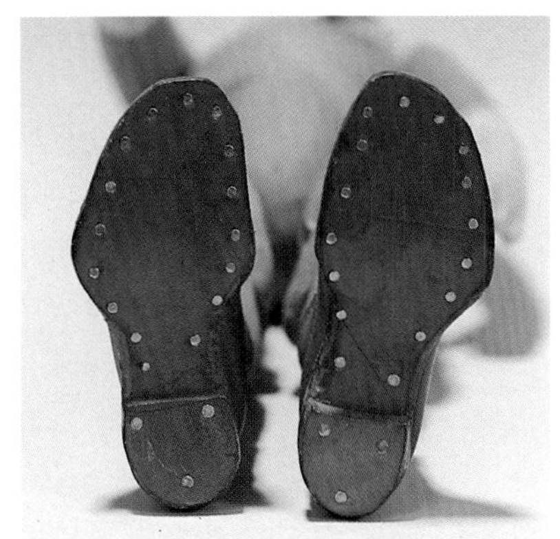

Illus. 865: *Trademark, early 1890*

Illus. 866: *Paper-label with printed elephant (from 1897/98).*

Illus. 867: *Elephant paper-label (1900-1903/04).*

Illus. 868: *Steiff house-sample button.*

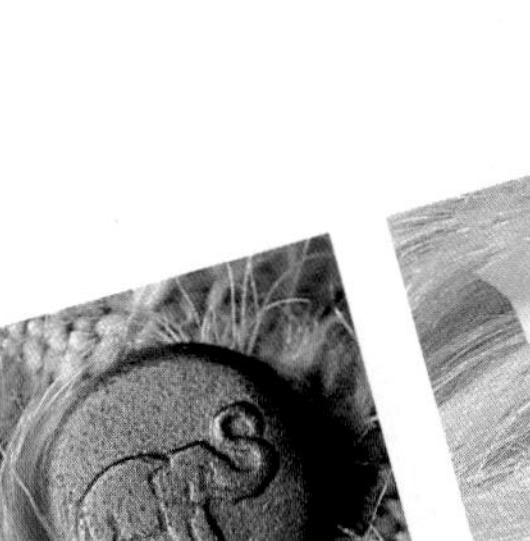

Illus. 869: *Elephant Button (1904-1905).*

Illus. 870: *Blank button 1904/05 with first label (circa 1908) probably trial series.*

Illus. 871: *Button (from 1905), label (1908-1910/11).*

Illus. 872: *Button (from 1905), label (1910/11-1925/26).*

Illus. 873: *Button (from 1905), label (1925-1934/35).*

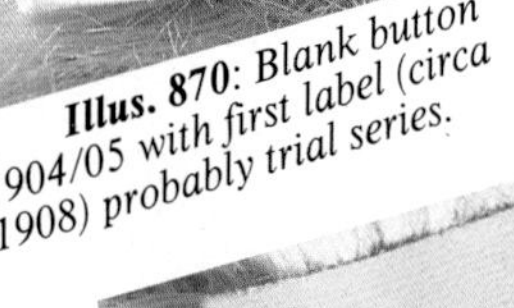

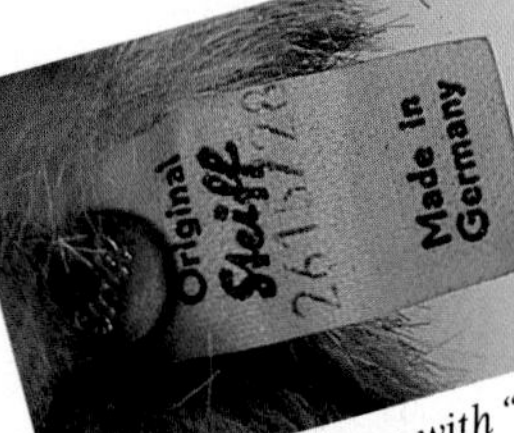

Illus. 879: *Button from old stock, label white or yellow (1950-1952).*

Illus. 880: *Button with "Steiff" in cursive script (lower-case letters), label in white or yellow (from 1952/53).*

Illus. 881: *Button with "Steiff" in cursive script, yellow label (1960-1972).*

Illus. 882: *Button with "Steiff" in cursive script, yellow label (1969-1977; until 1982 for wool miniatures).*

Illus. 883: *(1967-197*

Illus. 888: *Catalog photograph.*

Illus. 889: *Chest-label (1926-1928).*

Illus. 890: *Chest-label (1928-1950).*

Illus. 891: *Chest-label on special editions (1929).*

Illus. 892: *Ideal markings on button, ear-tag and chest-label.*

Illus. 898: *Bear button with blue label and gold writing (circa 1929, for special designs).*

Illus. 899: *Metal bear-head for scooters and pedal cars.*

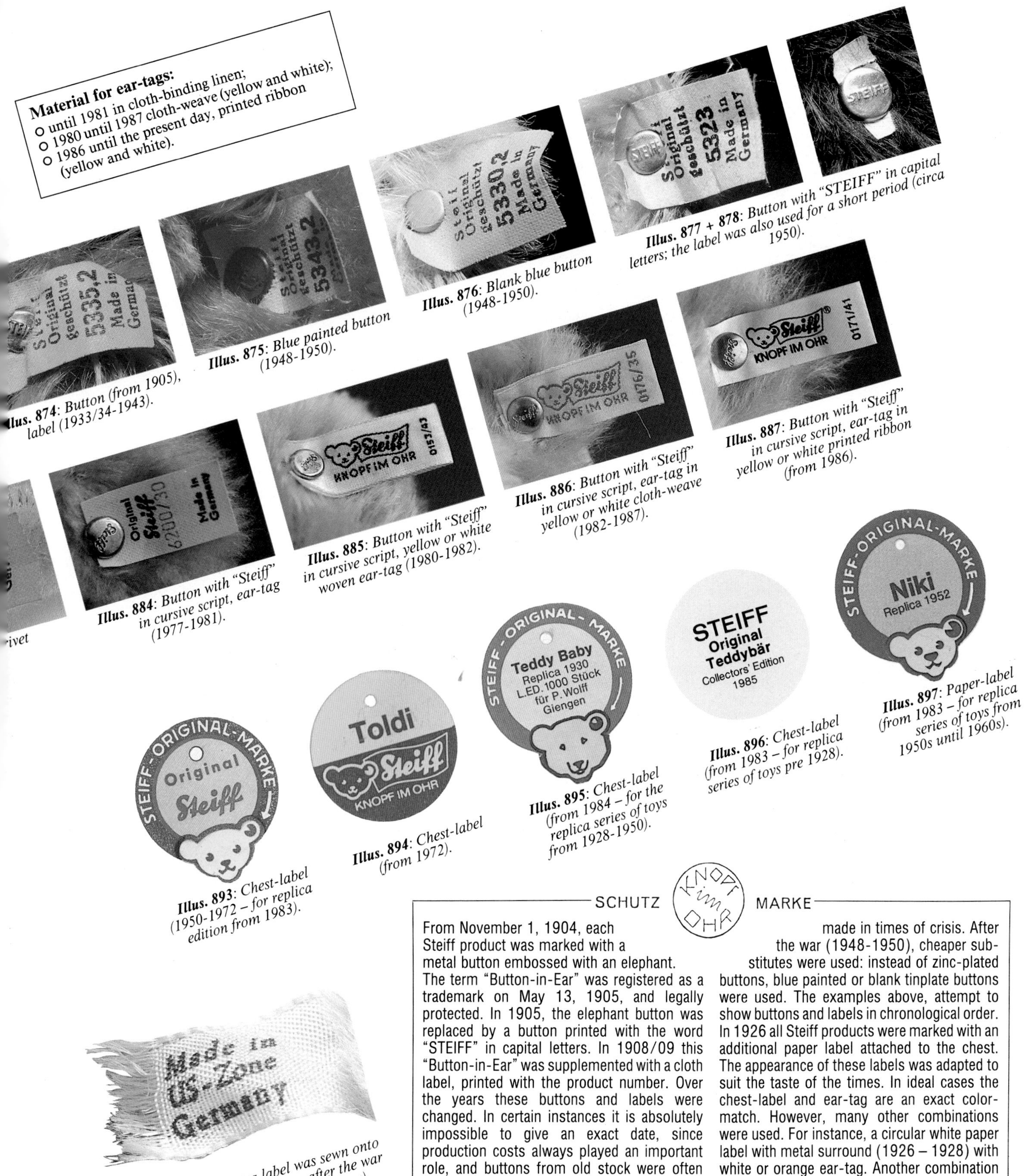

Material for ear-tags:
- until 1981 in cloth-binding linen;
- 1980 until 1987 cloth-weave (yellow and white);
- 1986 until the present day, printed ribbon (yellow and white).

Illus. 874: Button (from 1905), label (1933/34-1943).

Illus. 875: Blue painted button (1948-1950).

Illus. 876: Blank blue button (1948-1950).

Illus. 877 + 878: Button with "STEIFF" in capital letters; the label was also used for a short period (circa 1950).

Illus. 884: Button with "Steiff" in cursive script, ear-tag (1977-1981).

Illus. 885: Button with "Steiff" in cursive script, yellow or white woven ear-tag (1980-1982).

Illus. 886: Button with "Steiff" in cursive script, ear-tag in yellow or white cloth-weave (1982-1987).

Illus. 887: Button with "Steiff" in cursive script, ear-tag in yellow or white printed ribbon (from 1986).

Illus. 893: Chest-label (1950-1972 – for replica edition from 1983).

Illus. 894: Chest-label (from 1972).

Illus. 895: Chest-label (from 1984 – for the replica series of toys from 1928-1950).

Illus. 896: Chest-label (from 1983 – for replica series of toys pre 1928).

Illus. 897: Paper-label (from 1983 – for replica series of toys from 1950s until 1960s).

Illus. 900: An extra label was sewn onto the body of Steiff toys after the war (1947-1953; U.S. Zone, Germany).

SCHUTZ — KNOPF IM OHR — MARKE

From November 1, 1904, each Steiff product was marked with a metal button embossed with an elephant. The term "Button-in-Ear" was registered as a trademark on May 13, 1905, and legally protected. In 1905, the elephant button was replaced by a button printed with the word "STEIFF" in capital letters. In 1908/09 this "Button-in-Ear" was supplemented with a cloth label, printed with the product number. Over the years these buttons and labels were changed. In certain instances it is absolutely impossible to give an exact date, since production costs always played an important role, and buttons from old stock were often used irrespective of the actual manufacturing date of a product. The use of old and new buttons at the same time has been confirmed mostly for products made in times of crisis. After the war (1948-1950), cheaper substitutes were used: instead of zinc-plated buttons, blue painted or blank tinplate buttons were used. The examples above, attempt to show buttons and labels in chronological order. In 1926 all Steiff products were marked with an additional paper label attached to the chest. The appearance of these labels was adapted to suit the taste of the times. In ideal cases the chest-label and ear-tag are an exact color-match. However, many other combinations were used. For instance, a circular white paper label with metal surround (1926 – 1928) with white or orange ear-tag. Another combination is the Bear-head chest-label (1928 – 1950) with orange, yellow or white ear-tag. In the eighties the chest-labels for Steiff replicas were also modernized.

TRADE — STEIFF — MARK

INDEX of Illustrations

General

Animals

Dolls

Comic-Figuren